AGAINST
NATURE

SUNY Series in Social and Political Thought
Edited by Kenneth Baynes

AGAINST NATURE

The Concept of Nature in Critical Theory

Steven Vogel

STATE UNIVERSITY OF NEW YORK PRESS

Published by
State University of New York Press, Albany

© 1996 State University of New York

For information, address State University of New York Press,
State University Plaza, Albany, N.Y., 12246

Production by Cathleen Collins
Marketing by Nancy Farrell

The following publishers have granted permission
to reprint passages from the following works: From *Dialectic
of Enlightenment* by Max Horkheimer and Theodor W. Adorno,
English translation copyright © 1972 by Herder and Herder,
Inc. From *Negative Dialectics* by Theodor W. Adorno, English
translation copyright © 1973 by The Continuum Publishing
Company. From "New Science, New Nature: The Marcuse-Habermas
Debate Revisited," by Steven Vogel in *Research in Philosophy
and Technology* vol. 11, published by JAI Press. From
"Habermas and Science," by Steven Vogel in *Praxis
International* vol. 8, No. 3, published by Basil Blackwell
Publisher Ltd. From "Nature, Science, and the Bomb," by
Steven Vogel in TIKKUN MAGAZINE, A BI-MONTHLY JEWISH
CRITIQUE OF POLITICS, CULTURE, AND SOCIETY. Subscriptions are $31.00
per year from TIKKUN, 251 West 100th Street, 5th floor, New York, NY 10025.

Cover Photo © Ken Schles/Onyx
Cover Design: Ellen Roebuck/Onyx Design

Library of Congress Cataloging in Publication Data
Vogel, Steven, 1954–
    Against nature : the concept of nature in critical theory / Steven
Vogel.
        p.   cm.—(SUNY series in social and political thought)
    Includes bibliographical references and index.
    ISBN 0-7914-3045-6 (alk. paper). — ISBN 0-7914-3046-4 (pbk. :
alk. paper)
        1. Philosophy of nature.   2. Critical theory.   I. Title.
II. Series.
    BD581.V57   1996
    113'.09'04—dc20   95-41253
                                                                CIP

10   9   8   7   6   5   4   3   2   1

Contents

For Anna and Jesse, and for Jane

Introduction

This book offers a critical examination of the concept of "nature" as employed in the tradition of German Western Marxism often known as Critical Theory. It focuses on central figures in that tradition: Georg Lukács, Max Horkheimer and Theodor Adorno, Herbert Marcuse, and Jürgen Habermas. My claim is that the concept of nature has been a problematic one for Critical Theory from the very start, and that a consideration of the tradition's history reveals it as struggling with a series of difficulties about that concept which it has never found itself entirely able to resolve. But my point in arguing this is neither entirely historical nor entirely negative. Rather I will suggest that a reconsideration and re-evaluation of the problem of nature in Critical Theory can provide important insights relevant to contemporary discussions of nature, particularly those concerned with environmental issues and questions about the social role and meaning of science and technology. Yet those insights can be uncovered only by looking at subterranean strands in the history of Critical Theory's discussion of nature, examining hints and suggestions that were never fully taken up and following arguments further than their authors ever intended to go. The main strands, I am afraid, have been failures; the tradition finds itself caught in dilemmas that vitiate its most common claims about nature's status. And still I remain convinced that a careful study of the work of the figures mentioned can offer significant resources for rethinking the questions about nature that recent discussions have brought to the forefront.

Western Marxism defined itself from the start by its opposition to the "orthodox" tradition associated with writers such as Engels, whose accounts of Marxist philosophy it saw as impossibly simplistic. Engels appeared content to understand Marxism as a "science," methodologically similar to the successful natural sciences of earlier centuries, and to believe that by applying that honorific title to it all significant epistemological questions were resolved.[1] For Western Marxists such as Lukács, however, subtler and more steeped in Hegel as they were, the question of Marxism's own epistemological status was

1

considerably more complicated, and so too was the question of whether science and the scientific method were themselves to be understood so positively. Not science but scientism now appeared as an important topic for Marxist philosophical reflection, as the latter began to examine and criticize the unquestioning faith in science so characteristic of nineteenth-century views and to ask about the social origin and meaning of that faith.

Thus rather than seeing critical social theory as merely part of some broader and methodologically unitary Science, as Engels did, Western Marxism perhaps more consistently attempted to bring science, too, as a significant thought form of the contemporary world, into the ambit of the critique of ideology. If "the ruling ideas are the ideas of the ruling class," science ought not to be immune; and so the question of its own relation to the social must be raised and also problematized. Further, the methodological status of a critical theory no longer willing or able to call itself *scientific* in the older sense now requires an independent epistemological account and justification, while conversely "science" will now be criticized precisely for its failure to recognize its own rootedness in a (bad) social reality. In the course of the latter critique, it will be above all science's own claims to neutrality, objectivity, and "value-freedom" that will need to be unmasked.

Thus Western Marxism was marked from its beginnings by a critique of science and scientism. But what remains ambiguous—as we will see repeatedly below—is just how far that critique is supposed to reach. The critique of science involves a series of epistemological objections to the traditional conception of "scientific method," resulting in a clear-cut rejection of the idea that a critical social theory ought to take such a method as a model. Yet the validity of that method for the examination of the extrasocial realm, which is to say of *nature*, still requires clarification, and here the question becomes considerably more complex. Neo-Kantianism had already sharply distinguished on methodological grounds between the *Geisteswissenschaften* and the natural sciences; Lukács employed a version of this distinction in an attempt to argue that Marxist philosophy deals entirely with the social and has nothing to add, critical or otherwise, to the unexceptionable results of natural science.[2] (We will see the unhappy fate of this attempt in Chapter 1.) By the time of Horkheimer and Adorno's *Dialectic of Enlightenment*, however, the idea of the appropriateness of natural science's methods even "in its own sphere" had become considerably harder to accept; the technologically mediated horrors of fascism and of the Second World War seemed to confirm the sense that a critical theory methodologically precluded from speaking about natural science and technology was crucially incomplete. Natural science *itself* had to be criticized, not just the scientistic effort to remake social theory in its image. The "domination of nature" characteristic of science and technology, the Frankfurt School theorists began to argue, could not be separated from the *social* domination critical theory had always taken as its theme.

The tradition seems to vacillate between these two poles, sometimes accepting (natural) science as unexceptionable when applied to the sphere of nature and objecting only to its use as a methodological model for social theory, sometimes however wanting to go further and criticize natural science as such. The first approach, announced by Lukács, doubtless has the advantage of not requiring the apparently quixotic rejection of a technology and science whose massive material successes (and whose significance to any seriously envisaged socialism) seemed scarcely deniable; but on the other hand, it does generate a strange epistemological situation whereby something like a neo-Kantian dualism between nature and the social is uneasily grafted onto traditional Marxist materialism in a way that seems inconsistent with both. And indeed Lukács makes little attempt, as we will see, to justify or even explain this dualism or for that matter to indicate what epistemological account of *natural* science it might involve. The postwar Frankfurt School, as noted, moved in the opposite direction, applying the epistemological critique of science as "domination" even (or especially) to the case where that science concerns itself entirely with the world of nature. Habermas, the most recent figure in the tradition, moves back, returning to dualism while attempting (at least in his earlier work) to resolve some of its problems by actually offering an epistemological account of natural science that attempts both to ground it and to explain its differences from social theory. Yet as we shall see in Chapter 5 his project too faces significant problems.

In fact *none* of these views turns out to be stable; the difficulties they confront generate a constant tension in which positions shift, reveal inner contradictions, and even threaten to turn into their opposites. Lukács's assertion that critical theory must limit itself strictly to examining the social and can have nothing to say about nature is radically undercut when he goes on to define the "social" so broadly that, by the end, nature turns out itself to be a social category—which means that the supposed limit turns out to be no limit at all. Horkheimer and Adorno provide such a far-reaching critique of "enlightened reason" as domination that it threatens to swallow itself, because their own strong normative claims (e.g., that domination is wrong) seem grounded on the very Enlightenment values they claim to be questioning. They can avoid this circularity only by appealing to the "nature" that enlightened natural science is supposed to be harming; the trouble is that such an appeal itself requires a kind of knowledge of the nature being harmed that would substitute for the natural science they want to reject, and they have nothing to say about what this knowledge might be (beyond vague and unpersuasive appeals to animism) or how it might be justified. Adorno's attempt, in his later work, to sidestep this problem by replacing "nature" with a concept of the "nonidentical" about which, by definition, nothing can ever be known just exacerbates the difficulty, generating a systematic tendency to paradox that only his rhetorical brilliance prevents from appearing as a reductio of the whole position.

Later views fare not much better. Marcuse's ambivalence about science and technology is palpable, and his call for a "New Science" and "New Technology" that eschew domination involves the confusing notion of a technological transformation of nature that somehow leaves nature as it is, or rather "for the first time" lets it be what it "really" is (even though he also says that what it "really" is is *historical*); and all this further stands in an obscure relation to his curious tendency to insist that to stop dominating nature would require the acquisition by humans literally of "new instincts." And Habermas's more sober critique of objectivistic accounts of nature leaves him in his early work with an ambiguity about nature's ontological status that causes him to posit a quasi-noumenal "nature in itself" whose theoretical function appears hopelessly self-contradictory, while in his later work references to nature seem simply to disappear.

In each of these cases the question of the meaning and status of nature produces the difficulty. I will argue that, in fact, the tradition of Western Marxism is bedeviled by a fundamental tension lurking within its epistemological views, one that comes to the surface as soon as the question of nature is posed. On the one hand, the tradition's roots in classical German philosophy lead it to emphasize (more, for instance, than Engels ever would have) the active and social character of knowledge and to draw familiar Hegelian conclusions about the influence of the socially situated subject on the object known. But this emphasis stands in uneasy conflict with the tradition's equally strong (Marxist) commitment to something like a "materialism" that would insist on the existence of a substrate underlying social action making such action possible and not itself constituted by it. If we call that substrate "nature," the structure of the problem emerges clearly: Is knowledge of *nature* active and social? Does the socially situated subject influence *natural* objects? To answer yes is to remain true to the Hegelian epistemology but to reject any ordinary interpretation of the "materialist" ontology; to answer no is to retain the materialism while rendering problematic not just the activist epistemology but also the entire critique of objectivism and scientism it serves to ground.

The problem has something of the structure of an antinomy, produced by the attempt to combine an activist account of knowledge with a materialist view of nature. It will become clear in the course of the book that I do not think that this antinomy can be resolved and that I am also not particularly optimistic about the possibility of finding some clever synthesis of the two views in which it can somehow be sublated. My own sympathies, frankly, lie in the Hegelian direction, and here perhaps I differ from many who continue to interest themselves in the tradition of Western Marxism I believe that what is best in that tradition, what is most philosophically interesting and fruitful for the discussion of current issues about nature, comes above all from the former side of the dilemma just presented By insisting on the significance of what was the great insight of classical German idealism—that knowledge, if it is to be possible at all, must be *active* and understood as involved from the very start with the object known—such a view asks us to "deconstruct" supposedly natural and familiar phenomena into the hidden social processes by which they were produced It sees the relation of human subjects to the nature they inhabit as an active and world-changing one and wants therefore to take seriously the idea of nature as a "social category" or more precisely as something *socially constructed*

Putting the point this way perhaps throws a slightly different light on the tension just outlined I will be arguing that two quite different sorts of argument about nature can be distinguished within the tradition of Western Marxism One is the Hegelian one to which I have already alluded It insists on the active role of a socially situated subject in constituting the field that subject inhabits, it emphasizes the dynamic, the social, and the historically changing in its account of what the world is like and sees the static and putatively "natural" as standing for those aspects of the world whose social character has been hidden or forgotten and that have thus become "reified " The model here is Marx's account of the exchange value of commodities as consisting in truth of "congealed" labor The role of liberatory critique, for such an argument, is to dereify or "uncongeal"—to dissolve false immediacies, to reveal to human subjects that what they think of as "natural" is actually the product of their own socially organized activity The critique of ideology, for such a view, would then involve a critique of contemporary attitudes (including those associated with natural science and technology) for their failure to see the world humans inhabit as one that bears traces of their own actions [3] The other argument, conversely, has its roots not in Hegel but in Romantic and *Lebensphilosophische* traditions, for it, "nature" and more generally that which is Other than the human or social take on a *positive* sign, and contemporary science and technology are criticized on completely different and even opposite grounds—not because they fail to acknowledge the human character of the world that surrounds us but rather because they violate that world's otherness, its specificity as an ontological realm beyond the human and not finally graspable by it

The latter view is probably more familiar today Not only is it the view defended by the great figures of the classical Frankfurt School (i e , Horkheimer and Adorno) and by Marcuse as well, but its similarity to themes in the late Heidegger should also be clear And of course versions of this sort of critique of science and technology are common in contemporary environmental discussions associated with "deep ecology" and related positions. But it faces, I will argue, a series of deep and indeed ultimately fatal problems as a philosophical view, deriving fundamentally from the difficulty it confronts in explaining how it can itself come to *know* the nature that it claims dominative worldviews fail to comprehend. Its naturalism stands in conflict with its claims about the absolute otherness of nature, and the result is either incoherence or vacuity: either it grounds its critique in substantive claims about nature without being able to explain how such claims are possible or could avoid the trap of again denying nature's otherness, or else it makes no such claims and so leaves its critique utterly empty.

Habermas has recognized this kind of problem in the work of the postwar Frankfurt School authors; it lies at the heart of the normative deficit he has consistently pointed to as the central difficulty in their work. Their commitment to naturalism leaves them unable to provide the sorts of normative justifications necessary to ground the plausibility of their critique; by attempting to ground that critique instead in nature (whether internal or external) they both fall prey to the naturalistic fallacy and also leave themselves open to the objection that they offer no account of how nature is to be known if not by the standard natural sciences. Yet Habermas takes this difficulty as demonstrating that the real normative issues relevant to critical theory have nothing to do with nature at all, and arise only with respect to subject-subject interactions. (This is the sense in which his position is a throwback to Lukácsian dualism.) Thus he essentially bans nature from the realm of the normative; but that conclusion, I will argue, does not follow, or rather follows only if dualism has already simply been presupposed. I want rather to hold to the intuition of the Frankfurt School, and of contemporary environmental ethics as well, according to which deep and significant normative issues are indeed raised by our interactions with the natural world—but I want to do so without falling into the difficulties of a naturalism embarrassed about its own epistemological status.

My suggestion then is to consider the *other* line of argument just mentioned, the quasi-Hegelian one that sees nature as socially constructed and that criticizes contemporary views of the natural not for their attempt to dominate that which is Other but for their failure to recognize the human character of that which appears to be nonhuman. Such a line points (back) to something like a "philosophy of practice," to an older tradition in Marxist philosophy that saw the materialist reformulation of Hegelian epistemology as consisting in the substitution of concrete human labor for the abstract activity of *Geist*. This suggests the specific form in which the thesis that "nature is a social construction" will appear in this book: as a claim that emphasizes the way in which the environment that surrounds us and that we take for granted as "natural" turns out on investigation to be the product of human labor and hence *literally* socially constructed. The environment we inhabit is to a remarkable extent a "built" environment; the mark of the human can be found on almost everything we see. More generally, I will argue, it is through our practical activity, socially organized and historically variable as it is, that the world we inhabit comes to be, and for *this* reason that world and our relationship with it necessarily possess a normative component. To say this is to reject dualism: the "natural" world and the social one are not distinguishable, because the *Umwelt*, the surrounding world of "nature," is itself in various senses the product of social practices. If this is the case, then a critical social theory will indeed have much to say, and of a normative character, about nature—not because that theory is itself grounded in a naturalism but precisely because of nature's own sociality.

One trouble with Engels's epistemological discussions was that he simply took for granted without argument the validity of the natural sciences and of certain standard accounts of their methods; the strongly critical attitude with which he and Marx approached the results of contemporary political economy was never applied to the results of contemporary natural science. Western Marxism generally breaks with Engels, as I have said, but unfortunately tends not to break with this tradition of not inquiring too carefully into what natural science's methods or results really are as opposed to unquestioningly accepting that science's own ideological self-conception. Thus Lukács no less than Engels assumes that the (natural) Scientific Method is simply correct when applied to the realm of nature, whereas Horkheimer, Adorno, and Marcuse, too, seem to take for granted the truth of standard positivist accounts of natural science's method, wanting only to criticize the social meaning and consequences of the use of such a method. And Habermas's early epistemological work as well (e.g., in *Knowledge and Human Interests*) is badly flawed by an uncritical acceptance of "positivist" accounts of method that, by the time it was published, had already come in for significant critique even from within the supposedly positivist camp.

The truth is that, beyond generalized critiques of positivism, little serious consideration has been given to contemporary philosophy of science within the postwar tradition of Critical Theory, and this is a significant fault. Positivism, of course, is today quite dead, and I would argue that "postpositivist" or "postempiricist" developments in the philosophy of science over the past three decades have much to say about the issues involving nature and natural science with which Critical Theory has struggled, tending both to elucidate and fundamentally to complicate the epistemological and methodological accounts it has attempted to provide. In particular I think that such developments offer support to just the sort of account of nature as social and as "constructed" that I will be suggesting represents the best reformulation of the tradition's views.

By undercutting the older image of an objective and value-free (and asocial) science impassively examining an independent nature, postempiricism allows us to understand the senses in which natural science and the nature it describes to us must themselves be seen as practical, historical, and social products. Recent theorists such as Bruno Latour, Joseph Rouse, and others have emphasized the extent to which science itself has to be seen as a *practice*, as well as the extent to which the entities about which science reports are themselves again quite literally constructions—"real," doubtless, but "constructed" nonetheless. This book does not itself pretend to be a work in the philosophy of science but rather wants to begin by taking certain elements of these postempiricist and sociologically oriented accounts of science as read. What I see myself as doing here is beginning a conversation, one that has been long postponed, in which Critical Theory's discussions of science and scientism come into confrontation with discussions that have been taking place in a very different arena in a way that might be mutually beneficial to each.[4] Critical Theory has suffered too long from a failure to grapple directly with the philosophy of science as such, while much of the most "socially" oriented philosophy of science has tended to be notable for its failure satisfactorily to conceptualize the political and normative questions raised by its own accounts of method.[5] I hope this book may be a contribution in both directions.

The book is also driven by another concern with current issues, to which I have already made reference: environmental theory, and especially the debates over "deep ecology" and other anti-anthropocentric critiques of contemporary approaches to nature. Discussions of nature, and even the old-fashioned idea of a "philosophy of nature," are today back on the agenda because of the recognition that contemporary environmental problems require a philosophical response and can no longer be treated as unrelated to fundamental questions of ethics and politics and indeed even epistemology. I am convinced that environmental theory represents an important field for critical philosophical reflection. Yet I am equally convinced that environmental philosophy will require a *considerably* more sophisticated account of what it means when it speaks of "nature" than has in general heretofore been forthcoming if it is to achieve any important results; and here I think the tradition of Critical Theory I am examining has a great deal to offer. I share with theorists of deep ecology a serious concern about the meaning and consequences of the current environmental crisis, a crisis that I agree with them in seeing as a symptom of a deeper problem whose roots lie in the mistaken way the industrialized West views the world of nature. But I have already said enough to suggest that my account of that mistake will be quite different from the one more familiar from their arguments. My deepest purpose in writing this book was to begin at least to clear the way for a more serious and open examination among environmentally concerned thinkers about what exactly "nature" is and what in the current way it is thought about ought to be criticized and rejected.

Against Nature—the title of course is deliberately meant to be provocative. "Nature" has been a problem for the tradition of Western Marxism from the start, I will be arguing, and there are good epistemological reasons why this has been so. In this sense I suppose the title simply suggests that it might be better off simply dropping the concept. But by this I do not mean to make the tempting move we have already seen in Lukács, demurely asserting that a critical theory of society has nothing to say about nature. Instead I mean to suggest that critical theorists ought to learn to take seriously the telos toward which so many of their epistemological arguments seem to move—the thesis that a socially constructed nature must be seen as intrinsically connected to and even part of the social world, and hence that an adequate critical theory of society must at the same time quite literally be *a critical theory of nature*. In such a theory the "natural" would stand for that which still needs to be deconstructed into the social practices that make it possible, a deconstruction oriented by the hope that humans could take responsibility for the world they inhabit instead of believing that world to be determined by external forces they are unable to control. In this sense human liberation itself would be "against nature."

The last sentence sounds shocking only because *against nature* has also come to mean "normatively wrong." But it is exactly this equation, and the naturalism it involves, that it seems to me crucial to reject. Such a naturalism (characteristic, e.g., of much "radical" environmentalism) thinks it can resolve what are fundamentally *social* questions—about the sorts of practices we as a society ought to be engaging in, the sort of world we ought to inhabit, the sorts of people we want to be—by appealing to "what nature demands" of us or to the dangers of a dominated but powerful nature that might "take its revenge" on us. Yet in such appeals the social is not avoided so much as it is smuggled in: instead of allowing the human community to decide these matters democratically, those who make such arguments attempt to short-circuit democratic discourse by labeling as "natural"—and hence unquestionable—what are inevitably really their own socially situated normative claims. The naturalistic fallacy is a constant *political* danger, whether it takes the form (say) of critiques of homosexuality or of nuclear power. To call either of these *against nature* is to abdicate moral responsibility, pretending that fundamental questions about how to live can be answered by appeal to something other than the social realm that is in fact the only source of normative justification. Here is where Habermas's work, with its emphasis on the relation between ethics and language, is particularly important. To attempt to ground normative claims outside the realm of the social, which is to say outside the realm of communication, is to insulate such claims from the requirements of discursive scrutiny inherent in the very idea of normativity itself. To say that nature is "constructed," then, is in a sense simply a way of saying that an appeal to nature is always nothing other than an appeal to *us* and to our own discursive processes of justification.

Talk of nature as "socially constructed," or for that matter of the social realm as the only source of normative justification, tends to worry environmental thinkers; they hear in it the kind of anthropocentric denial of nature's otherness and value many see as the source of contemporary environmental problems. I plead guilty to something like anthropocentrism, at least if the latter is correctly understood, and will indeed suggest in Chapter 6 that Habermas's conception of discourse ethics provides a persuasive argument for the assertion that humans do possess a distinctive moral status as the subjects of normative discourse. To say that value comes to be recognized only in and through such discourse (and that as far as we know only humans can engage in discourse) is however not to say that only humans are *bearers* of value; in this sense nothing in my argument suggests that humans may not discursively determine that natural entities, or nature itself, possess value. We cannot read an ethics off "from" nature without falling prey to naturalism, but this does not entail that there is nothing normative to say about nature at all. I will argue indeed that to see the environment as *not* other than us but rather as something we shape and construct through our practices is precisely to see that our relations to nature are normative through and through. To view the environment as socially constructed is to see it as something for which we are literally *responsible*; it is in this recognition of our inextricable connection to and responsibility for the world we inhabit, it seems to me, that the source of a morally justifiable "environmental ethic" is to be found.

The arguments I have been anticipating here are developed in what follows by way of a critical study of each of the figures I began by mentioning. In Chapter 1 I examine the famous "problem of nature in Lukács": the basic ambiguity in his account of nature in *History and Class Consciousness* referred to earlier, according to which it seems alternately to be banished from social theory and then on the contrary to be entirely assimilated to the social. In Chapter 2 I argue that, although both positions can be found in Lukács's text, only the second one is really consistent with the (Hegelian) epistemology he develops, and I try to suggest a possible reading in which the claim that "nature is a social category" can be understood as a plausible one. Chapter 3 considers Horkheimer and Adorno's *Dialectic of Enlightenment*, suggesting that its difficulties with normative grounding stem from its own ambiguity about the role of nature, and in particular from its own tendency toward naturalism. Chapter 4 reads the later works of Adorno, especially *Negative Dialectics* and the *Aesthetic Theory*, as an attempt to resolve those problems by offering a highly sophisticated recasting of the arguments of *Dialectic of*

Enlightenment in the name of a "nonidentity" now explicitly distinguished from nature; yet even this attempt, I argue, does not succeed. In Chapter 5 I discuss Marcuse's own reformulation of the Frankfurt School view, and then consider Habermas's strong and epistemologically complex critique of it in his early work. I argue that *neither* Habermas nor Marcuse is sufficiently sensitive to the implications of the insight (to which they both pay lip service) that the "nature" of natural science is itself in some sense a construction and suggest that taking that insight seriously might allow us to understand Marcuse's notion of a "new" science in quite a different light—as a science that consciously acknowledges not only its own social meaning and origin but also that of the "nature" it depicts. And finally in Chapter 6, as already mentioned, I take up Habermas's more recent and very important notion of "discourse ethics" and of the need for a communicative turn in philosophy, and examine its relevance to questions about nature and the environment. Habermas is famously uncomfortable about such questions, but in fact (I will suggest) his views offer important resources for answering them, and in a way that helps to clarify both the very idea of a "socially constructed" nature as well as its normative status. The result is something like a "communicative theory of nature," which although it involves rejecting the kind of strict dualism between the social and the natural that Habermas constantly wants to assert, nonetheless I think offers a better account of nature and of environmental ethics than his own "official" view could ever provide. I try to sketch out such an account in the closing pages of the book.

My own background and training is in the tradition of Critical Theory and Habermas in particular, although as will become clear I am by no means an orthodox defender of its tenets. I do find within this tradition, however—and especially in Habermas's work, in fact—the strongest and most helpful arguments for thinking about social and political questions, a genus of which (as has already become clear) I believe environmental questions form a species. In recent years, due above all to Habermas's sustained critiques, this tradition has understood itself as in strong disagreement with more recent "postmodern" developments in philosophy, such as those associated with Foucault or Derrida, not to speak of the Nietzschean and Heideggerean traditions that underlie such developments. It will be noticed that on occasion here I have, as the saying goes, "coquetted" with some postmodern turns of phrase or forms of argumentation, for which I suppose some will criticize me. But I believe, as indeed I will try to show in what follows, that there are important points at which these two traditions have much to say to each other, although on other points they doubtless differ radically as well. At the same time, like Horkheimer and Adorno and of course Habermas too, I see no reason to apologize for a commitment to the values of enlightenment. I think that truth and normative rightness, understood in universalistic terms, ought to serve as the regulative ideals organizing both our intellectual life and our social practices. I do not, however, think (as Habermas sometimes seems to) that this requires positing any strong distinction between the natural and the social, nor the kind of careful immunizing of natural science from any admixture of the political that he sometimes defends. The argument for this, of course, will have to wait for the body of the book.

Conversations with many people over many years have helped me to develop and complicate the views expressed in this work, although few of them will agree with all (or even most) of what is said in it. I want to thank them here: they include James Bohman, Joseph Rouse, Andrew Feenberg, Georgia Warnke, Paul Stern, Kenneth Baynes, Johanna Meehan, Daniel Brudney, Harry Heft, Bill Nichols, Stuart Pimsler, Suzanne Costello, Marx Wartofsky, Robert Cohen, Michael Zimmerman, Thomas McCarthy, and Jürgen Habermas. My colleagues in the Philosophy Department at Denison University, including especially David Goldblatt, Ronald Santoni, and Anthony Lisska, as well as Philip Glotzbach (now of the University of Redlands), deserve special thanks for their support, their critical questions, and their friendship. Thanks, too, to Gary Baker and Barbara Fultner, who assisted on some of the translations; to Ellen Roebuck and Daniel Roebuck, for their generous help on the cover; to Pat Davis, whose aid has been invaluable in general; and to Kyle Hamilton. I am also grateful to the National Endowment for the Humanities, the Center for the Humanities at Wesleyan University, the Deutsche Akademische Austauschdienst, the Grawemeyer Foundation, the Humanities Research Center "Menneske og Natur" at Odense University (Denmark), the Denison University Research Foundation, and the R. C. Good Foundation for support in various ways and at various points in this project. Portions of this book appeared earlier in *Research in Philosophy and Technology*, in *Praxis International*, and in *Tikkun*.

My brother, Loring Vogel, has been a constant source of inspiration and encouragement and has been for many years a treasured fellow searcher in the attempt to understand technology and nature. And my father, Amos Vogel, is someone to whom I owe a deeper intellectual debt than I can even express— dating back more or less to the days he and my mother Marcia first dressed me in those (red) diapers. I thank all three of them. Finally, this book could not have been finished had it not been for the love, encouragement, and intelligence of Jane Henderson. To her, and to our children Anna and Jesse, I dedicate this work.

CHAPTER 1

The Problem of Nature in Lukács

1. THE PROBLEM

Andrew Feenberg, in his *Lukács, Marx, and the Sources of Critical Theory*, writes that "Lukács' fundamental difficulty is with nature," and most commentators seem to agree that this is so.[1] Yet as soon as they start to describe what that difficulty consists in, disagreement immediately arises. The most common criticism is that Lukács denies the existence of nature as something independent of the social: Lucio Colletti explicitly asserts this, and Alfred Schmidt too writes that Lukács in *History and Class Consciousness* "dissolves nature, both in form and in content, into the social forms of its appropriation."[2] Yet Schmidt himself also writes that Lukács "deserves recognition as the first to oppose Engels's fateful attempt to extend the dialectic to cover . . . nature, by pointing out how important it is precisely for materialism to restrict the dialectical method to the socio-historical areas of reality."[3] It's not at all clear, though, how both of Schmidt's characterizations can be true: if nature is dissolved into the social, why would a dialectics of nature not precisely have a place reserved for it *within* a dialectical method "restricted" to the socio-historical?

Similar critiques accuse Lukács of rejecting natural science. Gareth Stedman Jones says that *History and Class Consciousness* "represents the first major irruption of the romantic anti-scientific tradition of bourgeois thought into Marxist theory," and Colletti witheringly criticizes what he sees as the irrationalist elements in Lukács's thought, accusing it of falling into a tradition that "mistak[es] the romantic critique of intellect and science for a socio-historical critique of capitalism."[4] But on the other hand Feenberg writes that Lukács "has a quite banal respect for the sciences of nature," and "nowhere denies the independence of nature nor the validity of the sciences which study it"; and he produces persuasive textual evidence to show that this is so.[5] Andrew Arato and Paul Breines agree, writing against Jones that "the argument that [Lukács] meant to do away with the positive results of modern science . . . is groundless" and adding that in any case "it would be a mistake . . . to seek a fully developed critique of modern science . . . in *History and Class Consciousness.*"[6]

Lukács himself is not much help. In his self-critical 1967 introduction to *History and Class Consciousness*, he complains that the book's position implies "the disappearance of the ontological objectivity of nature."[7] But he also agrees with Schmidt that the book is marked by a desire to restrict Marxism's applicability to the social realm and "repudiate it as a theory of nature," yet unlike Schmidt he sees this as a failing that "strike[s] at the very roots of Marxian ontology," not as something to be praised.[8] His youthful mistake, Lukács famously writes, was to confuse objectification with alienation, resulting in a fundamental theoretical antipathy toward the objective as such. Colletti, Arato, Schmidt, and many others agree.[9] But Feenberg denies that Lukács makes this identification;[10] and Marković (who was a student of Lukács) concurs, adding that "it is a sad task to have to defend this extraordinary book, one of the most original philosophical works in this century, from its own author."[11]

What's a commentator to do, when those who precede him seem unable to agree (and seem indeed to disagree so radically) not merely about whether an author's theses are true but even what precisely those theses are, and when they are even prepared to reject the author's own self-criticism (not the only one Lukács ever performed, of course . . .) as based on a misreading? Does Lukács have a theory of nature or natural science at all? Is he a romantic critic of science or does he ignore it? Does he restrict his theory to human history and society and deny it any relevance to nature, or does his theory itself depend on "dissolving" nature *into* the social? Does he identify objectification with alienation or not? What is going on here?

In this chapter and the next I want not only to disentangle the various threads associated with "the problem of nature in Lukács," but also to examine why they got tangled in the first place. The truth is, I will argue, that Lukács's position is marked from the start by a series of deep ambivalences about the status of nature and natural science, and it is these that have led to such confusion among his critics as to what he really believes. Further, it is these ambivalences, as much as the particular theses he defends, that Lukács bequeaths as a difficult and ambiguous inheritance to the Western Marxist tradition he inaugurates. We will see the later career of this inheritance in the chapters that follow.

2. MARXISM AND THE DIALECTICS OF NATURE

It is of the first importance to realize that the method is limited here to the realms of history and society. The misunderstandings that arise from Engels' account of dialectics can in the main be put down to the fact that Engels—following Hegel's mistaken lead—extended the method to apply also to knowledge of nature. However, the crucial determinants of dialectics—the interaction of subject and object, the unity of theory and practice, the historical changes in the reality underlying the categories as the root cause of changes in thought, etc.—are absent from our knowledge of nature.[12]

With this apparently simple remark (deceptively placed in a footnote) Lukács founds Western Marxism. Despite the attempts at camouflage—the footnote is prefaced in the text by not one but two comforting quotations from Marx and Engels both, and appears in the middle of an essay supposedly calling for a return to "orthodox Marxism" and a rejection of revisionism—the radical theoretical implications are unmistakable. Here, in the first essay of *History and Class Consciousness*, Lukács announces the defiant repudiation of what were until then central tenets of Marxist philosophical orthodoxy—Engels's view that Marxism is a science of society on the model of the successful natural sciences and his further claim that, as such, Marx's "dialectics of history" is grounded on a more general "dialectics of nature" identified ultimately with the most advanced discoveries of those sciences. Lukács's critical point is not merely to demand a new ontological modesty in Marxist theory, as the reference to "limiting" might suggest, but rather radically to transform its view of method, questioning Engels's account of what is meant by "dialectics" and in particular renouncing the latter's identification of Marxist method with that of the natural sciences.

There are two noteworthy aspects to Lukács's rejection of the "dialectics of nature," one having to do with nature, the other having to do with dialectics. On the one hand, Engels's claim that Marxist method—the method of materialist dialectics—is applicable universally, and that indeed Marx's accounts of history and society are merely part of a broader dialectical view of the world as a whole that includes the world of nature, is here peremptorily denied.[13] Marxism is a social theory, Lukács is asserting, and as such is methodologically *sui generis*; it neither offers a method for the investigation of nature nor does it borrow one from that investigation.

On the other hand, Lukács here at the same time is rejecting Engels's account of what the dialectical method *is*. For the "crucial determinants" he mentions are not the ones emphasized by Engels in the latter's accounts of dialectics (e.g., in *Anti-Dühring* and the *Dialectics of Nature*). Lukács makes this clearer elsewhere in the essay. Although Engels emphasizes the role of "interaction" instead of one-way causality as pivotal to dialectics, Lukács writes, "he does not even mention the most vital interaction, namely the *dialectical relation between subject and object in the historical process*."[14] We might say that Engels's conception of dialectics is essentially *dynamic*, emphasizing motion, the fluidity and interconnection of objects, and the dissolution of the world of static things into one of processes. But all this takes place, so to speak, on the side of the object; the subject investigating the world—the scientist or social theorist—is concerned simply with describing it as it is, "*ohne fremde Zutat*," as Engels says.[15] Indeed, for Engels, just such a pure, objective description of nature leads to the discovery of its dialectical character; natural science in this sense is for him the proof of dialectics, but is not itself understood dialectically. Against this Lukács is calling for a return to the root Hegelian sense of dialectics as *epistemological*, emphasizing the interconnection between subject and object in the process of knowledge. On this view, knowledge is fundamentally active, which means that knowledge and that which is known are correlative from the very start. The "fluidity" and "interrelation" between objects Engels speaks of are only consequences of this, the primary dialectical relationship. Such a view clearly puts into question the very idea that knowledge ought to, or could, aim at the kind of pure description of an external state of affairs that Engels's view of natural science seems to take for granted.[16]

Thus although both Engels and Lukács distinguish "dialectical" from "metaphysical" modes of thought, they differ on how to draw the distinction. For Lukács the "bourgeois worldview" involves the taking up of a "contemplative attitude" by the subject toward the world with which it is confronted, an attitude whereby that world is viewed as separate from the subject and knowledge is seen as a passive reflection in the subject's mind of what is "out there" independent of it.[17] But this, Lukács believes, is just the attitude taken up by natural science. Thus the sign conferred upon natural science is reversed: whereas Engels saw it as providing a methodological model to be emulated by Marxist social theory, Lukács now sees it as methodologically associated at its core with bourgeois ideology and hence as subject to critique. Here nineteenth-century Marxism's essentially Enlightenment view of natural science as offering a paradigm for a liberating knowledge that might help overcome oppression is replaced by a new suspicion of natural science as in itself oppressive, a suspicion that will henceforth characterize Western Marxist discussions of science.

"There is something highly problematic in the fact that capitalist society is predisposed to harmonise with scientific method," Lukács writes in *History and Class Consciousness*, and the distrust this predisposition generates is a central theme of the work.[18] He sees a set of philosophical consequences in Marx's account of the fetishism of commodities whose implications Engels had missed. Under capitalism, Marx had claimed, human relations and human activities congeal into the form of things; the model, of course, is the way in which the exercise of human labor power to produce a commodity takes the form of an apparently objective property of the commodity produced, its exchange value. For Lukács this process of reification (*Verdinglichung*) suggested more generally a basic propensity for the institutions and policies of the capitalist social order to appear as eternal and unalterable givens, in which their source in human interaction is systematically hidden: they appear thinglike. But to say this is to say that they appear *like nature*—like a kind of "second nature," in the famous phrase, not in the Hegelian sense of a *sittliche* realm of Objective Spirit in which humans can feel at home but rather in the sense of a false consciousness in which the human origin of the human world has been forgotten.[19]

If this is so, it begins to become clear what is "problematic" about natural science. For the appearance of society as "second nature," Lukács argues, encourages the illusion that the way we achieve knowledge of society is the same as the way we achieve knowledge of things. This is why Engels's dream of Marxism as part of a more universal dialectical science based on a unity of method with the sciences of nature is, in Lukács's view, an ideological mistake. Contra Engels, Lukács wants to insist on the essential *difference* between radical social theory and natural science: they are different sorts of projects, employing different methodologies and concerned with different kinds of objects. And the failure to recognize this difference is not merely an epistemological error, but one with an ideological import, reflecting (and helping to perpetuate) the reification that forms the dominant fact of contemporary society.

But here an ambiguity starts to emerge. The argument about reification just outlined entails that the attempt to employ the methods of natural science to investigate "second nature"—that is, the realm of the social—is illicit and ideological. But what about the employment of these methods in the investigation of *first* nature? The quotation with which this section began asserted that "crucial determinants" of dialectics were missing from knowledge of nature; this seems to suggest that the critique of science and its epistemological presuppositions simply does not apply there. The methods of natural science extolled by Engels are inapplicable to "second nature" because those methods ignore the dialectical interplay between subject and object central to an understanding of historical and social processes, and hence they perpetuate the reified misunderstanding of such processes as things. But the things of first nature *are* things (aren't they?), and so for the examination of such a realm a natural science ignorant of dialectics is apparently unproblematic. Lukács's position combines something like a neo-Kantian dualism distinguishing *Natur-* from *Geisteswissenschaften* with a distinctively Marxist critique of reification and its ideology. "When natural science's ideal of knowledge is applied to nature," he writes, "it simply furthers the progress of science. But when it is applied to society it turns out to be an ideological weapon of the bourgeoisie."[20]

Yet there is something disingenuous about this. It seems to assert a kind of ideological neutrality to the methods of natural science when applied to their own proper realm—that of nature—while reserving its criticism for the misapplication of these methods to the realm of the social; we might call it the *misapplication thesis*. But *that* those methods are so easily misapplied and *that* they are "predisposed to harmonize" so well with the requirements of a reified society suggests that their "problematic" character might arise at a different level. We have already seen Lukács associate the methods of natural science with a nondialectical "metaphysical" standpoint, presupposing as they do a set of epistemological assumptions where knowledge ("science") appears as the pure and disinterested apprehension of external objects taken as independent of the knowing subject. It is these very assumptions and not simply their "misapplication" that Lukács criticizes as "problematic": might the methods of natural science *themselves* reflect the structures of a capitalist society in which the contribution of knowing and acting subjects to producing the objects they confront is systematically obscured?

Lukács, that is, wants to reverse the sign that traditional Marxism gave to natural science, now turning it into an object of critique, but his strategy for doing so takes the paradoxical form of splitting natural science off from the social and banishing it from any role in Marxist theory at all. Whether one emphasizes the desire to criticize natural science or the attempt to split it off determines which view of Lukács one takes—Lukács as radical "neo-romantic" critic of science or Lukács as modest limiter of Marxism's ontological pretensions. But this indicates the problem: Lukács's paradoxical strategy does not really resolve the question of the status of natural science so much as it drives it underground. The tensions and contradictions in the position are built in from the very beginning—indeed, in the very footnote I began by quoting.

For the methodological dualism Lukács asserts in *History and Class Consciousness* is highly questionable given his own assumptions. It seems to require for its own plausibility something like a fundamental *ontological* dualism as well, between the realm of nature and the realm of society.[21] This seems to run directly counter to Marxist "materialist" assertions about the continuity between nature and the human, and to reinstitute the very centrality of the category of *Geist* in social theory that Marx and Engels had so decisively rejected (a rejection Lukács shows no sign of finding questionable). But the dualism fits uneasily with Marxist "materialism" in quite another sense as well. For if "ideas" reflect "material conditions," and if "in every society the ruling ideas are the ideas of the ruling class," then it is not clear how natural science could in any case escape the charge of being part of the ideological superstructure even as an account of nature. In a book so centrally dedicated to criticizing the worldview of contemporary society, how could natural science, so closely tied to that worldview, be immune from critique?

Lukács recognizes this set of problems, although perhaps only obscurely, and they account for a strong underground *countertendency* in *History and Class Consciousness*, in which the misapplication thesis is de-emphasized and the suggestion arises that contemporary natural science, too, even in its "own" sphere, must be seen as part of the ideological superstructure of a society based on reification. Knowledge of nature itself is a social phenomenon, after all: why then should the "crucial determinants of dialectics" be missing there, as the footnote I began this section by quoting claims? Andrew Feenberg has remarked on a passage at the very end of the essay on reification that indeed seems to offer a significant modification of that claim, where Lukács writes that

> the dialectics of nature can never become anything more exalted than a dialectics of movement witnessed by the detached observer, as the subject cannot be integrated into the dialectical process, at least not at the stage reached hitherto. . . . From this we deduce the necessity of separating the merely objective dialectics of nature from those of society. For in the dialectics of society the subject is included in the reciprocal relation in which theory and practice become dialectical with reference to one another. (It goes without saying that the growth of *knowledge* about nature is a social phenomenon and therefore to be included in the second dialectical type.)[22]

This differs from the footnote in "What Is Orthodox Marxism?" first in the concession that there might be a dialectics of nature after all (albeit of a different form than that studied by Marxist social theory), but second and more important in the explicit appropriation of natural science (as *knowledge* about nature) to the dialectics of the social, and hence presumably also to the theory of reification. These two points are in some tension, however: if our knowledge of nature involves the second or social dialectic, it is not clear how the "merely objective" dialectics in nature could themselves ever come to be known. At least Engels had grounded his dialectics of nature on the results of empirical research; by drawing the dualist line in this new way—so that instead of separating social theory from natural science it now separates the latter from objective nature itself—Lukács leaves the assertion that nature is dialectical, and in a different way from the social, entirely without any foundation at all. Indeed, it is not evident how this new dualism could possibly be tenable—and in this context the obscure (and unexplained) hint that a "social" dialectics of nature is impossible only "at the stage reached hitherto" perhaps represents an interesting irruption of some other possibility into the text.

Lukács is drawn, I am arguing, more or less despite his explicit intention, to the claim that natural science's methods, even as applied in their "own" realm, have to be seen as social and ideological, and hence as subject to a critique that goes beyond the misapplication thesis. It is this secret telos to his position that accounts for the view of him as romantic critic of science (although Feenberg is nonetheless quite right to point out that Lukács never makes any such *explicit* claim). It also helps account for the widespread view of him as offering an idealist account of nature. "Nature is a social category," Lukács famously writes (forgetting his own stricture against offering a Marxist account of this "nondialectical" sphere); "whatever is held to be natural [*als Natur gilt*] at any given stage of social development, however this nature is related to man and whatever form his involvement with it takes, i.e., nature's form, its content, its range and its objectivity are all socially conditioned."[23] Here "nature" and "knowledge of nature" both are entirely relativized to the social, in complete disregard of the dualism supposedly instituted both by the misapplication thesis and by the rejection of Engels's dialectics of nature.[24] A very different thesis is now hinted at—and it too will shadow Western Marxism over the decades to come: that contemporary natural science is only *one* possible approach to nature, an ideological one corresponding to a reified society, and that a "new society" in which reification is abolished will possess a "new science" whose methods will differ radically from those of the science we know today.[25]

Lukács's position, I am claiming, is thus shot through with contradictory impulses, symbolized (but also heightened) by the paradoxical attempt to criticize natural science by expelling it from Marxism. They take clearest shape in the tension I have begun to trace between the methodological dualism Lukács explicitly asserts and the argument's secret telos in the claim that natural science is social, ideological, and subject to critique even in its "own" realm. It is this tension that is responsible for the "problem of nature in Lukács." But to see how this is so, we need to look further into the details of Lukács's account.

3. REIFICATION AND SELF-RECOGNITION

History and Class Consciousness is above all a work of epistemology. Lukács's audacious claim is that the social phenomenon of reification has an *epistemological* meaning: that Marx's account of commodities holds the key to the solution not only of practical and social problems, but of philosophical ones as well.[26] Part of Lukács's importance as a Marxist theorist is the way he radicalizes Marx's thesis about the connections between modes of thought and material life, going far beyond the crude functionalism that has typically characterized Marxist discussions of the relations between "base" and "superstructure." His concern is not to show the ideological function of particular (e.g.) religious or political beliefs, but rather to examine the connections between the deepest categories of contemporary thought and the social practices (and social contradictions) within which that thought arises.

The argument has several steps. The first we have already seen: it is the identification of commodity fetishism, or in its broader form reification, as the central structural fact of contemporary society.[27] The next step, in accordance both with the Marxist conception of "superstructure" and with Lukács's own methodological insistence on the category of totality, is to examine a number of contemporary social institutions and phenomena to show the ways in which reification works itself out all across the social field. Lukács, with much debt to Weber, here uncovers a set of striking *structural homologies* among a remarkably diverse group of areas—including the capitalist state, the legal system, journalism, economics, management techniques, factory organization, bureaucracy, and so forth. His claim is that these all share a deep structure, that this deep structure is simply that of the "bourgeois worldview" (and the bourgeois world) itself, and that ultimately its roots lie in the phenomenon of reification.

He names this worldview the *contemplative attitude* and subjects it to a detailed analysis and critique. For the contemplative attitude, the world that surrounds us is something independent of us, given, and immutable; we observe it but cannot change it. The investigator of this world and the actor in it alike relate to it as to something separate from them; knowledge is conceived of as the essentially passive receiving of information from a world external to the observer. The world is viewed as *objective*, as *subject to formal laws*, as *reducible by analysis*, and as *unchanging*. *Objective* means separate from the subject; we come to know the world by observing it "just as it presents itself" and taking care not to impose upon it our own "subjective" hopes and expectations (which are called "biases"). *Subject to formal laws* means (among other things) regular, general, predictable; individuals (the "content" that the formal laws are "about") appear as bearers of abstract properties that allow us to determine which laws apply and to predict, algorithmically, future effects. *Reducible by analysis* means subject to reductionistic explanation; complex wholes are to be understood by breaking them into the smaller parts of which they are made. *Unchanging* means essentially ahistorical: because the world external to us is separate from us and subject to universal formal laws, the only changes it can undergo are predictable and law-governed ones. The objects themselves may change, and thus have a "history" in a minimal sense (like the history of the solar system, say), but the laws they follow are eternal, and so no *fundamental* change is possible.

All this produces a deep division between the subject and the object of knowledge, recapitulated at the level of both theory and practice. To know the world is to be able to describe its laws through analysis without the imposition of the subjective; to act in it successfully is to manipulate those laws and the objects they govern in order to achieve one's goals. Such manipulation—which Weber had called *purposive-rational action*—treats the laws and objects as given and unchangeable, and as independent of the subjective (the "goals"); the ought and the is, what one wants and how one gets it, are kept entirely distinct.

The contemplative attitude is to be met with, Lukács believes, in a wide set of phenomena in the contemporary world—from the cult of "objectivity" in journalism to the bureaucracy of the modern social welfare state to electoral systems in which voters dutifully choose from among indistinguishable candidates without ever asking why these are the only alternatives they are offered. Formalism, passivity, a taking for granted of what is as what must be: they are endemic at all levels of our social world and our social discourse, and according to Lukács are ultimately the consequences of a contemporary social structure founded on a mode of production characterized by reification.

In each realm, he furthermore argues, the contemplative attitude finds itself faced by basic *antinomies*, problems of both a theoretical and practical nature that it cannot resolve. Objectivism finds itself unable to excise all traces of the "subjective" from its knowledge; formalism is stymied by an inability to grasp the real objects of the system in their specificity and concreteness; analysis cannot cope with holistic and emergent properties of systems; the search for eternal laws and predictable procedures is incapable of comprehending historical change as such. Is/ought, form/content, whole/parts, historical change/eternal verities—"bourgeois thought" is characterized throughout by a set of antithetical oppositions it does not know how to integrate. The society whose guiding presuppositions derive from the contemplative worldview constantly confronts a set of problems it is incapable of resolving, including (to name just a few) bureaucratization, a conflict between formalism and compassion in the law, a populace increasingly cynical about electoral politics and politicians, and so on.

Lukács's important claim is that these difficulties at the level of real institutions are connected to a set of *theoretical* difficulties that can be demonstrated within the worldview itself. It is in this context that he launches, in the second section of the essay on reification, into his remarkable rereading of the history of modern philosophy. This is the next step in his argument: to show that the tradition of epistemological thought from Descartes through Hegel represents the working out, on a highly abstract level, of the contemplative attitude and its predicaments.[28] The central problem for this tradition, Lukács argues, has been to understand how the subject comes to know the object. The tradition thus begins with the assumption of a division between the two (announced explicitly in Descartes), and then sets itself the task of explaining how this division can be overcome. Knowledge is understood as requiring the possession of a correct model of the objective world in thought, one that "reflects" or "corresponds" to what is out there and from which all traces of the "merely subjective" have been eliminated. Assumed from the start, Lukács asserts, is thus precisely the standpoint of contemplation: the world is separate from the knower, and knowledge is a process by which information from the world is passively received by the subject. (If the subject *did* anything to it, the result could no longer be called a "reflection," but rather would be "distortion" or "bias.")

Yet a model of the world *in thought*, of course, is inevitably already "subjective"; the great problem for the modern epistemological position is to discover how to guarantee that the model the knower develops is the correct one—which would require, in turn, having some other prior knowledge of what the world is "really like." Struggling with this dilemma, which Lukács thinks is in fact insoluble as posed, forms the central drama of modern philosophy. Its consequence is a set of antinomies of exactly the sort the contemplative attitude always confronts, Lukács argues. The most fundamental form these antinomies take—the one to which he claims they can all be reduced—is the one that finds its sharpest expression in Kant: the problem of the *thing in itself.* That which knowledge was supposed to achieve—a grasp of the objective world as it is independent of the knowing subject—is exactly that which "critical" epistemology discovers it to be absolutely incapable of attaining.

Now this account of modern philosophy is not particularly original, having roots in Hegel and elsewhere. What makes Lukács's version of it interesting is his attempt to relate the history he recounts back to the phenomenon of reification, which is to say to what Marx called the fetishism of commodities, and thus to trace the source of the epistemological antinomies confronted by modern philosophy in the "practical" contradictions of bourgeois life. Lukács speaks of "the antinomies of bourgeois thought," a phrase designed to indicate the (shocking) conjunction of post-Kantian epistemology and Marxist social theory that marks the location of his work. Both at the level of theory and of practical life, he argues, contemplation finds itself setting up abstract systems that attempt to capture concrete reality but that fail entirely; modern epistemology's inability to grasp the thing in itself is thus structurally related to, say, modern bureaucracy's callousness toward the real individuals whom it is supposed to be assisting or the modern economy's inability to comprehend the phenomenon of the periodic crisis. And all of these, he suggests, find their ultimate origin in "the commodity form"—in the processes of reification that underlie capitalism whereby human social relations appear as independent and immutable Things.

But if the real contradictions of capitalist society are what underlie the ideal problems of the philosophers, then perhaps the *solutions* to the latter problems might arise in the practical political sphere as well—which means for Lukács in the revolutionary processes of a proletarian seizure of power. To suggest this is the next and perhaps the most original step in Lukács's argument, whereby he rereads the post-Kantian history of classical German philosophy in a Marxist light, using the crucial idea of *knowledge as active* as his guiding thread.

Kant's "Copernican Revolution" of course introduced the idea that the problem of knowledge can be solved only if the subject is seen not as passively receiving information from an external and independent source but as actively involved in the constitution of the world of experience. Contemplative epistemology cannot explain how we could know the world to be structured and causally coherent; Kant sees that the answer is to show that we ourselves *constitute* it as such (although he is none too clear on how this constitution takes place). But Kant's view remains antinomical, due to his insistence on distinguishing the world of experience from the noumenal one—we don't constitute the "real" world, it turns out, only the world "as it appears"; the result is a doctrine of things in themselves that Lukács takes as paradigmatic of the bourgeois antinomies.

Hegel radicalizes the view of knowledge as activity and as world-creating, first by rejecting the notion of noumena as incoherent: the world we know is the only one there is. But he radicalizes it in a more significant respect as well, for he sees that the assertion that the world of objects is not external to and separate from the subject has to be supplemented by an account of why it nonetheless *seems* to be separate—which is to say, in Lukács's terms, by an account of the origin of reification. Hegel confronts this question (which earlier idealist philosophers had hardly noticed) by offering an historical account, a "phenomenology of spirit." The "objective" world *is* indeed actively constituted or produced by the spirit that comes to know it, but that spirit does not at first recognize it as such; both phylogenetic and ontogenetic maturation must be understood as a process in which the subject comes to recognize itself in the world it confronts— comes to see, that is, that that world is and always was its own product. In coming to this recognition, though, the subject changes, and so too does its activity: which means so does the world as well. This complicates the epistemology, requiring now a distinction between "in itself" and "for itself." At *first* the world is the product of spirit but only implicitly so—and in this sense, because "unconscious spirit" is a contradiction, is also *not* (yet) really its product. To this kind of "immature" spirit the world appears as an alien and incomprehensible power, an independent Thing which the subject seems incapable of ever comprehending. It must learn, through a complex process of self-reflection, that the world is indeed its own product. But the process whereby it comes to this self-recognition has itself to be understood as an active one: it recognizes itself in the world because it *puts itself there*, thereby making explicitly and self-consciously true what was in fact the case, but only implicitly, all the time.

The resulting *dialectic of reification and self-recognition* is crucial to Lukács (as it was to the early Marx). What Lukács rejects is the mystification it undergoes in Hegel, whereby the subject of this process is identified as a *Weltgeist* acting behind the backs of human agents and ultimately finding its self-recognition somewhere other than in mundane secular history. Lukács insists rather that human beings themselves are the subjects of this process; they make the world through their concrete practices, and the story of their coming to self-recognition is simply human history. To say that the problems of epistemology can be solved only by seeing the subject's relation to the world as an active one means not that humans magically create the world out of their own heads, but rather that they literally produce the world they inhabit with their hands and muscles, through a set of socially organized practices, and must come to recognize this fact about themselves. Their failure to do so is the phenomenon of reification, of a world that they think is other than them but in fact is really their own doing.

Hegel's mystification is itself to be explained by the same dialectic, Lukács believes; Hegel goes as far as bourgeois (reified) thought is capable, which is to say as far as pure thought can go without itself becoming practical. His thought points toward *practice* as the solution to the epistemological antinomies, now identified as the "antinomies of bourgeois thought," but insofar as it is itself merely "thought" it can do no more than point. Thus Hegel is ensnared in a paradox: for him it is not practice but the *thought* of practice that appears as the solution, with the result being that it is only the thought of a solution that is presented. No real subject, only the abstract idea of one, appears as the creator of history.

This is "the greatness, the paradox and the tragedy of classical German philosophy"[29]: that it brings philosophy right up to its very end, and then points beyond it. For if the solution to the problems of philosophy lies in human practice and not in a thought independent of the world, this means that it lies outside of philosophy itself. The "antinomies of bourgeois thought," that is, cannot be resolved by yet another thought, in fact cannot be resolved theoretically at all: they can be resolved only by an *act* in which the self-recognition Hegel imagined only in theory actually takes place. And this act, for Lukács, is of course nothing other than the proletarian revolution, which now turns out astonishingly to have an epistemological significance.[30]

Thus Lukács's attempt to take seriously the consequences of classical German philosophy's move toward practice leads him to a reinterpretation of the history of that philosophy in which the concept of reification now plays a central role. Several times Lukács quotes a famous early letter of Marx to Ruge: "the world has long dreamed of possessing something of which it has only to be conscious in order to possess it in reality."[31] The world we inhabit, the social order we believe to be natural and eternal, and the institutions we never think to question are in fact the product of our own social actions: reification is when we fail to recognize this—most crucially in the commodity fetishism where our own products appear as independent objects imbued with objective exchange values—and revolution is the act of self-recognition in which it is overcome.

Thus Marxist social theory is Hegelian philosophy gone practical; but that means too that the "recognition" and the "we" just mentioned have themselves to be understood in a practical way, not theoretically. There must be a *real* subject (not some *Weltgeist*) that discovers itself to be the author through its *real* practices of the actual social world we inhabit. This subject, Lukács believes, Marx had shown to be the proletariat, whose surplus labor was the foundation, both physical and institutional, of the capitalist social order. And this subject's self-recognition must be an *act*, not just a piece of abstract knowledge—an act in which what had heretofore been only implicitly true, taking place behind the backs of and despite the needs of the real subjects, now becomes an explicit truth that they themselves consciously posit.

Thus there must be a real revolutionary transformation of society, in which proletarians take control for the first time of the conditions of their existence and engage in the activity of constituting the social world for the first time in a consciously planned and communal manner: this is the sense in which communism appears as the abolition of reification. And the implications of this act include epistemological ones, for only in such an act will the world cease to appear as something alien, as external and thinglike. Only then, Lukács thinks, will the "contemplative attitude" cease to seem a piece of common sense—and only then will the "antinomies of bourgeois thought" find, not their resolution, but their dissolution.[32]

4. THE PROBLEM RESTATED

What can we say, in the light of the epistemological position just outlined, about Lukács's attempt to distinguish on methodological grounds between natural science and social theory, and especially about what I have called the misapplication thesis? It should be clear, first of all, that in the context of this position natural science as Lukács understands it has to count as a case of "contemplation" and that indeed in a way it is the paradigm case. It construes the world as objective and distinct from the subject; it understands knowledge as a description of objective reality from which all "subjective elements" have been expelled; it sees its goal as the discovery of formal laws that remain constant over time and model the world by breaking it into basic analytical elements.[33] Even scientific experimentation, which Engels had extolled as the "proof" of the correctness of our views of the world and thus as the decisive response to Kantian scepticism, is explicitly described by Lukács as contemplative: "Scientific experiment is contemplation at its purest. The experimenter creates an artificial, abstract milieu in order to be able to *observe* undisturbed the untrammelled workings of the laws under examination, eliminating all irrational factors both of the subject and the object. He strives as far as possible to reduce the material substratum of his observation to the purely rational 'product,' the 'intelligible matter' of mathematics."[34]

As we have already seen, this is why Lukács resolutely rejects Engels's attempts to take natural science as the exemplary method for social theory. If the socialist revolution represents the overcoming of reification, and hence also the overcoming of the contemplative worldview, then it cannot take its theoretical lead from a method in which this worldview is assumed from the start. But this explains only why Lukács asserts that when natural science's method "is applied to society it turns out to be an ideological weapon of the bourgeoisie"; what about the other side of the misapplication thesis—that when applied to nature it is not such a weapon but rather "simply furthers the progress of science"? Is this distinction tenable?

I think it is not, for reasons that by now should be clear: the broad epistemological character of the critique of contemplative thought that Lukács offers prevents it from being limited to the social realm, for it takes place at such a high level of generality as to be logically prior to any distinction between the natural and the social. It is important not to read Lukács through spectacles of the second half of the century: his argument for the inapplicability of natural science's method to social material is *not* the sort of argument one finds in Winch or Gadamer or Taylor or other Wittgensteinian or neo-Diltheyan thinkers.[35] *Those* arguments depend on showing there to be specific characteristics of the object field confronted by the *Geisteswissenschaften*—their meaningful character, perhaps, or their connection to rule following, or the curious fact that the very scientific theorizing that takes social action as its object is itself a case of social action—that render natural science's method inappropriate in that field. But Lukács's argument is Hegelian, not hermeneutic, which is to say it does not begin with the (phenomenologically grounded) assertion of an ineradicable distinction between two domains, but rather with a fundamental meditation on epistemology, deriving whatever distinctions it finds in the world only out of that meditation. This is why Colletti and Jones are wrong to identify Lukács's position simply with romantic or neo-Kantian ones that depend on assertions about the "organic" or the "irrational" or "life" as characteristics of the world which "analytic" techniques of natural science will inevitably fail to capture.[36]

For Lukács it is not some particular characteristic of the sphere of the social that explains why the methods of natural science cannot be used to come to know it—after all, that particular characteristic would have first itself to be *known* beforehand (and by what method?) for the argument to be successful. Indeed, it follows from his view that whatever is taken as constitutive of the specifically human realm will always be historically variable and that any account of this realm that fails to recognize the historical processes underlying that variation would itself be a case of reified thought. Instead any discussion of the limits of natural science's methods would have to derive from an epistemological examination of those methods themselves, in something like an immanent critique, without (that is) any presuppositions about the kinds of objects they might be used to investigate.

Lukács's Hegelian strategy is thus to engage in an examination not of the various realms to which knowledge will be "applied" but rather of knowledge itself—an examination, that is, of the conditions for the possibility of there *being* a realm of objects to investigate at all. Only this can provide an answer to fundamental questions of method. This examination, as we have seen, claims to discover a deep incoherence within contemplative epistemology, one that leads to the "antinomies of bourgeois thought." These antinomies derive from the mistaken way in which contemplation understands knowledge—from its failure, that is, to see its own knowing as active and as changing the object. But they then derive from the contemplative epistemological standpoint itself, not from some particular characteristic of the objects to which it is applied, which means in turn that natural science *even in its "own" realm* must be subject to the same critique. And by the same token, if a "dialectical" method that recognizes the contribution of the subject to the object known is appropriate for knowledge of the social realm, it must be equally appropriate to the realm of the "natural."

Here then is the deep tension in Lukács's position I am indicating: that the specifically epistemological argument he offers simply *contradicts* the methodological dualism he explicitly asserts. Indeed any such dualism seems itself to betray symptoms of just the sort of "reified thought" Lukács wants to oppose. For one thing, it gives up the intention to totality that Lukács believes to be crucial.[37] It is characteristic of contemplative theory, Lukács claims, to break up into "partial systems" or *Teilsysteme*—into formalisms that deal only with particular limited fields, analyses that stop only at a certain level, predictions that make liberal use of ceteris paribus clauses. Although these are always presented as provisional and temporary limitations to be overcome when the system is complete, in fact this is a necessary characteristic of contemplative thought, Lukács argues, which is constantly running up against a barrier of irrationality: the impossibility of entirely banning the subjective from knowledge, of developing a formal system to deal with every eventuality, of deducing every aspect of a whole from an exhaustive account of its parts, of explaining the real unpredictabilities of historical change.

Despite their totalizing intentions, therefore, contemplative systems of knowledge are always more modest in practice, demurely claiming validity only in some limited sphere or other and unable to answer questions about items external to this sphere or about their own connection with other "neighboring" systems dealing with different ones.[38] But this critique would seem to make us suspicious about Lukács's own "modesty" in limiting his theory to the sphere of the social, not to speak of his failure to offer any mediating account of how a method like that of natural science, so useful to "the progress of science" in one sphere, could come to be such a dangerous "ideological weapon" in the sphere next door.

Second, it would be astonishing for natural science to be excluded from Lukács's critique given the dominant role played in that critique by the problem of the thing in itself—a problem raised in Kant's work (as Lukács obviously knew) precisely in the context of a discussion of the epistemological foundations of *natural science*. The obstacle thus produced for Lukács's dualism is so glaring as to suggest that we are dealing here less with a mere "difficulty" or oversight than with a conscious or unconscious occlusion of the real tendency of the argument. Indeed, if Lukács's entire critique of bourgeois thought as inevitably foundering on the problem of the thing in itself and his apotheosis of proletarian revolution as offering the resolution of this problem turn out to be relevant only to social theory and have nothing to say about nature, the argument begins to take on a kind of comic aspect: he has labored long and hard and brought forth a mouse. It is not the noumenal character of *social* reality that worries Kant, after all; and so if despite all the bluster about practice solving the dilemmas of bourgeois philosophy it turns out that this practice has no relevance to the objects of nature, then Lukács leaves the classical problem of the thing in itself just where he found it—unsolved.[39]

Indeed, if nature is excluded from the account, Lukács seems to fall prey to just the criticisms he offers of Kant's own dualistic move to "practice" in the second *Critique*. By positing real practice only in the inward realm of morality, so that the "activity" in which subject and object coincide is identified with the *ethical* act, Kant explicitly leaves nature outside the practical realm and treats it as subject only to the workings of objective and determinate laws. "Activity" is thereby limited to some mysterious inner noumenal sphere, Lukács argues, and the world of nature appears as even more alien to the moral subject than to the theoretical one. The effect, though, is that now every aspect of the *real* "phenomenal" subject (as itself a natural being), including its own psychology, its moral sensibility, and even its motives for acting ethically, appear as external facts given independently of the moral domain and hence under the sway of the "inexorable necessity" of the laws of nature. The consequence, he writes, is that "freedom and the autonomy that is supposed to result from the discovery of the ethical world are reduced to a mere *point of view from which to judge* internal events." Hence "the hiatus between appearance and essence . . . is not bridged"; instead (and worse) the dualism that was supposed to be overcome by the appeal to practice is now rather introduced directly into the subject itself, divided now between its own empirical psychology and some mysterious moral soul. No real ethics can be derived from such an account except one that is "purely formal and lacking in content," Lukács concludes (following Hegel); the result is the kind of impotent assertion of an abstract and formal *Sollen* against an implacable and unyielding *Sein* characteristic of all utopianism.[40]

Yet this seems exactly the fate that befalls Lukács's own appeal to practice if it is banned from nature. For the proletarian subject he calls to action is after all fundamentally tied to nature, precisely by being tied to work. Lukács seems crucially vague on the connection between the "practice" he posits as central to the proletariat's revolutionary overcoming of contemplation and the ordinary work—which is to say, the physical labor on nature—proletarians actually perform. His materialist critique of Hegel, demanding a conception of real practice instead of the mysterious activity of a disembodied *Geist*, would seem to demand a role for nature and natural processes within the dialectical epistemology, and yet it is just that role that appears to be missing. The danger is clear: by leaving the realm of nature untouched by the critique, Lukács threatens to leave real life, and real practice, untouched as well.[41] The result here as in Kant is to introduce the dualism into the subject itself, now split between noumenal and empirical self—a split that I would argue reappears in *History and Class Consciousness* in a more sinister form, precisely as the famous distinction between empirical and "imputed" class consciousness, and so between the proletariat and the Party.[42]

I began by quoting Schmidt's two remarks about Lukács—criticizing him on the one hand for dissolving nature into the social but praising him on the other for limiting his theory's applicability to the "socio-historical"—and asking how Lukács could consistently do both things at once. I have now argued in more detail that he could not, because his epistemological argument and in particular his critique of contemplation take place *prior* to the drawing of a distinction between the social and the natural, in such a way as to vitiate the possibility of the kind of methodological dualism required by the misapplication thesis. In this sense Colletti and Jones are surely warranted in seeing Lukács's argument as tending toward a critique of natural science as such. Feenberg and Arato's defense that the misapplication thesis is explicitly asserted in order to block such a critique, although doubtless textually justified, remains disingenuous, depending as it does on what Feenberg calls a "saving inconsistency"[43] in the position; and indeed each admits that the misapplication thesis is inconsistent with certain elements of the epistemology.[44] This wins the textual battle but loses the philosophical war: one defends against the charge of idealism by copping a plea to a charge of inconsistency. It's not clear, though, that that's a lesser charge.

What Colletti and Jones and Feenberg and Arato all seem to agree on (and Lukács the self-critic of 1967 does, too) is that the dissolution of the boundary between the natural and the social, which is seen to follow if the critique of contemplation is applied to natural science, would represent a reductio ad absurdum fatal to Lukács's epistemology. I want rather to argue quite the contrary, that what would be fatal would be to try to graft a dualism onto the epistemology that the latter rather simply contradicts, and that Lukács's interest as a thinker lies in just the position denying the independence of nature from the social that Feenberg calls "rigorously consistent and obviously absurd."[45] I want, that is, to accept that the most coherent reading of Lukács's epistemology indeed entails a critique of natural science, and that this does indeed render problematic the attempt to draw a boundary between natural science and social theory or for that matter between nature and the social. But I want to deny that this commits him to a romanticism or even an "idealism" of the sort that would render his position unacceptable. The distinction I have drawn above between the Hegelian and the neo-Kantian versions of the argument against natural science is crucial here.[46] Lukács's critique of science (a critique that I think is justified) is not that it fails to grasp some aspect of the external world, but rather some aspect of *itself*—namely, the fact that it is itself a human practice. This is not, I think, idealism, at least in any ordinary sense; and it is certainly not romanticism or vitalism. But to understand this further we need to examine in more detail the role of "nature" in the critique of reification.

CHAPTER 2

Nature and Reification

1. THE CRITIQUE OF NATURE

I have been arguing that Lukács's attempt to remove any analysis of nature or of natural science from his epistemological critique of "contemplation" is a failure, because strong elements in that critique tend to render incoherent the methodological dualism such an attempt requires. The misapplication thesis tries to interpret the category of "nature" as an ideologically neutral one, objecting only to its illegitimate transfer into the social realm ("second nature"). My claim is that given Lukács's epistemological position "nature" cannot be a neutral term, but rather necessarily appears in a negative light. Let me try to explain this further.

J. M. Bernstein, in his highly interesting article "Lukács' Wake: Praxis, Presence, and Metaphysics,"[1] reads Lukács as a kind of proto-deconstructionist with strong affinities to Derrida, thus giving Lucien Goldmann's well-known thesis of a secret connection between Lukács and Heidegger a further twist. "Reification," Bernstein writes, "is a process whereby the world as world comes to appear as present-to-hand";[2] the "things" that appear in place of social relations under the sway of reification are like the *vorhandene* objects that Heidegger criticizes the tradition of metaphysics for taking as ontologically primary. For Lukács and Heidegger both, the appearance of the world as consisting of independent objects known by passive observation obscures the fact that such objects are possible only on the basis of a background of practical engagement by humans in a world of what Heidegger calls the *Zuhanden*, "ready-to-hand" objects whose significance and ontological status arise out of that engagement itself.

The suggestion is a fruitful one, although there are clear disanalogies between the positions, too. It may indeed not be entirely misleading to see Lukács as engaged in a kind of deconstruction, attempting through his critique of reification to dissolve the apparent simplicity and immediacy of the "things" that surround us into the complex human practices that in fact make that (illusory) simplicity possible. The point is to show that that which appears as immediately given is actually the product of a hidden and intricate process of construction and hence of mediation. But if it is a deconstruction it is a Hegelian one, which gives it a historicity and a directionality Derridean deconstructions sometimes lack—involving on the one hand (as we have seen already) an account of false consciousness (and hence also of the genesis of reification in real social processes), and on the other a quasi-ethical imperative whereby views of the world that have *seen through* the social processes of construction are to be preferred to those that have not yet done so.

Thus Lukács views the Marxist project as one whose goal is the breaking down of all false immediacies, revealing them to be the product of hidden constructions or mediations and bringing such mediations to the surface. But the point of dissolving false immediacies is not somehow to get to some deeper level of *true* ones—to some ultimately given reality on the basis of which all these constructions take place. That's the traditional metaphysical move that Lukács (like Heidegger and like Derrida) wants to renounce. It ends antinomically—either in a dogmatism that arbitrarily asserts that a particular apparent immediacy is indeed the "real" one (and thus cuts off further analysis that might show this immediacy, too, to be the product of a construction) or else in a Kantian scepticism that despairs of our ability ever to know the immediate, "noumenal," foundation of our mediating activities (but just as arbitrarily asserts that one exists).[3] Lukács's more radical move, which does bear similarities to Derridean ones, is to criticize the category of immediacy as such, to reject (that is) the idea that mediations must always be mediations *of* some pre-existing immediacy, and to insist instead that every supposed immediacy can be shown to be the result of previous constructions, thus dynamizing and dissolving all static givens into the social processes that make them possible. ("Reality is not," Lukács writes; "it becomes."[4])

The Hegelian twist, though, is to perform this deconstruction not in the name of irony but rather of a process of mediation that *knows itself as such*—in the name, that is, of self-recognition.[5] Processes of construction appear as external "things" (i.e., are reified) precisely to the extent that those who engage in them do not recognize them *as their own practices*. To come to this recognition, which however cannot be merely a theoretical one but rather must itself be a matter of a new kind of practice, is to be liberated from the oppressive power of social processes congealed into things, from what Marx called *alienation*. This removes the danger of relativism that seems to inhere in the deconstructive discovery that an ultimate immediacy underlying our acts of mediation does not exist. "Truth" does not consist now in some correspondence between the mediated objects we have to do with and an ultimate reality underlying them, nor in our principled (but doomed) refusal to engage in mediations; rather, it consists in our acknowledging to ourselves what it is we are doing—producing our reality through mediations, which is to say, through our practices—and in doing so thereby transforming those practices so that we no longer engage in them blindly. This is the directionality mentioned previously: Lukács's argument leads, as already noted, to the call for a practical act of self-recognition, the revolutionary act that produces a social order in which humans' own responsibility for the world they inhabit has become a matter of self-conscious choice.[6]

Thus Lukács's critique of reification has its core in a critique of immediacy. But a critique of immediacy cannot avoid a critique of nature. For nature is the final given to which one tries to appeal when attempting to avoid the universality of the deconstructive moves; "the natural" is exactly that which appears most immediate, most directly given, most independent of and prior to any social practices of construction. It was on nature that traditional Marxism wanted to ground its social theory: this is what was meant by "materialism," and was the motivation for Engels's claims for a dialectics of nature. But Lukács rejects these very claims and precisely because of their basis in immediacy: by appealing to "scientifically established" facts about nature prior to any epistemological investigation of the status of such facts or the sciences that claim to discover them, Engels misses the relation between subject and object, which is to say the crucial dialectical-deconstructive moment of asking about the practices of mediation through which a subject constitutes a field of objects as something to be known at all. Lukács does not want to repeat this mistake: his theory will be based not on nature but on self-recognition.

But then "nature" will inevitably have a negative sign for him and will stand exactly for those false immediacies that are to be deconstructed, resolved into their human origins. Lukács attempts to get around the implications of this, as we have seen, by attempting to banish "first" nature from the theory, but as we have also seen that will not work—nature is not so easily excluded. The distinction between the social and the natural on which Lukács's methodological dualism rests simply reproduces the distinction between the mediated and the immediate that his critique is meant to overcome. This last dualism, too—between "society" and "nature"—must be deconstructed. *This* is what it means to say that "nature is a social category": that nature, too, "first" nature, is itself another false immediacy—or rather that there is no first nature, that all "nature" is second nature, that the givenness of the present-at-hand is always founded upon practices of creation and mediation.[7] I want to indicate four senses in which this is true.

1) The Lukácsian-Marxist radicalization of Hegel offers the key to the argument, suggesting that we look toward the real practical processes by which the environment around us is *constructed*, the processes through which our

own actions help produce and shape the world we inhabit. That world, the *Umwelt* that surrounds us, cannot be neatly divided into the "social" and the "natural"; we live in one world, not two. In particular, it does not consist of a "physical" realm on the one hand, investigable by science, and a "social system" on the other, the product of human practices. Rather the social system appears to humans within it in the form of physical things: the checkbooks, automobiles, voting booths, postage stamps, living rooms, clocks, and so on that make up the real environment of our daily lives and in which and through which the sociality of our existence is articulated. The "social realm" is not something mysterious and ethereal, separate from the world of objects: it exists *in and through* the objects that surround us. It is by means of those objects that our social practices are organized, and such practices take their meanings from those objects themselves.[8]

The objects are "social," then, but they are of course "natural," too—both in the sense that they are real, physical, concrete and in the sense that we find them familiar and obvious, that we cannot imagine a life without them (even though most or all of them actually do not exist in other social orders) and often do not recognize their role in defining and organizing our own practices. They are thus "reifications," objects that appear to be independent of us and whose social meaning is obscured by their very "naturalness." This is the *first* sense in which the natural and the social cannot coherently be distinguished, and in which nature has to be seen as a social category.

2) The social character of the objects that surround us is not simply a matter of their function in structuring and reproducing social practices and institutions, but also, and crucially, a matter of the practices that structure *them*. For each such object comes into existence as the result of real socially organized processes of labor: each is the product of a number of human beings working together on the basis of some plan, and in the context of another set of social practices and institutions (again mediated by objects) associated with factories, the economy, the "market," and so on. Marx said that the commodities that surround us are social hieroglyphics, and this I think is what he meant: that the *Umwelt* is almost always a built environment, built by humans through socially organized labor.[9] As I look about me there is no object in my environment (including the tree out the window that I watched being planted last month) that is not in this sense literally a social "construct." To choose a single object in my immediate *Umwelt*, like this wooden paperweight for instance, and to think of all the humans involved in producing it—not just those who labored on it directly, but those who built the tools that made their labor possible, those who transported the raw materials, not to speak of those who marketed it, made the financing possible, advertised and sold it (and recall that at every step of the way more tools were employed—lathes and photocopiers, trucks and computers, telephones and wastepaper baskets—which

themselves must be built, must be transported, must be sold) is to begin to recognize, in the image of human solidarity suddenly revealed by this geometrical series of acts of labor that must have already taken place simply to produce *this thing*, the depth of the sociality of the world of objects that surrounds us.[10]

3) But it is not only the urbanized world of "man-made" (and woman-made, too) objects that is produced by social processes of mediation. "Nature" in the sense of the "natural" world around us—the world of countryside, mountains, wilderness, the world that is "not yet" urbanized—is social, too, in yet a *third* sense. The extent of real "wilderness" is considerably less than one might guess: writers such as William Cronon, René Dubos, and J. Donald Hughes have pointed out the degree to which the "natural" landscapes of places like New England, France, Greece are the consequences of centuries of human habitation and transformation, so that much of what we take as their intrinsic characteristics are in fact the result of human action.[11] The Niagara Falls whose flow is regulated for the pleasure of tourists, the Mississippi whose course is controlled by the Army Corps of Engineers, the Yellowstone whose fires are extinguished or allowed to burn in accordance with current social fashions in thinking about nature: all of these bear traces of the very reification under discussion here, where what is in fact socially mediated appears as immediate, "real," "natural," independent of the human.[12] And even "true" wilderness remains so only by virtue of a complex set of social mediations: the acts required here are Acts of Congress, by which we socially decide to remove areas from the sphere of transformation, thus revealing the extent to which for us wilderness is now founded upon and carved out of the world of the social and not vice-versa.

Of course in a wider sense there "is" still nature as untouched by human action: the oceans, the atmosphere, the cosmos beyond, though in each case we are doing our best (which is to say often our worst) to "humanize" these too. Yet even to the extent these have not yet been transformed it would be incorrect to see them as a horizon of immediacy within which our social actions take place. For the ocean we view as a potential mineral resource or jump over in our transcontinental jets is not the ocean of the great days of the Cunard Line or of Columbus or Homer or the Polynesian travelers; and the stars we look at, with eyes transformed by moonwalks and exploding shuttles and talk of light years, black holes, big bangs, are both nearer and further, but in any case different, than those seen by Blake, by Kepler, by Copernicus, by Ptolemy. Nature never appears as it "is" but rather always as already the nature of a particular social order, in a particular context, subject to a particular set of mediations. And this applies to "our" nature too, the one revealed to us by our proud and impressive natural science; it even applies, although we sometimes forget that this is so, when we speak of a cosmos that "is" out there, stretching infinitely far beyond us and dwarfing the realm of the social. Even then, even when we speak of that which is other than us, Absolutely Other even, it is still *we* who are speaking, we who cannot escape our sociality or our boundedness by history.

4) This suggests the *fourth* sense in which nature is a social category. Even the nature that science tells us about—not just the cosmic nature surrounding us but even more primarily the underlying material nature of which everything is said to be made: ocean, cosmos, Mississippi, tree out my window, microchip in my computer, polyester in my socks, even and finally me myself—even this nature cannot escape the claim for the priority of mediations, of the social. Scientists have no access to nature "in itself" but rather act within a "view" of nature that they themselves have a central role in generating, through their theories, their language, and above all their practices; I take this to be the cardinal conclusion to which more than thirty years of postempiricist philosophy of science has been led. These practices are socially and communicatively organized ones, which means that a budding researcher learns about what the world is like above all by learning "what one does" as a scientist, and so the world of science is from the very start socially and practically structured. The "community" of scientists, further, cannot be coherently separated from the broader social community they belong to as citizens, and so more general "views" of nature and practices regarding it will necessarily play a role in scientific work as well.[13] And this is a two-way process: scientific work in turn deeply influences and transforms the society in which it arises, affecting not simply how members of that society view the world—as the previous examples suggested—but even what that world itself *is*, as Bruno Latour with his analyses of laboratization has emphasized.

The objects "naturally" surrounding us have social roles and meanings; they are literally "social constructs," built by human labor; the "natural environment" is never encountered independently of its social context; and the "nature" revealed by natural science cannot be separated from the socially organized practices through which such a science operates—these are, then, the four senses in which "nature is a social category." These four senses can be seen as stages in an argument in which the desire for nature as an ultimate immediacy on which our practices are founded is shown to be systematically frustrated. The conclusion is a hard one to accept. Mediations, we believe, must come to an end somewhere, and "nature" is the name we give to that somewhere. The social, we think, *must* be based on the natural; practices *must* take place on the basis of something pre-existing; labor can only *transform* the world, it cannot create it. Yet when we try to grasp that nature that is prior to the social, we always fail. The "nature" we want to get to, the ultimate immediacy, is always deferred, always subject to a further deconstruction into the social.[14] At first it is asserted to be the obverse of the social, the constant "real" environment as distinct from the historically varying social one; but then it turns out that social institutions are instantiated in quite "real" objects, which make up the single and undivided (and historical) "environment" in which we live. Then it is asserted that the social lies in the *meanings* we grant to these objects in contradistinction to their physical existence; but it turns out that even their physical existence is the product of socially organized labor. Then it is claimed that nonetheless such labor is only the modification of a "nature" that exists prior to our transformative acts and that much of the wider environment in fact consists of this not-yet-transformed nature; yet examples of this pure nature prove on examination to be remarkably difficult to find—not Yellowstone, not the Mississippi, not even "outer space." Then comes the decisive move, in which it is asserted that, after all, everything physical, even those things that have been transformed by labor, is "made" of some ultimate *Urstoff*, the matter of modern physics. Yet even that matter turns out not to be so ultimate, as we discover that its very existence as something about which we can meaningfully speak depends on a particular scientific community and a particular set of practices.[15]

We are left, frustrated, with Locke's "unknown X"—"nature" as an unconstructed immediacy whose existence we almost obsessively feel the need to assert but which we find ourselves amazingly unable to say anything about. This, of course, is just the problem, and just the fate, that Lukács had predicted for a thought grounded, as ours is, in a social order marked by reification—a thought that wants to separate objects from subjects and that sees mediation, practice, as destructive of an object's "true being" instead of as creating it. In its frustration, such a reified thought reveals its preference for the static, the congealed, the *Vorhanden* over the practices that make the objective world possible—and reveals, too, its failure to engage in a self-reflection that might dissolve false immediacies and so free humans from the rule our own objects have come to exert over us. It pays for these failures by its conceptual incoherence, its entanglement in antinomies of just the sort we have traced—antinomies based finally on the desperate need, and yet at the same time the inability, to uncover a "nature" independent of the social (that is, of us), a nature that always seems at just the last moment to elude our grasp, beckoning us toward it but mocking us at the same moment—as we keep tearing back what we think will be the last veil, and keep finding, shockingly, ourselves.[16]

2. AMBIGUITIES

I have been arguing that Lukács's position is at bottom a critique of immediacy, and hence also a critique of nature, and that in this context the distinction between the social and the natural cannot hold. Yet Lukács, with his limitation of dialectical method to society and his assertion of the misapplication thesis, unquestionably wants to maintain it; it is the final dualism, the one he cannot bring himself to give up. He writes of bourgeois philosophy that its difficulties are "revealed at least as clearly by what [it] does *not* find problematic as by what it does,"[17] but the remark seems to apply to him as well: he assumes without examination that the social realm and the natural one can be distinguished and so fails to see the very radicality of his own claim that "nature is a social category." We might at this juncture ask the question of why this is so.

One reason, doubtless, has to do with his a priori commitment, as a Marxist, to something called "materialism." To assert that nature is a product of our practices (of social mediations) seems to stray too close to the sort of idealist theses that Marxists from the very start always wanted to avoid. I do not think it really does—or rather it only does if "mediation" and "practice" are themselves understood in idealist ways, as mysterious events in which a disembodied subject somehow "creates" a world of objects. But to say this is to begin to suggest a deeper reason for Lukács's own ambivalence here—for (as I have already suggested) I think he operates with a less than satisfactory conception of practice, in which elements of idealism do indeed tend to predominate.[18] Thus I want to argue that in a curious way it is his idealism more than his materialism that accounts for his failure to grasp the implications of his own position with respect to nature.

"The principle that would enable contemplation to be overcome," writes Lukács, is "namely *the practical*";[19] yet there is remarkably little detail in *History and Class Consciousness* about what exactly the "practice" that will overcome contemplation would consist in. The pivotal insight is that "we have made our own history";[20] to recognize this is to begin to overthrow reification. But *how* have we made our own history? Lukács does not really have much to say about this. What is surprisingly missing from his account—as he conceded in 1967—is the category of *labor*.[21] It is important not to read concepts from Marx's *Paris Manuscripts* into Lukács's work, despite the well-known connections between the two.[22] Whereas Marx explicitly associates the phenomenon of alienation with a labor process in which workers quite literally produce objects that (in the form of capital) turn into an independent and alien power over and against them, Lukács never actually does so, and certainly never identifies this process as the origin and conceptual core of reification.[23] Most of the discussions of labor in the book involve generalized references to its technological aspects or to modes of organization such as Taylorism; the structure of labor under capitalism is taken as an *example* of reification, not as its central phenomenon.

To inquire more closely into the real structure of labor, however, would have caused the buried tensions within Lukács's position to emerge. For labor is not some abstract and ideal "practice" in which somehow history is myste- riously "made," nor some "interaction" in which social "institutions" are "con- stituted," it is rather a *real* activity in which *real* concrete objects are produced. The production is physical and real, and so is part of "nature." But it is also "social"—both socially organized (in the factory) and socially effective (pro- ducing the objects that make up our real social world). In this process of "metabolic exchange" or *Stoffwechsel* (as Marx calls it), the natural and the social are woven together in an inextricable connection—a connection that is fatal to the Lukácsian dualism we have been examining.

Lukács was therefore right in 1967 to criticize the book on the ground that "labor, as the mediator of the metabolic exchange between society and nature, is missing." But he was wrong to conclude from this that it entails "the disappearance of the ontological objectivity of nature which forms the real basis [*seinsmässige Grundlage*] of this exchange,"[24] at least if "objectivity" and being a "basis" are understood to refer to nature's supposed independence from and ontological priority over the social. This self-criticism is doubly misleading. First of all, as Feenberg has pointed out, Lukács's own method- ological dualism strictly speaking prevents his account of social practice from having any implications for nature at all and indeed serves as a guarantee of nature's "objectivity" and priority from the very beginning.[25] But secondly I have been arguing that it is just this idea of "the ontological objectivity of nature" as the "basis" of our mediations that *ought* to disappear, and that a correct understanding of the epistemological and ontological significance of labor's role as "mediator of the metabolic exchange between society and nature" reveals the incoherence involved in taking either side of this (false) opposition as the "basis" of the other. Thus, although the Lukács of 1967 and I agree that *History and Class Consciousness* is flawed by its failure to grasp practice as labor, we see the consequences of that failure in diametrically opposed ways: whereas he thinks that it leads to the denial of the ontological independence of nature, I think on the contrary that it makes possible just the (illegitimate) *assertion* of this independence, via a methodological dualism that a serious analysis of practice would have shown to be untenable, and that this very assertion leads to the problems about nature in the book we are tracing.

Similarly the failure to offer an adequate analysis of labor produces a weakness in Lukács's account of why the *proletariat* is the privileged subject- object of history and not some other group. For Marx, the epistemological significance of the category of labor stemmed from its role as the concretiza- tion of the mystified Hegelian idea of knowledge as actively producing the object known: in labor such production takes place literally and materially. But because Lukács systematically underestimates the role of labor he never really says this and so has trouble identifying what about the proletariat's own practices render it uniquely capable of overcoming reification. Thus all the emphasis is put on the *revolutionary act*, which takes on a quasi-Kierkegaardean character, and not on the prerevolutionary practices that make it possible.[26] Marx has no such problem: it is the process of labor, in which the workers literally produce the world by building its objects and generating its wealth, that identifies them as the essential agents of social change. The world already is their product; they need only become aware of and take conscious control over this process to abolish alienation.

Indeed, in the last analysis, Lukács's argument for the superiority of the "proletarian standpoint" over the bourgeois one depends on nothing other than *immediacy*, the very category I have been arguing he needs to reject. The proletariat, he writes, "obtains its sharpest weapon . . . from its clear insight into reality," its access to what he calls *"hüllenlose Wahrheit"*—that is, reality as it is, not hidden or distorted by any ideological veils—while on the other hand "the survival of the bourgeoisie rests on the assumption that it never obtains a clear insight into the social preconditions of its own existence."[27] What is it that makes this "clear insight" possible for the workers? When one examines the passages in which Lukács tries to answer this question, one is struck by a series of locutions emphasizing, not the productive power of labor, but the way in which the proletariat is *driven* to an understanding of capitalist society by the empirical (immediate) facts of its position in the production process. The proletarian's experience "drives him beyond" (*hinaustreibt*) immediacy, it "forces" (*aufherrscht*) knowledge of alienation upon him; "for the proletariat to become aware of the dialectical nature of its existence is a matter of life and death." Its "social existence . . . is far more powerfully affected by the dialectical character of the historical process" than is that of the bourgeoisie, Lukács writes; in its daily existence "the reified character of the immediate manifestations of capitalist society receives the most extreme definition possible."[28] Reification is always hidden, merely implicit, to the bourgeois, whereas for the proletarian it is a real and directly experienced force in every element of his or her life; what appears for the former in the form of the magical (and gratifying) fact of profit, for instance, appears to the latter in the form of a direct struggle over the length of the working day.[29] Thus, for example, "the quantification of objects . . . makes its appearance in the life of the worker immediately as a process of abstraction of which he is the victim"; similarly, "in every aspect of daily life in which the individual worker imagines himself to be the subject of his own life he finds this to be an illusion that is destroyed by the immediacy of his existence."[30]

But then *immediacy* turns out after all to be the source of truth. The proletariat, because of its position in the production process, is able to see capitalism in all its (immediate) naked brutality, whereas the bourgeoisie, protected by a complex cocoon of mediations, both intellectual and social, is prevented from achieving such insight. Immediacy here has returned as the decisive epistemological category, with the brute facts of the world impinging upon a subject in such a way that they can neither be avoided nor denied and serving then as a guarantor of the subject's claim to veridical knowledge. With this move Lukács retreats to the pre-Hegelian dogmatism we saw him earlier trying to reject. Now the revolutionary potential of the proletariat derives from the fact, not that the workers through their practice produce the world that oppresses them and thus through self-recognition can achieve the *hüllenlose Wahrheit* in which they find themselves behind the last veil, but rather that this truth is, as it were, right before their noses. And the reason for this, I am suggesting, is that Lukács does not see what this practice would be: labor.

This capitulation to immediacy is the flip side of the subtle idealism in Lukács's conception of practice, an idealism secretly suspicious of anything as concrete and "natural" as real work. This is the sense in which Lukács has quite rightly been taken to task (again, not least by himself forty years later) for identifying objectification with alienation: it is almost as if labor seems to him too "thing"-bound, too reifying from the very start, to be the foundation of revolutionary praxis, and so instead his appeal is to some vague other sort of "practice" through which history is somehow "made" without his ever fully defining what this is. Feenberg is right, of course, to point out that Lukács's methodological dualism formally protects him against the charge of confusing objectification with alienation, since by treating our interactions with nature as nondialectical it renders the category of alienation ipso facto inapplicable to them. The trouble, though, is that, at a deeper level, even this dualism appears as an expression of a fundamental antipathy toward the real: its hidden message is that every practical interaction we have with nature plunges us into a realm so profoundly alien that not even dialectical method can grasp it.

Lukács's idealism is apparent in other ways too. Sometimes one glimpses in the background of his arguments the workings of a speculative metaphysics that is quite dogmatically asserted, as if the applicability of categories from Hegel's *Logic* to historical processes were something known a priori.[31] And there are further ambiguities in the text, places where the pre-Marxist roots of Lukács's thought in the neo-Kantianism and vitalism of Lask, Rickert, et. al. plainly show themselves. Even in the sections criticizing the "bourgeois worldview," one can surely see the subterranean traces of arguments that owe more to the *Lebensphilosophie* the Marxist Lukács had supposedly left behind than to the arguments about mediation and self-recognition I have highlighted.[32] Indeed, despite his critique of what I have called Engels's "dynamic" conception of dialectics, there are places where Lukács's own account bears some resemblances to it; to this extent Colletti's criticism is justified.[33] At those places Lukács turns away from the insight that the resolution to the problems of contemplation is to be found in practice and toward a claim which he does not sufficiently distinguish from the former—that merely seeing the world as dynamic, as a process of "becoming," would solve those problems. "In this Becoming, in this tendency, in this process," Lukács writes toward the end of the essay on reification, "the true nature of the object is revealed. . . . [T]he transformation of things into a process provides a *concrete* solution to all the *concrete* problems created by the paradoxes of existent objects [*seienden Dinges*]."[34] This is at best ambiguous, its meaning depending on whether one emphasizes the subject who puts these processes into play or looks at "process" as simply an objective characteristic to be "discovered" in the world, as Engels did. Only the first offers a real break with contemplation.

Lukács's problematic assertion of the virtue of "totality" produces similar difficulties. Sometimes he speaks as though it is the unavoidable inability of "bourgeois formalisms" to be able to comprehend the *whole* that is their essential failing.[35] By breaking up into partial systems, contemplative thought finds itself essentially limited, unable to achieve a holistic knowledge of reality as such; dialectical thought, on the other hand, is oriented from the beginning toward knowledge of the totality. This is the "essence," Lukács writes, of Marxist method, the "decisive difference" between Marxism and bourgeois thought.[36] But this way of speaking is not so much a critique of the contemplative desire finally to grasp the "objective" world in all its truth as it is the most extreme form of that desire. We can see this now more clearly, thanks to the postmodern tradition from Heidegger on, which has rightfully made us much more suspicious of such aspirations toward totality. There is again an ambiguity here: does "grasping the whole" mean "seeing every object at once" or "seeing the role of the subject in the constitution of objects"? The two meanings are perpendicular to each other—the one dreaming of a total knowledge of all objects, the other unconcerned that some objects might not yet be understood but insistent on a recognition by the subject of its own place in the world it "sees." This latter is not so much a matter of holism as it is a matter of practice and self-recognition; by emphasizing "totality," Lukács allows this point to be obscured and falls back into a bad metaphysics.

He shows, too, a tendency toward organicism in which the *Lebensphilosophische* influence is particularly evident and in which once again a nostalgia for immediacy can be sensed. Capitalist modes of production are criticized in the early pages of the essay on reification for breaking up "organic unities"— the technologized division of labor, Lukács writes, exacerbated by Taylorization, leads to "the progressive elimination of the qualitative, human, and individual attributes of the worker," while at the same time it "break[s] with the organic, irrational, and qualitatively determined unity of the product." It "declare[s] war on the organic manufacture of whole products based on the traditional amalgam of empirical experiences of work." Organic communities too are destroyed: workers become "isolated abstract atoms whose work no longer brings them together directly and organically."[37] All of this, he argues, also arises at the level of bourgeois thought, which is marked as we have seen by a formalism that finds itself intrinsically unable to grasp the specificity of its own content.

But this organicist insistence on the "irrational," "qualitative," "individual," and "traditional" stands in an uneasy relation with the rationalistic Hegelianism of the main argument, since the organic is clearly nothing other than the natural, the immediate, the uncomprehended, that which even self-recognition cannot recognize. Capitalist production "conceals above all," Lukács writes in a remarkable passage, "the immediate—qualitative and material—character of things as things." Commodification produces in them a "new substantiality [Dinghaftigkeit] . . . which destroys their original and authentic substantiality."[38] The whole set of adjectives here—unmittelbaren, qualitativen, materiellen, ursprüngliche, eigentliche—refers back to and expresses nostalgia for a world of the not-yet-mediated, not-yet-constructed: for a world of objects left to themselves, unconcealed, free to be what they really are. This nostalgia is potent, and we will see it more than once in the chapters that follow, but in the context of Lukács's epistemology it has no place. Here the overcoming of reification is founded not on the recognition of ourselves as responsible for the objects we produce, but rather somehow on these objects's own "immediate" and "authentic" qualities. This does not overcome reification so much as it repeats it, once again seeing the objects as independent of and prior to our own acts.

Earlier I pointed to four elements Lukács emphasized in his account of the "bourgeois worldview": its formalism, its reductionism, its ahistoricity, and its objectivism. Each, as we have seen, is associated with a critique: formalism cannot grasp the content of knowledge, reductionism cannot grasp the world as a whole, ahistoricism cannot grasp the fact of historical change and unpredictability, and finally objectivism cannot grasp the role of mediation in the production of that which appears as immediate or "natural." It turns out that only the last of these critiques is unambiguous; the others are capable of an "idealist" reading of which indeed Lukács himself is sometimes guilty. Thus the critique of formalism can turn into an organicism with roots in romantic attacks on reason; the critique of reductionism can turn into a holism that makes a fetish of "totality"; the critique of ahistoricism can turn into a mystical celebration of the "creativity" and "uniqueness" of historical developments. Interpreted in this way all three exhibit a dangerous affinity with just that which they try to renounce, finding the solution of philosophical problems simply in the substitution of one (dialectical, Heraclitean, dynamic) metaphysics for another as the "correct" way to understand an "objective" world still seen as beyond us.

Only in the context of the last critique, I am suggesting—the critique of forgotten mediations, of social constructions that have come to look like nature—

can the other three be adequately understood, as critiques not of a mistaken metaphysics but of the absence of the mediating subject. To say analysis "cannot grasp the whole" means not that some other method *could* comprehend all of objective reality at once, but rather that the subject's role in that reality is always left out; to say formalism "cannot grasp the content" is not to suggest that there is always something irrational in the object that passeth beyond our understanding, but that the object must be seen as the product of a subject's practice; to say the search for eternal laws "cannot grasp change" does not involve the assertion of some Heraclitean essence to history but rather the recognition that history is made in and through the practices of the very subjects who experience it.

Yet both sets of readings can certainly be found in Lukács's text, as he vacillates between what might be called the *Lebensphilosophische* and the Hegelian version of the critique of modern thought. One version criticizes it for ignoring "life" or "holism"; the other, for failing to deconstruct the false immediacies it has itself produced. The one leads to a critique of contemplation on romantic grounds (for its inability to comprehend the "organic" or "irrational"), while the other leads to a critique on what are really Hegelian ones (for blocking the possibility of self-recognition). Here again we find an ambiguity in Lukács's view, just as we did with respect to the status of natural science. His "idealism" *is* the culprit, I have been arguing, but not in the sense usually meant—for by leading him to misconstrue "practice" as something other than labor, it renders him too easily persuaded that nature and the social are distinct, and that natural science can therefore somehow remain untouched by the critique of "bourgeois thought."

3. SCIENCE AND REIFICATION

But with the abandonment of the distinction between the social and the natural, it should be clear, the basis for Lukács's critique of the idea of a "dialectics of nature"—the critique I began by quoting—collapses. Instead the possibility opens up of returning to that idea, albeit in an entirely new sense. A social theory oriented toward the overcoming of reification would have now to be one that also subjects our interactions with "nature" to a dialectical interrogation, with the intention of revealing the socially organized practices of mediation that help to produce the "natural" world of physical things surrounding us and stripping that world of its apparent immutability and independence from the human. The project of such a dialectics of nature would therefore be to understand the sense in which Lukács was right to assert that "nature is a social category." I have already attempted to sketch the outline of an argument for that assertion. It involves grasping the world as a human world, constructed by us through our practices, and sees "reification" in our failure to recognize ourselves in our *Umwelt*, our failure (that is) to see it as the product of human transformative practices.

Obviously science and technology today play an enormous role in these transformative processes. Lukács, as we have seen, explicitly denied that natural science was a form of practice, identifying it rather with contemplation; this, too, was important to his critique of Engels.[39] But this denial rests not only on his idealist misunderstanding of practice in general, but also of scientific practice in particular. "The experimenter creates an artificial, abstract milieu in order to be able to *observe* undisturbed the untrammelled workings of the laws under examination," we saw him writing; the emphasis on *observe* obscures the other significant word here, *creates*. It was central to the argument I made earlier about the social character of the nature revealed to us by science that science is itself a practice, and creates a world—the world inside the laboratory that is literally built with tools and labor, the broader world outside the laboratory that authors such as Latour and Rouse have argued is fundamentally transformed by scientific practices, the world of "phenomena" whose creation Hacking has suggested is the primary goal of experimental work, the new world that scientists live in according to Kuhn after they take part in a scientific revolution.[40] By taking science to be merely a matter of undisturbed observation in which no subjective element, and hence no element of practice, is permitted to intrude, Lukács here is accepting the very kind of story about science that postempiricism over the past thirty years has done so much to debunk.

Yet this is not all there is to say here. There remains "something problematic" about the fit between capitalist society, on the one hand, and natural science and the technology associated with it, on the other; they seem to stand in a remarkable relation of mutual support, as the more politically oriented of recent philosophers of science among others have begun to acknowledge.[41] Lukács's misapplication thesis, as we have seen, understands this merely as the result of a kind of border violation, in which the appearance of reified society as second nature encourages the mistaken attempt to apply the worldview of natural science to the social realm; but this account (which in any case as I have argued is incoherent on Lukács's own terms) misses the extent to which natural science and technology themselves have become not only crucial to contemporary society's legitimation but also constitutive of its very structures. The alternative to the misapplication thesis that I have been suggesting sees the problem not in the violation of a border but in the dualism that thinks there is a real border there to be violated; what it objects to in *Verdinglichung* or reification is not that some entities (human practices and the social institutions they produce) that are not really *Dinge* are treated as if they were, but rather that the category *Ding* is treated as though it refers at all—as though there were *any* entities whose characteristics could be identified independently of human practice. But this is exactly what contemporary natural science does believe about the entities with which it deals.

This is the sense in which there is something right about Lukács's claim that natural science is not a practice but rather a mere contemplation of something external to the human: it does indeed think of itself this way. The objects it investigates are assumed to exist independently of and prior to the activities of the investigators, and the purpose of the investigation is assumed to be to come up with objective, formal, eternal, analytical laws. Postempiricism has done much to reveal the errors in positivist stories about how science operates, but it has never successfully faced the question about why such stories are so widely believed, not least by scientists themselves. Kuhn speaks of the "invisibility of revolutions," and Latour and Woolgar point to the processes by which scientists attempt to establish "facthood" for their own assertions and so obscure the local and constructed ("artifactual") character of what are taken as facts,[42] but the implications of these claims—which amount after all to claims that, on basic methodological issues, scientists simply do not know what they are doing, and further that they *could not* know it without ceasing to do science as currently practiced—are never really examined.[43]

Yet this is what it means to say that natural science, too, even within its "own proper realm," is part of what Lukács calls "bourgeois thought": its own self-understanding employs the categories, and confronts the antinomies, of contemplation. If science is intrinsically social and if something like Lukács's account of reification is right as a description of contemporary society, then science, too, will be marked by a reification in which the role of its own mediating practices in the production of the "immediacy" it thinks it is "observing" will be systematically obscured. And this, I am suggesting, is just what postempiricist accounts of scientific practice have revealed. Science's traditional self-understanding (which is at the same time the most common view of science among non-scientists too) is of a value-neutral observation of an external physical world independent of the social, oriented toward the discovery of eternal truths and the removal of the subjective, the artifactual, the mediated so as to reveal "Nature" as it is. The practices science engages in, which (if the argument so far has been correct) are nonetheless still social and still mediating, will therefore have to be *self-obscuring* ones, practices that paradoxically work to prevent themselves from being recognized as such.

But in this sense we are thereby returned to the very dialectic of reification and self-recognition I have suggested is central to Lukács's epistemology. Engels was right to call natural science a practice, but wrong to take it as a model of a liberating one. Rather it is a practice taking place under the sign of reification; *this* explains its "problematic" fit with contemporary society. The hint raised here is of the possibility of a different kind of scientific practice, one that somehow knew itself to be practical and social and that could therefore begin, as *part* of its practice and not separately from it, to ask questions about the social sources and the social implications of its work. The Lukácsian critique of natural science would thus be like the Lukácsian critique of reified practices in general: they must come to be recognized as such by those who engage in them, in an act of recognition that must itself be *practical*, and so involve a social transformation in which the practices themselves would be transformed. This idea, of a nonreified science as one that knew itself in a different way and so engaged in its investigations differently too, is one to which we will return several times in what follows.

I have been drawing from Lukács's text a set of conclusions that he doubtless would himself have had trouble recognizing and probably would have rejected both in 1922 and again in 1967. I am trying to grasp rather a *tendency* in a work that standing on its own is certainly deeply flawed. We have traced out one flaw in detail, by examining the self-contradictory character of the text's account of natural science and the nature it studies. Another flaw is probably more significant (and more obvious) and derives from the concrete political purpose the book had at the moment it was written—I mean its Bolshevism, its paeans to the Party, its ungrounded "wager on the proletariat," its antidemocratic and metaphysical conception of a class consciousness that can be "imputed" to those who do not in fact possess it. I am suggesting that nonetheless a substantial and meaningful intellectual core can be extracted from the text which offers a useful way to think not only about science but also about social change in a manner relevant to contemporary questions. This core results from holding on to *one* side of the contradictory account of science (the side that represents, I have argued, the work's "secret telos") and stripping it of its direct relation to Communist politics (a relation not logically required, I would claim, by the particular epistemological arguments we have examined).

History and Class Consciousness does not present this position in an univocal manner so much as it points toward it—toward, that is, a liberation based on a self-recognition become practical, in which the apparent immediacy and givenness of that which is taken as "natural," including (first) nature itself, are exploded and the processes of construction that underlie that false immediacy are revealed. In this liberation those processes themselves, through which we make and remake our social *Umwelt* (the world we inhabit), are transformed and subjected to conscious social control; and in it natural science too is "liberated," coming to know itself as practical, as social, as world changing. In its practical overcoming of reification, this liberation would also liberate us from any dualism between the "natural" and the "social," and from any limitation of our knowledge, which is to say our self-knowledge, to a particular realm, in the manner of what I have called the misapplication thesis.

Lukács of course never got this far, remaining stuck as we have seen at the last step, unable to move beyond the dualism between nature and society. To dissolve that dualism would be to transcend even the categories of "materialism" and "idealism" so central to Marxist thinking, both in the form it takes in Engels and in Lukács himself as well. Lukács himself, as I have suggested, fits nowhere simply in that opposition: his "idealism" keeps him from seeing practice as labor, while his "materialism" keeps him from seeing that first nature, too, must be understood as a false immediacy whose constructed character requires recognition.

Thus finally it is his inability to confront the real implications of his argument that results in the famous "problem of nature in Lukács" with which we began. By failing to solve it, he bequeaths it to the later tradition of Western Marxism, as the next chapters will show. Expelled from the critique of reification, nature continues to appear as the uncomprehended Other of the tradition, the shadow of the social that social theory could not, yet had to, incorporate—the problem that bedevils Western Marxism just as Lukács argued the problem of the thing in itself bedeviled bourgeois thought. (It follows, of course, from the argument here that the two problems are indeed really the same.) It reappears in two forms, as we will see: on the one hand, as a romanticized past of nonidentity, of memory, of mimesis, of the Id, on which all (meager) hopes for liberation are now placed; and on the other in the inverse form of a natural science now reintroduced (contra Lukács) into the ambit of social theory and roundly castigated as "instrumental reason" oriented toward the domination of inner and outer nature. What will be missing is the dialectic of reification and self-recognition. The Frankfurt School will see that Lukács's position about science is untenable as stated and will move to extend the critique of reification into a critique of science. But the source of the critique will lie more in romantic and *Lebensphilosophische* thought than in the Hegelian tradition Lukács represented; the new critique will be performed in the name of a repressed nature itself, not of a subject who needs to recognize its own practical role in generating the "natural."

CHAPTER 3

Horkheimer, Adorno, and the Dialectics of Enlightenment

1. ENLIGHTENMENT AND THE DOMINATION OF NATURE

"In the most general sense of progressive thought," Horkheimer and Adorno begin *Dialectic of Enlightenment* by writing, "enlightenment has always aimed at liberating men from fear and establishing their sovereignty. Yet the fully enlightened earth radiates disaster triumphant."[1] The tone is set from the start. Instead of Lukács's optimism about the imminence of the revolutionary transformations his theory requires (requires, that is, even to be verified), here—two decades later—all that seems imminent is further catastrophe; and it is "enlightenment" that has failed, which is to say exactly the tradition of "progressive thought" of which Marxism had always seen itself as being a part. "We are wholly convinced," Horkheimer and Adorno also (and paradoxically) write, "—and therein lies our *petitio principii*—that social freedom is inseparable from enlightened thought. Yet we believe as well that the concept of just this thought . . . already contains the seed of the reversal universally apparent today."[2] It is this paradox of an "enlightenment" both necessary for human freedom and yet also the source of a "universal reversal" that *Dialectic of Enlightenment* intends to investigate. Enlightenment, Horkheimer and Adorno argue, is a double-edged phenomenon: in its implicit commitment to truth, to clarity, and to freedom it remains the indispensable presupposition of social critique and the best hope for social change, but at the same time it also and inevitably works to subvert and invalidate these very goals, and hence to abolish itself.

By deliberately (and provocatively) identifying the contemporary crisis with a dialectic in the very idea of enlightenment itself, Horkheimer and Adorno locate the origins of that crisis considerably further back in time than the standard Marxist accounts, including Lukács's: "capitalism" and the "rule of the bourgeoisie" are now merely the latest (and most harmful) forms of a development whose roots are much older. Underlying the book's arguments is the (pseudo-)historical account developed in its first chapter, which attempts to trace the process whereby the human relations to nature expressed in myth and magic are transformed into a new set of "enlightened" ones. The distinction thereby drawn between myth and enlightenment is central to the text. Myth is marked by a "mimetic" relation to nature, in which humans consider themselves a part of nature and express their connection to it through rituals of imitation and assimilation. It is an animistic stage, characterized by a sense of the natural world as sacred (as, e.g., the home of the gods) and hence by worship of it. Enlightenment, on the other hand, is associated with the emergence of a new kind of relation to nature in which the latter appears as a tool for humans to be employed in their own interests. Thus enlightenment is marked by the "disenchantment" of nature, its transformation from something sacred into mere matter available for human manipulation.[3] No longer populated by the gods or by any trace of intrinsic meaning, nature now becomes purely the object of human instrumental action: "what men want to learn from nature," Horkheimer and Adorno write, "is how to use it in order wholly to dominate it and other men. Nothing else counts."[4]

Thus the project of enlightenment aims above all at the *domination of nature*.[5] Disenchanted and objectified nature, appearing now in the guise of meaningless matter, is seen by enlightenment simply as something to be overcome and mastered for human purposes and not as something to be imitated, propitiated, or religiously celebrated. The movement is from magic to science, from ritual to technology. In this movement, further, humans implicitly set up a radical distinction between the natural and the human realms: the position of humans as themselves *part* of nature that mythic thought insists upon and mimesis acts out is thereby forgotten. The result is a fundamental separation of humans from nature, an "alienation" that for Horkheimer and Adorno is pivotal to the fatal dialectic of enlightenment they trace. "Men pay," they write, "for the increase of their power with alienation from that over which they exercise their power."[6]

But the contrast between mythic and enlightenment views is in fact more complex. True to their dialectical intentions, Horkheimer and Adorno see the two poles as also mutually complicit, writing that "myth is already enlightenment; and enlightenment reverts to mythology."[7] Even magic has a secret and technological goal: humans of the mythic era engaged in mimetic acts so that the crops could be encouraged to grow, the hunt could be successful, the illness could be cured. Here too, already, the barely conscious purpose was to control nature in the interest of the satisfaction of human desires. On occasion Horkheimer and Adorno speak as though in fact *three* stages should be distinguished: a primeval and purely mimetic one marked by belief in "local spirits and demons," followed by a transitional magical stage where mimesis is organized in an institutionalized religion (and a corresponding hierarchy of magicians or priests) positing gods whose powers extend universally, and only then by enlightenment with its explicit ban on mimesis and assertion of human control over nature as the highest goal.[8] Each stage already bears the seeds of the next. But enlightenment reverts to myth, too: its radically instrumental approach to nature, its adamant refusal to countenance any ascriptions of meaning or teleology to nature, Horkheimer and Adorno write, "is mythic fear turned radical," producing "no more than a so to speak universal taboo."[9] In its desire to dominate nature enlightenment reveals its own fear of nature, and at the same time itself *turns into* something like nature: it promises humans a power over natural forces that will give them happiness and autonomy in their lives, but ends—in the catastrophes of the twentieth century—by submitting them to forces (now of *second* nature) that crush them ever so much more strongly.[10]

In the tour de force that is the first excursus in *Dialectic of Enlightenment*, Horkheimer and Adorno offer an interpretation of the *Odyssey* as the story of the production of the enlightened individual out of and against the mythic and natural powers of the past. Most remarkable is their retelling of the episode of the Sirens. In the tale of Odysseus having himself tied to the mast of his ship in order to be able to hear the song of the Sirens without succumbing to its fatal spell, they see an allegory for the relationship of enlightenment to nature. The Sirens represent pleasure, the past, all the mythic forces of nature that Odysseus must overcome. He asserts himself against these forces by separating himself from them, in a self-chosen act of bondage. The epic celebrates this self-alienation, emphasizing the necessity of such an arrangement if the self is to be preserved. What Horkheimer and Adorno see in the story, though, is its tragedy: for the bound Odysseus, when he finally hears the song, does of course change his mind. His desperate cries to be released are heartfelt ones; he calls to the oarsmen to ignore his earlier command, to let him go. He has outwitted himself, and only through this outwitting does he save himself. The oneness with nature that the mythic era expresses through mimesis appears under enlightenment as a tempting and everpresent possibility, but also as death, as loss of the self. The unquenchable desire for a reconciliation with nature that Odysseus's "passionate call for liberation" represents must in the interest of his own continued existence be carefully suppressed, and by his own action. Natural bonds are exchanged for social ones, self-imposed.[11]

The moment of renunciation is crucial here. "The title of hero is only gained," Horkheimer and Adorno write, by "the abasement and mortification of the impulse towards complete, universal, and undivided happiness."[12] It is not only external nature from which the enlightened man has alienated himself: he must renounce and suppress his own innermost desires (like those for the pleasures of the Sirens' song) as well and so is alienated at the same time from his own *inner* nature. The implicit debt Horkheimer and Adorno owe here to Freud, and specifically to his pessimistic social theory, is plain.[13] The ego is constituted only through the suppression of that out of which the ego arose—the undifferentiated unity of the infant's world. But this means that something central to its own existence is necessarily lost. "The subjective spirit which abolishes animation [*Beseelung*] from nature," Horkheimer and Adorno write, "can master this inanimate [*entseelte*] nature only by imitating its rigidity and abolishing its own animism in turn."[14] The paradox of enlightenment, then, is that only in the denial of self (which is to say in particular the denial of inner *nature*) does the self become possible. In this sense when Odysseus saves himself by telling the Cyclops that his name is "Nobody," he is saying something truer than he himself recognizes.[15] But then it is no longer clear what enlightenment was supposed to be saving: the alienation of the enlightened man from nature turns out to be an alienation from himself.

It is this moment of renunciation that stamps Odysseus as the "prototype of the bourgeois individual."[16] The heroism of the *Odyssey*, according to Horkheimer and Adorno, is quite different from that of the *Iliad*, which they interpret as belonging to a different and earlier era: the proud and self-assertive warrior gives way to the wily and cautious bourgeois, unashamed to call himself Nobody if it will help him get out of a tight spot. "Odysseus does not try to take another route that would enable him to escape sailing past the Sirens," they write. "And he does not try, say, to presume on the superiority of his knowledge and to listen freely to the temptresses, imagining that his freedom will be protection enough." Instead "he abases himself," denies himself, renounces his claim to happiness or reconciliation with nature—and thereby survives.[17] "All bourgeois enlightenment is one," they add, in this "requirement of sobriety and common sense, a proficient estimate of the balance of forces."[18]

Odysseus is *der Listige*, the cunning one, "wily Odysseus." Cunning or *List* is the other principal element in Horkheimer and Adorno's account of Odysseus as the prototype of enlightenment.[19] The hubris of the pre-Odyssean hero had consisted in the attempt to defy, and indeed to supplant, the natural forces or the gods in a heroic but doomed act of self-assertion. The sobriety of cunning, on the other hand, involves a recognition of the impossibility of supplanting these forces and instead undertakes the remarkable (and fateful) project of *overcoming them by submitting to them*. "Cunning is defiance become rational,"[20] Horkheimer and Adorno write. The enlightened self defeats the older forces by using them: it beats them at their own game. The letter of the law, natural and divine, is scrupulously observed; indeed the cunning hero expends an almost obsessive amount of energy on a careful examination of every detail of the law's requirements, searching for the loophole he knows he must find. Thus the laws set down by the mythic powers (the "laws of nature"), which for the earlier heroes were threats that had to be abolished, become for the Odyssean hero the very means for his salvation. "He satisfies the sentence of the law," Horkheimer and Adorno write, "so that it loses power over him, by conceding it this very power."[21]

Horkheimer and Adorno see in this cunning, with its literalism, its compulsive concern with detail, its submission to the law in order to find a loophole in it, a metaphor for modern science and technology. Science too wants to discover the laws of natural processes by investigating them in detail, never dreaming of course of supplanting them and knowing that all it can do is obey them, hoping through this curiously ambivalent "obedience" at the same time to overcome the natural powers so as to achieve human goals. But this very metaphor shows the situation to be more complex than phrases about science as the "domination of nature" or enlightenment as "alienated from nature" might suggest. If there is domination here it has a curiously masochistic edge: we "dominate" nature only by studying it in detail, obsessively following its requirements, and keeping to the letter of its laws. And if there is "alienation," it too takes a peculiar form: can one be said to be alienated from something one so desperately needs to know?

There is after all a dialectic to cunning. When one defeats nature by strictly obeying its laws, it remains ambiguous who the victor really is and in what the victory actually consists. "The very spirit that dominates nature repeatedly vindicates the superiority of nature in the competition," Horkheimer and Adorno write. "Only consciously contrived adaptation to nature brings nature under the control of the physically weaker. . . . The schema of Odyssean cunning is the mastery of nature through such adaptation."[22] The "domination of nature" that cunning allows enlightenment to achieve, that is, is made possible only by a *submission* to nature, and to "the requirements of sobriety and common sense" we saw earlier—by renunciation, destruction of the instinct for happiness, loss of the self. The curious outcome of the project of dominating nature by obeying it then is that *nature wins*—and that its victory turns out to have been implicit in and even presupposed by the project from the very beginning. Nature, in the crucial phrase, has its revenge on those who attempt to master it. "Every attempt to break out of natural constraints [*Naturzwang*] by breaking nature enters all the more deeply into those constraints," Horkheimer and Adorno assert, adding ominously, "Hence the course of European civilization."[23]

2. THREE DIALECTICS OF ENLIGHTENMENT

The story of Odysseus serves as the guiding metaphor of the book, underlying the various "dialectics of enlightenment" Horkheimer and Adorno describe as they analyze the dilemmas of the enlightened world from the point of view of ethics, science, art, popular culture, psychology, and so forth. In each version of the dialectic of enlightenment a victory over nature, or over quasi-natural forces of tradition, is achieved by a separation from nature and the construction of a self based on reason and cunning. The struggle to overcome those natural forces promises to enhance human life and save humans from being subject to the dangers posed by that which is other to them; but the victory when it comes always turns out to be deeply ambiguous, and indeed finally to contradict itself. We can briefly trace three forms this dialectic of enlightenment takes in the book: an epistemological one, an ethical one, and a political one. They all have the same structure.

1) *Epistemology.* A science that disenchants nature so as to satisfy human interests, denying it any status other than an instrumental one and rejecting the ascription to it of subjectivity or meaning, has trouble coping with the fact that humans themselves are natural, and hence their interests too would seem to require disenchantment. Hence although enlightenment begins by positing humanism as its guiding value, enlightenment science cannot explain why that (or any) value should guide it. The positivist insistence on the value-neutrality of science follows from this. A well-known consequence is the dilemma of decisionism: enlightened reason can determine how best to achieve certain goals, but in principle can have nothing to say about what those goals ought to be. The choice of ultimate goals appears as an arational one; only *self-preservation* appears as a value whose rationality requires no further justification, precisely because it is presumably "natural." But then what exactly has been disenchanted—nature, or the humanistic values in whose name disenchantment was supposed to be working?

From the very beginning, Horkheimer and Adorno claim, enlightenment grants enormous powers to human thought (in contrast to myth's humility before the gods) but only so long as that thought carefully restricts itself to the severely circumscribed sphere of the instrumental, and so admits itself to be incapable of serious reflection on ultimate values or meaning.[24] This tendency is evident in Kant, the great founder of enlightenment epistemology, who on the one hand praises the capacity of autonomous human reason to know the world but on the other limits what is thus knowable to a world other than the *real* (noumenal) one.[25] Kant's epistemology asserts that the world is guaranteed to fit our perceptions of it, not because our perceptions are so brilliantly attuned to reality but because what we take as reality has already been structured to accord with our perceptions. Only what has been so structured, he argues, can be thought, thereby magically "proving" our thought to be veridical but only at the cost of banning any thought that tries to go beyond such structures.

Yet one such thought, as positivism discovered, is just the thought of such a restriction. The very sentences in which the enlightenment account of reason is phrased are, strictly speaking, ruled out as meaningless by that very account, and so too are any sentences in which the humanist values connecting reason and freedom or autonomy might be articulated. "The notion of the self-understanding of science contradicts the notion of science itself," Horkheimer and Adorno write.[26] But self-knowledge in the broadest sense was just what enlightenment had promised.

It was the individual subject in whose name enlightenment humanism claimed to be working, but that subject's individuality turns out to be part of what enlightenment reason ruthlessly disenchants—it, too, is nature. The formalism of such a reason means that qualitative uniqueness can be understood only when subsumed under some general law and so is no longer so unique at all. "Science in general," Horkheimer and Adorno write, "treats nature and humans no differently than actuarial science in particular treats life and death. . . . The law of large numbers, not the individual detail, is reproduced in the formula."[27] They see this as the real function of Kant's schematism of the understanding, which carefully preforms the material of experience so as to assure the applicability to it of the categories; in this way the possibility of subsuming individuals under general concepts is assured from the outset, but so too is the impossibility of anything ever being experienced as unique or unexpected, and hence as individual.[28]

Thus "everything—even the human individual . . . —is converted into the repeatable, replaceable process, into a mere example for the conceptual models of the system."[29] But this means the end of the subject qua individual. "World domination over nature turns against the thinking subject himself," Horkheimer and Adorno assert; "nothing is left of him but that eternally same *I think* that must accompany all my ideas."[30] Science then turns into nothing but a compulsive accumulation of facts, unable to answer the question of why they are collected or to whom they are addressed; the result is that "what appears to be the triumph of subjective rationality . . . is paid for by the obedient subjection of reason to what is immediately given."[31] Enlightenment was supposed to dominate nature in order to aid the individual, honoring the autonomous subject and turning its bondage into mastery; but by the end of the dialectic the subject has entirely disappeared, its power and autonomy replaced by a blind function of self-preservation, dissolved into the very nature over which enlightenment had promised it control.

2) *Ethics*. Enlightenment's values, including its humanism, thus seem rendered void by its own argument. This is the problem of enlightenment

ethics. Kant attempts to solve it in the second *Critique*, but only (Horkheimer and Adorno believe) at a significant cost of intellectual rigor. Kantian ethics, they claim, is itself entirely formal, unable to offer any concrete content for ethical thinking; and furthermore its argument cannot get off the ground without the assertion of an arational "fact of reason"—the psychological fact of ethical feeling. Such an assertion falls into a sentimentality quite at odds with the stringency and depth of the arguments of the first *Critique*. All that is necessary to refute it is a counterassertion, and one more in keeping with the radical and progressive (and anti-bourgeois) enlightenment insistence on personal autonomy—the assertion that one honestly does not find this feeling within oneself. "Facts have no validity when they simply are not there," Horkheimer and Adorno write.[32] And so instead of Kant, they provocatively choose Nietzsche and the Marquis de Sade in the second excursus to *Dialectic of Enlightenment* as representative enlightenment moralists. Sade and Nietzsche face consistently and unsentimentally the conclusion that Kant tries to avoid— that a purely formal reason can posit no substantial goals, and that a genuinely enlightened view must reject any appeal to supposed psychological "facts" of moral feeling as a mere residue of the very illegitimate authority enlightenment is dedicated to overthrowing. They recognize what follows from this as well—that the only truly categorical imperative for an enlightened and autonomous man or woman is to *make* his or her own "morality."

In the complex, bureaucratized geometries of the sexual combinations arranged by Sade's heroine Juliette, Horkheimer and Adorno suggest, one finds the perfect metaphorical expression of a totally formalized reason unencumbered by substantial goals or moral "facts."[33] The true conclusion to be drawn from Kant's arguments against heteronomy, once the sentimental appeal to a fact of reason is withdrawn, is that reason in itself is essentially indifferent, "a purposeless purposiveness which for just that reason can be bent to any purpose."[34] This is where enlightenment thought ends up, Horkheimer and Adorno claim: with the discovery of "the impossibility of deriving from reason any fundamental argument against murder."[35]

Here again a dialectical reversal switches the roles enlightenment had intended for Reason and Nature. The formalized, systematizing reason of enlightenment stemmed according to Horkheimer and Adorno from the attempt by humans to distance themselves from nature and dominate it, replacing the power of natural laws over humans by the power of autonomous thought legislating for itself. Yet, as we have seen, it follows from that formal concept of reason that the positing of any substantial goals cannot appear to enlightenment as anything other than heteronomy, which is to say as the illicit reintroduction of "nature" (in the form of impulses or biases) into the pristine processes of pure reason; and so reason ends up not merely indifferent to goals but also itself incapable of criticizing them (since any critique would have to be in the name of some *other* goal). But then paradoxically reason ends up capable of putting itself to work for any goal whatsoever, which is to say it ends up under the rule of heteronomy after all. But the rule of heteronomy is the rule of nature.

"Formal as it is, reason stands ready at the service of any natural interest," Horkheimer and Adorno write.[36] Since no values are rationally justifiable, nature itself becomes the only value: the subversive morality of enlightenment, which wished to oppose traditional authority in the name of individual autonomy, finds itself at the end of its long road defending the authority of nature. But that means the authority of the status quo; unable to choose among values, enlightenment has to accept whatever values empirically show themselves, and to support those strong enough to "posit" them.[37] In the work of enlightenment "moralists" like Sade and Nietzsche, once again, nature turns out to be victorious, whether this be in the form of an ethics that wants to release "natural" impulses supposedly repressed by traditional religious ethics (without the sentimental Rousseauian illusion that such impulses will always be good ones) or in the form of a cult of those "naturally" strong enough to impose their own values upon the world.

3) *Politics*. Marx and Engels in a famous discussion in the *Communist Manifesto* had written about the double-edged role of a revolutionary and world-transforming bourgeoisie whose rule makes "all that is solid melt into air" but at the same time appears as a conservative force convinced of the immutability of the conditions of its own power. Horkheimer and Adorno take up this idea in the middle of the second excursus to develop a specifically political form of the dialectic of enlightenment. The eighteenth century Enlightenment associated with the rise of the bourgeoisie, they argue, was marked by a radicalism that set it apart from earlier demythologizing enlightenments. Whereas those earlier movements tended only to replace one set of ruling myths by another one, bourgeois enlightenment took up a principled opposition to *all* myth: *no* beliefs were to be accepted except those that had been vindicated by pure autonomous (and formal) reason. Once the bourgeois revolution was successful, though, this radicalism turned out to have ambiguous consequences.

On the one hand, the principled assertion of the need to examine and question all beliefs that claim objectivity for themselves was soon turned against the beliefs underlying bourgeois rule itself. The ideas espoused by the enlightened revolutionaries in the course of their struggle with entrenched tradition became, after the revolution, a means by which their own rule could be criticized: "The instrument by means of which the bourgeoisie came to power— liberation of forces, universal freedom, self-determination—in a word, the Enlightenment itself, turned against the bourgeoisie once it was forced, as a system of domination, into suppression."[38] Thus enlightenment, despite its original role as apologist for the assertion of bourgeois authority, possesses a subterranean antiauthoritarian moment; this is its "secret utopia," and the source of its continued worth.[39] If all values are to be questioned and all authority is suspect, then bourgeois values and authority are no exception: that eighteenth-century revolutionaries decried the injustice of the ancien régime, and ultimately brought it down, does not make it any less necessary to ask about the degree of justice in the regime they installed to replace it. This is the positive side to the Enlightenment.

Yet, on the other hand, Horkheimer and Adorno argue, this anti-authoritarian (and implicitly anti-bourgeois) moment at the same time also takes the form of an irrationalist moment—of a fall into relativism: this is the negative side. As we have already seen, by formalizing reason and rejecting substantial goals as heteronomy, enlightenment is unable to defend any ideals at all, and hence the inability of bourgeois society to live up to the original revolutionary standards of freedom, justice, and equality perversely appears as something that enlightenment, which had originally promulgated those standards, is now prohibited from criticizing. *Every* belief is "just a belief"; no grounds for choosing one set of institutional arrangements over another are ever rationally justifiable.[40] Although enlightenment shows faith in authority and tradition to be ungrounded, its role is purely negative and sceptical: it cannot demonstrate any reason to believe in anything else either. The result is again that it ends up, despite itself, by supporting the status quo. "Ultimately," Horkheimer and Adorno write, "the anti-authoritarian principle must turn into its very antithesis—into opposition to reason: the abrogation of all inherently binding obligations which it produces allows domination to decree and to manipulate whatever bonds and obligations are appropriate to it."[41]

The relation of enlightenment to bourgeois society thus exhibits the familiar fatal dialectic. It begins, as the ideology of revolution, by supporting and leading to the establishment of the new order, but soon also serves as that order's potentially harshest critic, comparing the ideals for which the revolution was fought with the realities of "really existing" capitalism. Yet paradoxically the critique, taking as it does the form of a critique of "values" in the name of "facts," ends up turning *against* the positive ideals of the revolution, and of enlightenment, themselves, and hence also against notions of freedom, justice, and indeed truth and knowledge as such. Enlightenment's self-abolition—its implicit argument against the possibility of any social critique whatsoever—thus turns it, in a final twist of the dialectic, into the strongest supporter of the new order, and of the domination it originally wished to criticize: its relativism and scepticism with respect to values make it the handmaiden of whatever status quo exists. If no values are justifiable by reason, because all turn out to be forms of ideology, then even the core enlightenment values of truth and reason, of autonomy and solidarity, come under the same ban.

The result is an unresolvable—the word Horkheimer and Adorno use is *unaufhebbar*—contradiction within the very notion of enlightenment itself.[42] And it is one in which nature once again returns, for now the legitimacy of a social system cannot be distinguished from its de facto currency, and so political ideals are justified only by being derived from biological instincts or else because "naturally" powerful groups or individuals support them. The naturalistic cult of strength, like that of the status quo (which is to say, of *second* nature) is the sad last gasp of enlightenment's original radical liberatory principle. Thus finally enlightenment, Horkheimer and Adorno write, "abrogates itself."[43]

3. NATURE'S RETURN

Each of the "dialectics of enlightenment" Horkheimer and Adorno discuss turns out to have the same deep structure. In each an older, pre-enlightened order—the mimetic, the heteronomous, the traditional—is renounced in the name of an enlightenment that asserts the value and the power of human reason against the dangerous forces of the past. In each case, these older forces are identified as "nature," which is to say as the Other of reason. A new order is promised in which the natural will be overcome by enlightenment— the order of a science that can solve human problems, of a mature autonomy legislating for itself, of a society marked by freedom and justice. In this promise one hears the "secret utopia" of enlightenment, its call for a world in which human happiness can be achieved and the power of a massive and indifferent nature over finite and frightened humans can be overcome.

Yet in the attempt to implement this utopia—in science, in ethics, in politics—something goes awry, and with an apparently fateful necessity. The natural, that which enlightenment was attempting to dominate, seems inevitably to return. Odysseus's dialectic is recapitulated: the *separation* from the past and from nature, the autonomy of the rational self from the external, can be assured only by a willing (if cunning) *submission* to externality, to nature. Science, in disenchanting nature, ends up disenchanting any human values beyond the "natural" one of self-preservation; ethics too cannot find an argument against the expression of sadistic "natural" impulses; political theory can do no more than defend the "second nature" of the status quo.

Thus in each case, it is *nature* that reveals itself as the master. The attempt to dominate nature ends up only perpetuating and ratifying the latter's power: "the subjugation of everything natural under the purely autonomous and autocratic [*selbstherrliche*] subject," Horkheimer and Adorno write, "culminates ultimately in the domination [*Herrschaft*] of the blindly objective and natural" over that subject.[44] The original mimetic unity with nature that enlightenment destroyed for humanist reasons ends up after enlightenment's victory (now revealed to be a pyrrhic one) restored—except not as any happy dialectical negation of the negation, but rather as a dark and ominous world in which human individuals and human reason have put in place the institutions and the technology (the second nature) that render individuality and substantial rationality obsolete.

But this common deep structure to the "dialectics of enlightenment" in the text suggests a basic ambiguity in it, stemming from a significant ambivalence about nature. On the one hand, as we have seen, the critique of enlightenment thought seems to take place *in nature's name*: the hubristic attempt by humans to dominate nature by separating themselves from it is responsible for enlightenment's failure, and the very harm done *to* nature indicates the depths of that failure.[45] But on the other hand, as we have also seen, nature seems to function in the account exactly as that which is to be criticized: it is the return of the natural in enlightenment thought, the way in which enlightenment reverts to myth despite itself, to which Horkheimer and Adorno seem most to object—as though nature really were an enemy to be feared. The phrase "domination of nature" begins to appear ambiguous: one usually assumes that the *of* means "over," pointing us to the way humans exert mastery over the natural world, but might it not also be interpreted as a possessive, suggesting conversely that a vengeful and unforgiving nature dominates *us*, inevitably mocking our desperate attempts to overcome it? What conclusion should we draw from the "dialectics of enlightenment" whose paradigm is Odysseus—that contemporary society dominates nature and should not, or that it (so to speak) unfortunately doesn't dominate it *enough*, because nature in fact always returns to outwit us and take its revenge?

These issues arise most directly in the (often overlooked) chapter of *Dialectic of Enlightenment* entitled "Elements of Anti-Semitism," which unexpectedly contains what turns out to be the central epistemological argument of the book. In the fifth and sixth sections of that chapter, Horkheimer and Adorno draw a connection between anti-Semitism in particular and the "enlightened" attitude toward nature in general. It is nature that the anti-Semite is reminded of by the Jew, they argue—the nature that enlightenment thought constantly struggles to dominate—and that is why the latter is so loathed by the former.[46] The very powerlessness of Jews (like that of women, whom Horkheimer and Adorno also mention in this context) makes it easy for them to stand as exemplars of the Other, the natural, that which threatens to slip through the conceptual net of enlightenment thought and so must be the more ruthlessly suppressed. It is the attempt finally to extirpate any hint of the natural, an attempt that forms an inherent telos to enlightenment thought from the very start, that explains the ferocity with which the Nazi confronts the Jew.

But that ferocity is itself *like a force of nature*; enlightenment, as we have seen, reverts to myth, unconsciously revealing the strength of the mimetic element it thought it had so thoroughly suppressed. Enlightenment hates nature and wants to dominate it, but—as in the story of Odysseus—it is tempted by nature, too, and tormented by an ongoing and desperate desire to return to it. By setting upon those powerless figures who remind it of what it secretly wants to be, and by imitating nature's own ferocity in its attack, it is perversely able to have it both ways; the dialectic is of a fundamental sadomasochism at the heart of enlightenment.[47] The fascist torturers, Horkheimer and Adorno write, "identify themselves with nature by producing over and over again in their victims the cry that they dare not themselves emit."[48] The argument here again is influenced by Freud: the suppression of the id (or inner nature) by the superego is paid for by a projection of aggressive impulses toward the outer world. But it also has the same structure identified previously, of an enlightenment based on the domination of nature that however turns into its opposite—turns in fact *into* the very nature that it thought it was destroying (and that it did not really want to destroy). Again, though, the ambiguity as to what status nature really has in such an argument arises, identified as it is here at various points both with fascist terror *and* with that upon which that terror is exercised.

For it is not just the torturer who has something of nature about him; it is also the tortured through whom nature speaks, in the cry of pain. Thus Horkheimer and Adorno write in a remarkable passage that "in the chaotically regulated escape reactions of the lower animals, in the shapes of a swarm, in the convulsive gestures of the martyred, appears what in poor old life can despite everything never be completely overcome [*beherrschen lässt*]: the mimetic impulse. In the death struggle of the creature, the very opposite of freedom, freedom still irresistibly appears as the thwarted destiny [*Bestimmung*] of matter."[49] Here nature's role is clearly paradoxical: the opposite of freedom, it yet contains and promises freedom, revealing this promise in just those chaotic moments, like those of bodily pain and terror and death, where freedom seems most distant. For those are the moments where the rigor of the system, the orderliness of the second nature that we have constructed to protect us from the first, is stripped away— and they offer a glimpse of the "thwarted destiny," our own, that we have given up.

In the chapter on anti-Semitism, Horkheimer and Adorno offer an account of what they call *false projection*, explicitly contrasting it to mimesis, writing that "whereas mimesis makes itself like the environment, false projection makes the environment like itself. For mimesis the external is a model to which the internal conforms—the alien becomes familiar; but false projection transposes . . . inner and outer and stamps the most familiar as enemy. Impulses which the subject will not admit as his own although they are indeed his own are attributed to the object: to the prospective victim."[50] False projection is thus inverted mimesis: instead of imitating the world, I make the world into an imitation of myself. As a psychological phenomenon this is a kind of paranoia, but epistemologically, Horkheimer and Adorno think, it is nothing other than classical idealism, and the hubris of domination: the ego appears as master of all it surveys, as dominator of externality, remaking the world in its own image. It is also, they suggest, the secret to the anti-Semite's boundless hate.

For there are two moments to false projection, as the preceding passage indicates. In the first, the ego turns the world into a reflection of itself; but then in the second, it refuses to recognize itself in the world thus reflected and turns instead against it: "the familiar is stamped as enemy." The reason seems to be that the "self" that wishes to remake the world in its own image, having begun by disconnecting itself from anything external to itself or "natural," paradoxically finds itself entirely empty of content: uncoupled from the natural, it turns out by itself to *be* nothing. Or rather, the only real content of such a disconnected ego is the content it "naturally" finds in itself—which is to say, its inner nature. Hence it is the self's own *naturalness* (and so its entwinement with nature) and nothing else that ends up being projected onto the outer world, and this at the very moment when the deluded and hubristic self imagines itself to have transcended nature and the external. There is a further paradox here as well: for what the anti-natural self now finds in the external world that it confronts (and that is really the product of its projection) are precisely the very ("natural") impulses and drives it is unable to acknowledge in itself and so now proceeds to try to annihilate, never dreaming that this very desire for annihilation might itself be nothing other than yet again one of those impulses.

The situation is like the one described earlier in Kantian ethics, where a pure practical reason based on autonomy can find no content for itself because anything that would serve as content would ipso facto be heteronomous.[51] Here it gets a Freudian twist (whose ethical analogue is the Nietzschean one): the only content available to the ego is the impulse to separation from and rejection of externality itself, an impulse whose character is essentially destructive. Thus false projection, in its desperate need to furnish itself with content, turns outward as aggression, attempting to destroy anything that reminds it of otherness. But, as we have seen, then it simply *becomes* nature, turning into the very otherness it was trying to exclude.[52] The deep structure here is the same as the one examined in the previous section, and once again nature turns out to have a fatefully ambiguous status within it, serving both as that which is denied and oppressed by the enlightened self but also (secretly) as the source of that self's aggression.

Ultimately Horkheimer and Adorno believe there to be a deeper epistemological origin to this dialectic. For *all* perception, they argue—employing
what they call an anthropological Kantianism—contains this moment of projection. The sensory data always underdetermine the object perceived, which
must therefore be constructed by the subject from traces. "Between the true
object and the undisputed data of the senses, between within and without,
there is a gulf which the subject must bridge at his own risk."[53] Hence, more
is always projected onto the object than is actually sensed there: although
perception is always perception of an object that is other than the perceiving
subject, still it can never gain access to this object as it is in itself, which means
it always requires the moment of imagination. This is Kant's great discovery.
Projection becomes "false" only when this fact is forgotten, and what is perceived is taken as equivalent to the object itself without any recognition of the
inevitable contribution of the subjective. "The morbid aspect of anti-Semitism,"
Horkheimer and Adorno write, "is not projective behavior as such, but the
absence from it of reflection [*Reflexion*]."[54]

Reflection here means the difficult acknowledgment by the subject both
of its own complicity in what is perceived as outer but also of the necessary
difference between what it perceives and what is. Neither the positivism that
wants simply to record sense experience without interpretation nor the idealism that sees the world simply as an image of itself is reflective in this sense,
Horkheimer and Adorno believe, a sense that requires a thought that can hold
onto both sides of the paradox at once. Yet such a thought seems hard to
achieve, particularly because the argument suggests that the paranoiac-idealist
element is intrinsic in all cognition. They write:

> Whenever intellectual energies are intentionally concentrated on the
> world outside—that is, wherever it is a question of "pursuing," of
> "ascertaining," of "grasping," of functions whereby primitive con-
> quests over animals have been intellectualized into scientific meth-
> ods of dominating nature, the subjective process is easily overlooked
> in the schematization, and the system is taken to be the thing itself.
> Objectifying [*vergegenständlichende*] thought contains just as sick
> thought does the arbitrariness of a subjective purpose foreign to the
> thing; it forgets the thing itself, thus already committing the act of
> violence which later takes place in [fascist] practice.[55]

Thus ultimately, it is objectifying thought itself which sets the fatal dialectic in motion. "Perception is mediated immediacy," Horkheimer and Adorno
write; in it, thought is captured by "the seductive power of the sensory." The
very clarity and distinctness of perception blind thought to the subjective
element hidden within perceptual acts, thereby producing what Horkheimer
and Adorno call a "necessary illusion," and which they describe as "a consti-

tutive element of all judgment."[56] Any judgment, to the extent that it asserts something, must begin by assuming that that which it asserts is true; the very self-certitude the judgment needs simply to be able to be stated stands in the way of a reflective modesty that would try to distinguish what is objective and what is subjective (that is, what is projected and what is not) in the judgment itself. Judgment is thus always threatening to ossify into the false (and paranoid) claim that whatever I perceive is objectively true.

"Only the self-conscious labor of thought can escape from this hallucinatory power," Horkheimer and Adorno write, calling for a self-reflective and properly modest thought that tries to separate out in its perception what is due to the world from what is subjective in origin.[57] The idea is not to overcome the distinction nor to dissolve it, but simply to grasp and know it, accepting the tension between the poles and not trying to reduce one to the other. Yet nothing in their account suggests that this will be easy, and indeed nothing really suggests that it is even possible at all. They use the term *Besinnung* for that self-conscious labor of thought, but they acknowledge too that although "in a healthy person [it] breaks the power of immediacy, [it] is never so compelling as the illusion it dispels. As a negative, reflective [*reflektierte*], and indirect movement, it lacks the brutality inherent in the positive."[58] The fatal dialectic of false projection, which is implicit in the attempt to dominate nature and which ends in idealism, paranoia, and fascism, is set into motion by the first act of judgment and is perpetuated in all that follow—and note that it is not so much the unavoidable subjectivity of thought as the "seductive power of the sensory" that is at fault. Here, I want to suggest, once again nature returns and once again it plays a negative role: for it is nature, that which is external to thought, that provides the sensory element of perception with the vividness and "brutality" that frustrate the attempt through *Besinnung* to separate subjective from objective in cognition. The hope for a self-conscious labor of thought that might achieve this seems a meager hope indeed.

Indeed in each of the "dialectics of enlightenment" we have been investigating hope seems meager, a slender reed to be grasped at in the face of an overwhelming and fatal dialectical movement put into motion by nature itself. The *petitio principii* Horkheimer and Adorno ironically admit to in their introduction, after all, remains a logical fallacy no matter how proudly it is proclaimed; it is simply not clear how enlightened thought on their account can avoid its own fatal consequences, nor for that matter how an alternative to it could ever arise. The grounds they offer for hope seem tenuous. Whether it be the memory of a pre-enlightenment mimesis that was itself never entirely free of *List* (and was demonstrably unable to protect humans from illness, pain, or death), or the "secret utopia" in Kant's conception of reason that in Horkheimer and Adorno's own view ends up by abrogating itself, or the un-

flinching refusal of Sade and Nietzsche to accept the hypocrisy of enlightenment ethical theory, in each case it is hard to believe in the possibility (always
hinted at and obviously devoutly desired, but never very clearly stated) of a
reconciliation that might avoid or transcend the fatal dialectic. The wonderful
"Quand Même" section in the last part of *Dialectic of Enlightenment* soberly
surveys the reasons to believe that "terror and civilization are inseparable" and
that "it is impossible to abolish the terror and retain civilization"; instead of
accepting the various pessimistic consequences that follow, however,
Horkheimer and Adorno write, "there is another conclusion: to laugh at logic
when it runs counter to humans."[59] This sounds fine, but is really nothing
other than whistling past the graveyard; logic is not so easily done away with.

Adorno especially loved these sorts of paradoxical formulations; they form
the internal structure of whole works such as *Minima Moralia*. But despite the
rhetorical brilliance, it is not clear they do much except obscure the situation.
The *petitio principii* is more harmful than Horkheimer and Adorno let on; the
criticism of any asserted moral or political claim that it is "just a belief" is not
answered by pointing to its baleful consequences, because it is just the possibility of rationally distinguishing the baleful from the beneficent at all that
such a criticism is questioning. If Horkheimer and Adorno are part of enlightenment thought, and if enlightenment thought finds itself unable to justify its
own appeal to truth and freedom and autonomy, then they too face the same
predicament; pointing it out is not the same as solving it.[60]

This is the fundamental conceptual problem faced by the Critical Theory
of *Dialectic of Enlightenment*. Horkheimer and Adorno's position abrogates
itself too: since from within enlightenment no critique of enlightenment is
possible (because the ethical values needed for such a critique are illegitimate
to an enlightenment view that has seen through the heteronomy of all values),
their critique must come from a standpoint external to enlightenment. But
what sort of standpoint could this be? Horkheimer and (especially) Adorno
resolutely abjure the thought of presenting a systematic theory on the basis of
which their critique might be legitimated because to engage in systematic
thinking would, they think, simply be to find themselves again enmeshed in
the fatal dialectic; but as a result it becomes impossible to decide, when they
"laugh at logic," which of their criticisms represent principled objections to the
harm enlightenment has done to human beings and which represent merely
the dislikes and crotchets of mid-century central European intellectuals dis-
placed to southern California and shocked by what they find there.[61]

The dialectic of enlightenment here has run into a cul-de-sac. Its fatality
is built in from the start—for myth is already enlightenment, as we have seen,
and judgment is already paranoid projection. It seems to be the human condition; no escape, historically or conceptually, is possible. And the culprit,

never explicitly identified by Horkheimer and Adorno as such, turns out (I have been suggesting) to be nature itself—the nature that enlightenment wanted to dominate and in whose name Horkheimer and Adorno seem to be writing but that somehow seems always at the end of the dialectic to return and frustrate human desires. Nature's status is not only ambiguous, but also unavoidable: it stands in this theory as the great given fact, in the face of which humans can do nothing, except perhaps engage in a hope without much basis in experience. Its "revenge" for the attempt to dominate it, it turns out, is total.

CHAPTER 4

Adorno and
Nature as the Nonidentical

1. NONIDENTITY AND THE PRIMACY OF THE OBJECT

Despite some superficial similarities between Horkheimer and Adorno's concept of "enlightenment" and Lukács's discussion of the "contemplative attitude," as far as nature is concerned the two accounts are quite different. Horkheimer and Adorno's view depends above all on a kind of materialism or naturalism that stands in considerable conflict with the Lukácsian notion of nature as a social category developed in Chapter 2. Ultimately, as we have seen, enlightenment's greatest sin on Horkheimer and Adorno's account lies in its attempt to dominate or even abolish nature. That this project is doomed to failure really follows for them from the fact that humans are themselves natural beings, something that they claim enlightenment in its profound alienation from nature always tries to deny. But *this* "alienation" is very different from the "reification" of *History and Class Consciousness*. Although both positions doubtless involve a critique of any view separating humans from nature, they disagree altogether about why such a separation is problematic. Thus while Horkheimer and Adorno see the problem as lying in enlightenment's failure to acknowledge the rootedness of human beings within nature, for Lukács (as I have argued above) the problem lies rather in contemplation's failure to see the opposite—that nature is a social category and that therefore what we take as nature is in fact always already the consequence of our own practices. Thus whereas Horkheimer and Adorno want to emphasize the naturalness of humans, Lukács emphasizes instead so to speak the humanness of nature.[1]

I will return in the next section to an explicit comparison between these two views. At the moment however we can use Lukács's arguments to provide a clue as to a possible weakness in those of Horkheimer and Adorno. The problem is that their account seems to require the possession of some sort of objective theory of nature (the nature that we "are part of" and are "alienated from") that somehow escapes the inevitable sociality of our knowledge of nature to which Lukács had pointed. A surprising reversal has taken place here. We saw Lukács wanting very much to exclude natural science from his critique of contemplation; "scientistic" thinking only becomes ideological, he wanted to say, when applied to social phenomena. But as I argued earlier this exclusion is inconsistent with the real trajectory of his argument, whose critique of immediacy must turn into a critique of nature, and further seems unavoidably to entail that there is no access—not even through science—to *any* "immediate" nature independent of the social.[2] Horkheimer and Adorno, on the other hand, do not share Lukács's reluctance to criticize natural science. They have no trouble asserting its social character: on the contrary to them natural science and its methods form a major element of the enlightenment worldview they are concerned to criticize. What they do have trouble with, though, is the critique of immediacy, the one that asserts that all views of nature are always social in content.

Their critique, unlike Lukács's, carried out as it is not in the name of self-recognition by the subject but in the name of nature itself, requires just the sort of appeal to immediacy that Lukács's argument throws into doubt. In the thought-form of a nature repressed on the one hand by enlightenment's attempt at domination but also on the other always eventually returning to frustrate that attempt, implicit appeal must be made to a nature that is prior to, or at least other than, the social—the nature before disenchantment, the nature imitated in mimesis, the nature of the unique individual over and against the system, and above all the inner nature of humans suppressed by enlightenment renunciation. Underlying *Dialectic of Enlightenment*'s critique of the enlightenment approach toward nature is the implicit call for a different approach, in which nature is left alone and allowed to be what it really is—immediately, in itself, independently of the social.

But then everything will depend on the account of what nature "really is." The Lukácsian critique is self-sufficient; this other one however requires its own theory of nature, independent of and superior to the enlightenment theory being criticized—the one whose sociality is revealed in the critique. In the context of *Dialectic of Enlightenment* this means that everything depends first of all on the speculative anthropology of the first chapter—the story about mimesis, magic, and the transition to enlightenment—and second on the appeal to Freud's theory of the instincts. To point this out is immediately to show how unlikely such a strategy must be: for how could these particular theories themselves be expected to escape the objection that they too are social, are mediations, do not provide access to nature in itself? The whole work depends on a *particular* conception of nature, implicit in Horkheimer and Adorno's accounts of that which animistic magic mimetically recalls, or of the inherently destructive character of "inner nature" when it is projected outside itself, or of that which distorts judgment through the "seductive power of the sensory"; it is this conception that underlies both the critique of false projection and domination of nature on the one hand and the repeated assertion that nature cannot be dominated and will always have its revenge on the other.

The trouble is that given the far-reaching character of the epistemology examined above it follows from Horkheimer and Adorno's own position that this view of nature *too* will have something of a false projection about it, that it too has already failed to take account of the subjective element contained within it. Thus it too will partake from the start of the secret and destructive desire for domination and of the "necessary illusion" that mistakes its own perspective for an account of independent truth. Here is the deepest, and most inescapable, *petitio principii* in *Dialectic of Enlightenment*, and the one that explains its failure: it depends essentially on a conceptual mythology that first of all receives no independent confirmation in the text, and that second must claim for itself the very kind of "objective" knowledge of what nature is like prior to the mediating activity of humans whose possibility the text itself denies.

But Adorno's later work, to which I now want to turn, is marked by a much more sophisticated understanding of this problem; one might even surmise that part of the motivation behind it is the desire to find a philosophical framework for a critique of enlightenment in which the speculative anthropology and the implicit appeals to nature of *Dialectic of Enlightenment* are no longer required. Certainly in Adorno's major postwar works such as *Negative Dialectics* and the unfinished *Aesthetic Theory* the speculative anthropology has disappeared, and Freud's theory too takes on a greatly reduced role. "Mimesis" remains as a central concept, especially in the *Aesthetic Theory*, but with a much less anthropologically specific meaning. And in *Negative Dialectics* the critique of Heidegger's archaism and historical inventions might well be read as a self-critique of tendencies in the earlier Frankfurt School as well. Adorno's attempt in these later works to develop an account of nature that avoids the problems we have traced in *Dialectic of Enlightenment* certainly rivals Lukács's both in its brilliance and in its influence on later thinkers. I shall argue, however, that finally it is not successful.

In these works epistemological considerations, which played a somewhat secondary role in *Dialectic of Enlightenment* as compared to anthropology and psychology, move explicitly to the center of concern. As in the earlier account of the function of "false projection" in judgment, Adorno here emphasizes the inevitable failure of cognition fully to grasp the objects it wants to know and hence the inevitable difference between thought and the object it is thinking. The consequent "nonidentity" between concept and object is the fulcrum for the "negative dialectic" he proposes. "The name of dialectics says no more, to begin with," he writes, "than that objects do not go into their concepts without leaving a remainder. . . . Dialectics is the consistent consciousness of non-identity."[3] This consciousness is like the *Besinnung* mentioned earlier: the difficult and yet crucial task assigned to thought is rigorously to think this nonidentity, which is to say to think its own limitation, its own difference from the object it tries to know.

This conception of a dialectic that results from the necessary difference between thought and that which it thinks owes much of course to Hegel; but Hegel, Adorno believes, goes in for a premature reconciliation, positing an identity of identity and difference in which the nonidentity of thought and object is said to be *aufgehoben* but in fact is simply canceled. Difference, the motor of the dialectic for Hegel and Adorno both, is too quickly passed over in the former, dissolved always and again into a higher identity that ends in absolute knowledge. Thus although Hegel believes he has overcome the "identity thinking" that fails to grasp difference, finally (Adorno believes) he is still caught in it, and even in a sense more so than those whom he criticizes: his megalomaniac hope is for an identity in which nonidentity too would be encompassed—like Odysseus's desire to hear the Sirens' song and yet survive.[4]

Adorno wants rather (and he thinks more consistently) to assert the *nonidentity* of identity and difference, thereby positing difference rather than identity as primary. The result would be a paradoxical "nonidentity thinking" that would take place in the name of what is missed in the concept, what thought (including Hegel's thought) always leaves out. Adorno writes that

> At this historical moment, philosophy's true interest lies in those areas about which Hegel, at one with the tradition, expressed his disinterest: the nonconceptual, the individual, the particular—that which since Plato has been dismissed as transitory and insignificant and to which Hegel gave the label 'poor existence' [*faulen Existenz*]. Its theme would be the qualities it denigrates as contingent into *quantités négligeables*. Of urgency to the Concept would be what it cannot reach, what escapes its mechanism of abstraction, what is not already an instance of it.[5]

Such a philosophy would be an "anti-system," concerned not with achieving Absolute Knowledge but rather with redeeming the idiosyncratic, the neglected, the detail.[6] It would function as a truly "negative dialectic," abandoning the Hegelian dream of an ultimate negation of the negation that would issue in a positive result; its task rather would be in each particular case to show the difference between concept and object and hence to reveal the *impossibility* of a positive result—of a thought that, having ultimately attained full knowledge of something, could finally stop and rest.[7] It would thus have to be a modest thought, a thought that knows its own limits and does not mistake its ability to show how the object escapes the concept for an ability to comprehend the object itself after all; restless and rigorously negative, it must be a "thought thinking against itself," always on guard against its own tendency to believe it has finally grasped the object it thinks.[8]

Rejecting system, rejecting positive result, it must then also reject the notion of *totality*, of the possibility of knowing the world as a whole. "A changed philosophy would have to . . . cease persuading others and itself that it has the infinite at its disposal" and so is capable of understanding everything, Adorno writes. But in another sense, he adds, such a new philosophy "would itself *be* infinite, insofar as it would scorn being fixed into a corpus of enumerable theorems. Its substance would lie in the diversity of objects that impinge upon it or that it seeks, a diversity not patterned after any schema; it would truly give itself to such objects, rather than using them as a mirror in which to reread itself, mistaking its own image for concretion."[9] Not identity, not the one system or one method or one equation that can comprehend everything at once, but rather difference, nonidentity, would be the center of this negative thought.

But there is a great danger here, one that Adorno says he recognizes, for "difference" and "nonidentity" too are after all themselves concepts. The temptation will be to hypostatize them, to produce yet another System founded now on the nonidentical. (This is just the problem that I have argued *Dialectic of Enlightenment* faces with respect to the concept of "nature.") Adorno cautions that "in criticizing ontology, we do not aim at another ontology, not even at one of being non-ontological. If that were our purpose we would merely be positing an Other as the downright 'first'—this time not absolute identity, not Being, not the concept, but rather nonidentity, entity [*Seiende*], facticity. We would be hypostatizing the concept of nonconceptuality and thus acting counter to its meaning."[10] This is the basis of his sharp critique of Heidegger, despite the many clear similarities between their views. Adorno objects above all to what he sees as Heidegger's tendency to take "that which is left out" of the concept and turn it into something mystical—Being, the Nothing, *Lichtung*— as though the nonidentical were some specific and most mysterious thing that no thought could get to, and not rather simply an indication of the more mundane fact that each particular thought fails to grasp *some* particular aspect of its object (a different aspect, so to speak, in each case). Thus Adorno writes that

What echoes in the word "Being" as opposed to τὰ ὀντα—that everything is more than it is—means entwinement [*Verflochtenheit*], not something transcendent to entwinement, which is what Heidegger makes of it: something added to the individual entity. He follows dialectics so far as to say that neither the subject nor the object are immediate and ultimate [*Letztes*]; but he goes beyond it in reaching for something beyond subject and object that is immediate and primary [*Erstes*].[11]

Entwinement here means that neither subject nor object may be reduced to the other, and yet that there is nothing other than subject and object, nothing behind or prior to them.[12] The temptation to return to positivity, to achieve a *knowledge* of the nonidentical beyond the modest (and infinite) negativity that simply shows, in each case, how thought fails to reach its object, is one that for Adorno must be carefully resisted.

Positivity's hubris lies not merely in its faith that thought can grasp objectivity and cover it entirely by concepts; it also believes thought to be self-sufficient and thus itself free of the taint of objectivity. But in truth thought is always already itself objective, because it is always thought of *something*, thought with a content, and the content is always other than it. "*Kein Sein ohne Seiendes*," Adorno writes against Heidegger and Hegel both: *Etwas*, something, not *Sein*, being, is the logically primary category for thought.[13] All thought has a content, which means there is no such thing as "pure" or self-identical thought: "thought" too goes beyond *its* own concept. Only a negative dialectics, Adorno believes, can start to deal with this paradox. Thought—as the thought of a real thinker, herself a natural being—is enmeshed in the world from the very beginning; thus negative dialectics insists not simply that there is more to the object than the concept can grasp, but also that there is more to the *subject*, and hence for that matter to the concept, too.

This is Adorno's highly sophisticated reformulation of the old Marxist idea of a materialist dialectic, one that had been thrown into disrepute in the Western Marxist tradition by Lukács's critiques of Engels. Engels's mistake, probably Marx's too, had been to assert what Adorno calls the *Vorrang des Objekts*, the primacy of the object over any subjective attempt to know it, but then immediately to talk of a set of theories (natural science, historical materialism, the theory of surplus value, etc.) as correctly "representing" the objective world, not realizing that in so doing any claim for objectivity's primacy over all subjective endeavors to grasp it had promptly been forgotten. Adorno understands that a consistent materialism necessarily would have to be more modest and further could also only be negative in form, in acknowledgment of the paradox inherent in a thought that asserts the "primacy" of something other than thought.

Vorrang des Objekts means that the subject is necessarily linked to objects from the very start, and in a way that objects are *not* necessarily linked to subjects. The asymmetry is crucial to this kind of materialism. "An object can only be thought by a subject yet always remains something other than the subject," Adorno writes, "whereas a subject by its very nature is from the outset an object as well. The subject cannot be thought independently of the object, even as idea; but the object can be thought independently of the subject. To also be an object is part of the meaning of subjectivity; but it is not equally part of the meaning of objectivity to be a subject."[14] Indeed, only for this reason can the subject come to know the object at all: only because the subject is also object, mediated by the objective, is knowledge of the objective possible for it. This is not to deny that the object, too, as it immediately presents itself needs the mediating power of thought to be known, but only to assert that the situation is not symmetrical: "Mediation of the object means that it must not be statically, dogmatically hypostatized but rather can only be known in its entwinement with subjectivity; but mediation of the subject means that without the moment of objectivity it would literally be nothing."[15] The mediation of the subject by objectivity—the fact that all thought is the thought of a conscious living human in a specific physical and social situation—thus has a primacy over the very different mediation through which objectivity comes to be known.

Dialectic of Enlightenment's anthropological assertion that humans are first of all part of nature is thus here transformed into the epistemological assertion that subjects are always also objects, just as its concept of "enlightenment" here returns as the identity thinking that fails to recognize the difference between object and concept. As in the earlier work, idealism here is identified with paranoia, and with rage—with subjectivity's hatred for that which is other than it, an otherness upon which it stands but which it wants to repress.[16] Idealism rejects the primacy of the object, wanting rather to reduce the object to the subjectivity that knows it. But even to assert the goal of this reduction is implicitly to admit the object's primacy, Adorno notes, since "every statement to the effect that subjectivity 'is' this or that already includes within it an objectivity that the subject pretends to ground by means of its Absolute Being."[17]

But if classical German idealism falls under Adorno's critique as an identity thinking that fails to recognize the primacy of the object, so too it would seem does the theory of reification, in the form given to it both by Lukács and by the Marx of the section on fetishism in *Capital*. That theory, on Adorno's reading, sees "objectivity" as negative and something to be overcome, denying its "primacy" and instead (as we have seen in Chapter 2) concerned rather with dissolving static objectivities into the active and subject-initiated processes from which they derive. In so doing, Adorno thinks, it reveals its own dislike for objectivity as such. He is careful to acknowledge the positive value of the critique of reification: it helps to deconstruct the false objectivities of contemporary society that make the particular historical conditions of bourgeois rule look like eternal facts of nature. But it is itself a *"Reflexionsform"* of those false objectivities, he asserts, more caught in them than it realizes; by offering a critique of what is ultimately only a form of consciousness—by remaining, that is, on the level of subjectivity—it deprives critical theory of its objective content, as a critique of the real sufferings that real people undergo.[18]

The discovery that much of what the contemporary world calls "objective" is really "congealed society" misleadingly turns in the theory of reification into a critique of objectivity itself, and in so doing misses the primacy of the object that should be dialectical thinking's central theme.[19] Still thinking that liberation comes from overcoming that which is external to the subject, reification theory shows itself tied to identity thinking and to idealism's rage, Adorno believes; it wants to abolish anything alien to itself, rather than finding a way to acknowledge and accept the alien *as* alien, which is to say as nonidentical.[20] Its dream as we have seen is that of a humanity recognizing itself in otherness, but for Adorno this is not at all what utopia would involve: "the reconciled condition," he writes against such a conception, "would not be the philosophical imperialism of annexing the alien. Instead, its happiness would lie in the fact that the alien, in the proximity it is granted, remains what is distant and different, beyond the heterogeneous and beyond that which is one's own."[21]

Thus for Adorno "the category of reification, which was inspired by the ideal of unbroken subjective immediacy, no longer merits the key position accorded to it, overzealously, by an apologetic thinking happy to absorb materialism."[22] It is not the philosopher's stone, he says; "we can no more reduce dialectics to reification than we can reduce it to any other isolated category."[23] At best it is a kind of epiphenomenon, pointing to something important about contemporary society but misleading if taken as the center of the critique. Gillian Rose, in her study *The Melancholy Science*, has argued that "Adorno's thought depends fundamentally on the category of reification," but I think this cannot be accepted, at least if reification is taken in the standard (Lukácsian) sense as referring to a process in which human practices and relations are mistakenly viewed as external objects.[24] On the contrary such a category must appear from Adorno's standpoint as dangerously infected with idealism and the hubris of identity thinking; much more important for him is to point out cases where objects that *really are* external are mistakenly viewed as merely *for humans*.[25]

Rose tends not to see how radical is the break with Lukács (and with Hegel) entailed by Adorno's "nonidentity thesis"; she writes as though the nonidentity of concept and object were for Adorno merely an unfortunate characteristic of contemporary "reified" society, and even talks of a "rational identity thinking" pointing toward a utopia of reconciliation where concept and object finally and joyfully *would* correspond—an idea that would make sense to Lukács and Hegel both, but would seem anathema to Adorno's conception of the nonidentical.[26] This theme is no doubt there in the passages

Rose quotes: "the ideal of identity must not simply be discarded," Adorno writes, and adds that "living in the rebuke that the thing is not identical with the concept is the concept's longing to become identical with the thing."[27] But there is no hint that this longing could ever actually be satisfied, and instead one finds the usual (and paradoxical) claim that "nonidentity is the secret telos of identification."[28] To be sure, according to Adorno critical social theory must work through "immanent critique," which is to say through a critical unmasking of the gap between ideals and the real world, but in such critique the "longing" for identity can serve only a tactical function. Real identity is not achievable and in any case would be no utopia. Rather, he writes, "utopia would be above identity and above contradiction; it would be a togetherness of diversity [ein Miteinander des Verschiedens]."[29]

It seems to me that Horkheimer and Adorno's materialist critique of enlightenment, particularly as modified in Adorno's later critique of "identity thinking," represents a fundamental *alternative* in the Western Marxist tradition to Lukács's theory of reification as I have reconstructed the latter. We have seen something like this alternative before, though—for it has much more in common with the *Lebensphilosophische* themes in Lukács that I have argued stand in at best an uneasy conflict with the more sophisticated Hegelian ideas that underlie his account of reification.[30] Those themes, recall, had to do with the formalism of bourgeois thought, its inability to comprehend its own content, its failure to take account of qualitative difference among formally comparable "cases," its incapacity to understand change or the organic.[31] Such *Lebensphilosophische* lines of argument, as Colletti has pointed out, go back in the Marxist tradition to Engels's critiques of "mechanical materialism" and indeed back further to romantic critiques of *Verstand.*[32]

Adorno represents this tradition at its apogee. Central to its view is the notion that there is "always something left out" by conceptual (nondialectical, bourgeois, contemplative, formalistic, identity-oriented) thought—something in the object that static and systematic thinking can never grasp, that like quicksilver always escapes its clutches. Sometimes the argument suggests the possibility of some other ("dialectical") mode of thinking, some *Vernunft*, that *would* be able to grasp what *Verstand* cannot; but in Adorno—more consistent and more pessimistic—it takes a more radical form, leading to the sceptical assertion that no cognition at all is capable of grasping the object and offering instead a critique of cognition as such, precisely in the name of that which it leaves out. The opposition between this view, brilliantly developed by Adorno in the works we have been discussing but already present in *Dialectic of Enlightenment*, and the Lukácsian one we examined in the previous chapter, is central to the history of Western Marxist discussions of nature and alienation. I began this section with some general remarks about it; we now need to examine it more explicitly.

2. REIFICATION AND THE NONIDENTICAL

The one side, as we have seen, emphasizes materialism and the nonidentity of concept and object; the other emphasizes practice and the dialectic of reification and self-recognition. On one level the views have much in common. Both theories make the audacious move of attempting to derive social theory and social critique from epistemological considerations, and it is the same set of considerations in each case—the insights of classical German philosophy regarding the active involvement of the subject in the constitution of the object perceived. "All reification is a forgetting,"[33] write Horkheimer and Adorno, in words Lukács might well have written; for both views, the *epistemological* failure of the subject to recognize its contribution to what is perceived is taken as the paradigmatic phenomenon of contemporary society, and one that can serve as the guiding clue for understanding the *social* failures diagnosed by standard Marxist theory. This epistemological failure is central to what Horkheimer and Adorno call "enlightenment" on the one hand, and to what Lukács calls the "contemplative attitude" on the other.

The two views differ radically, though, when it comes to an account of how this epistemological failure is to be remedied and what such a remedy would look like, thus revealing that, from the very start, they each understand something very different by talk of "contribution," of "object," and of "forgetting." For the theory of reification (by which I now specifically mean the version of Lukács's view I defended in Chapters 1 and 2), recognizing the irreducibility of the subject's contribution to the object known translates into a call for the subject consciously to *acknowledge* that active contribution—not with the hope of eliminating it and somehow capturing the objective world "as it is in itself" (because that is impossible), but rather in order to dissolve the illusion of immediacy, objectivity, and otherness in the world perceived. The call here is for self-reflection and self-understanding: what has been "forgotten" on this view is the subject itself, deeply implicated from the outset in the production of a world that appears to be external to it but is in fact rather always already the consequence of its own transformative and mediating acts. Thus talk here of a "contribution" of the subject to what is perceived is actually somewhat misleading, for it suggests that there is something immediate, something other than and prior to the subject's transformative acts, *to which* those acts "contribute"; rather this theory interprets the discovery of the subject's active involvement in the world it inhabits in the most radical possible sense, suggesting that "objectivity" has the "subjective" (meaning here the active) within it from the very beginning.

For Horkheimer and Adorno, on the other hand as we have seen, what has been "forgotten" in cognition is precisely *nature*—which is to say, that which underlies cognition and makes it possible but is itself other than cognition and the subject.[34] Their account of false projection, and its further development in Adorno's account of identity thinking, sees the fundamental error as arising when the subject forgets its own contribution to the object known, forgets (that is) the nonidentity between concept and object, and so mistakenly and dangerously takes the experienced object to be identical with the real one. The call here is not for self-conscious self-assertion, but for a modesty in pretension, for a thought that knows its limits and does not take what it thinks as identical with what is. "Contribution" here *is* the right word, and furthermore has a negative sign: the subject must remember that in the cognition something has been added, something that is ultimately distorting. This view is reminiscent of some very traditional enlightenment epistemological positions, according to which real knowledge of an object is knowledge from which the "subjective component" has been eliminated:[35] in Horkheimer and Adorno it is merely given a pessimistic and sceptical twist, since on their account such an elimination is in fact impossible.

But here a regression behind the insights of classical German philosophy takes place; for it is just this aspect of precritical epistemology that the post-Kantian tradition most strongly criticized. To speak of a "contribution" by the subject to the object cognized, and especially of one that ought to be avoided— even with the despairing admission that such avoidance is impossible—makes sense only if one can give meaning to the idea of the object prior to and independent of this "contribution"; the trouble is that there's nobody around to give meaning to such an idea except us subjects. What is required here is an implicit appeal to an immediacy underlying the subject's acts of mediation to which those acts might be said to contribute, but it is not clear how such an appeal to immediacy could possibly be justified. This was the problem we identified earlier in *Dialectic of Enlightenment*; it is the deepest sense in which "nature always returns" in that work.[36] But even Adorno's more sophisticated reformulation does not avoid this problem. To say, as the theory of nonidentity does, that "the object always escapes the concept's grasp" requires being able to make sense of an object independent of the conceptual, which in this sense means independent of the subject's activity; yet this "making sense" would itself have to be an operation of thought and hence yet another activity of the subject.

Thus at bottom both accounts, Horkheimer and Adorno's in *Dialectic of Enlightenment* and that in Adorno's later work as well, face the same problem, because both require an appeal to immediacy to get their critique off the ground. There must *be* this immediacy if identity thought can legitimately be criticized for "forgetting" it, yet of course at the same time it is this very immediacy that the critique shows cognition to be incapable of ever knowing. It (and the "nature" that stands for it) appears then as a kind of deus ex machina, necessary for the critique to function yet not deriving from it immanently. We saw an example of this earlier, in Horkheimer and Adorno's account of false projection which depended on the positing of an "inner nature" repressed by enlightenment rationality and then projected onto the external world in the form of aggressive impulses. But that such an inner nature existed or would necessarily take that particular form was not required by the epistemological argument itself but was rather external to it, derived from a Freudianism whose own epistemological status and relation to enlightenment remained unclarified.

It is important to note that whereas the theory of reification here would speak about the subject's involvement in *constructing* the world around it—both literally thorough practical labor, and more abstractly through the mediations of cognition—this materialist theory speaks instead of the subject as *projecting* that world, finding the implications of "construction" to be too idealist. But then it needs an account of the origin of that which is projected, of the internal model that is externalized in the projective act. "Inner nature" is the obvious candidate for this model—a "nature" both within the subject but also other than it. Yet in the context of Adorno's later writings this seems problematic at best: the nonidentity thesis makes it unclear how such an "inner nature" could be conceptually grasped, and thus also unclear how it could be spoken of as a "model" for "projection." Instead of inner nature one would have perhaps rather only to assert the existence of a kind of nonidentity between ego and id, meaning simply that the "self" finds itself with "impulses" it does not recognize as its own; to identify those impulses with "nature" (or for that matter with any kind of hypostatized id) would be to try once again to grasp them conceptually, and in that sense to be subject to the critique of identity.

It is not only projection, furthermore, that turns out to be difficult to understand on this view; a similar problem arises with respect to the normative foundations of critical theory itself. We saw earlier the difficulty faced by Horkheimer and Adorno in their blithe assertion of a *petitio principii* according to which the standards they employ to judge enlightenment are precisely those of the enlightenment they are criticizing, as well as their injunction to "laugh at logic when it runs counter to humans."[37] Later Adorno faces an equivalent problem: he wants to criticize identity thinking in the name of that which it fails to grasp, but because he has to acknowledge (at pain of falling into his own identity thinking) being equally incapable of grasping it himself, it is hard to see how it could ever really function as the foundation of his critique.

He ends up in a regression, asserting in *Negative Dialectics* that critical ethical judgments have their basis ultimately in the *somatic*. Horrors like Auschwitz, he claims, cannot be criticized on the basis of some abstract principle; to do so would only increase the horror—for Auschwitz was precisely the revenge of the abstract and universal, of identity, upon the concrete and nonidentical. Rather it is "the practical abhorrence of the unbearable physical agony to which individuals are exposed" that by itself and alone grounds the critique.[38] Elsewhere he writes that our direct somatic impulses against torture and genocide must be understood as just that, as particular impulses: "they must not be rationalized; as an abstract principle they would fall promptly into the bad infinity of proof and validity." Such impulses, he adds, are "immanent in moral conduct and would be denied in callous attempts at rationalization. What is most urgent would once again become contemplative, mocking its own urgency."[39] "The smallest trace of senseless suffering in the empirical world," he writes in another place, "belies all the identitarian philosophy that would talk us out of that suffering. . . . The physical moment tells our knowledge that suffering ought not to be, that things should be different."[40]

Here the "self-conscious labor of thought" elsewhere so eloquently called for in nonidentity thinking is explicitly abdicated in the name of an intuitionist appeal to brute physical reaction. Adorno does not remark on what he otherwise is quick to acknowledge—that even our most apparently "direct" physical responses are always already the product of the social and even of the conceptual and hence can offer no magical access to the land of the immediate. But the reason for his move, inconsistent though it is, should be clear. For how else could an ethics be founded? It cannot be founded in mediation, since to try to do so (for Adorno) would be to reproduce identity thinking's illusory dream of a self-sufficient thought that could fully master and even guide the real. But then unless it can be founded in something immediate like the body it cannot be founded at all. The danger opened up, that is, is of a sceptical relativism that denies that any of our moral insights have objective validity, because each can be shown to be based on social processes of mediation and so immediacy cannot be reached. Since Adorno shares with this sceptical view the belief that only that which is immediate could be objectively valid, he can escape its anti-critical consequences only by finding something immediate on which to ground his own critique—and so claims to find it in the natural and the somatic, in our immediate revulsion at murder and pain. But this is just a rhetorical flourish, utterly at odds with the rest of his view, which would otherwise suggest that the somatic can no more be immediately grasped than anything else.[41] The "impulses" Adorno speaks of are social ones; to ground the critique of Auschwitz on a physical aversion to genocide is to leave it vulnerable to the Nazi attempt to produce a generation of hardened *Hitlerjugend* who simply did not feel that aversion. The point is the one we saw Horkheimer and Adorno making earlier about Kant's appeal to a fact of practical reason: "facts have no validity when they simply are not there."[42]

This helps, though, to clarify the differences we are examining. It should be clear that although both the nonidentity thesis and the theory of reification recognize that we have no access to any realm of immediacy, the former view unlike the latter takes this as a failing of thought to be lamented, seeing the source of contemporary problems in the deleterious effects of this (necessarily unseen and unknown) immediacy upon us when it is "forgotten." Nature always returns, the somatic has its revenge. But to speak this way is to pretend despite everything to *know* something about that immediacy. Such a view really secretly imagines a moment at which we can catch a glimpse of the immediate (or can "feel" it in our bodies), sneaking a peek at it when thought (the faculty of mediation) isn't paying attention.[43]

What lies beneath the surface here is the hope for some access to immediacy other than the cognitive one, a hope that marks this kind of theory finally as romantic. Even if there were some such access, of course—mystical or somatic or mimetic—it would still have to be known as such; cognition is not so easily done away with. Against this the theory of reification is more consistent: it does not dream of the immediacy it proves not to exist but rather of *a mediation become conscious to itself*—and sufficiently self-confident that it does not believe itself to need any basis in anything external to it.[44] The one view finds in mediation only distortion and violation of the immediacy it admits it cannot ever know (yet still pines for); the other view sees distortion only in the constantly repeated yet in principle never redeemable claim that *now*, finally, immediacy has been achieved. If cognition is irreducibly active from the outset, and so offers no access to the immediate, then this is not something to be deplored (as though we secretly did know what the immediate is like and wished we could attain it) nor even to wish to escape (since "escape" only makes sense if there is some place, a heaven of immediacy, to escape *to*). Rather, as I argued in Chapter 2, it is the very category of immediacy itself that has to be questioned, and finally given up.

Thus the theory of reification answers the theory of nonidentity with an old Hegelian argument, one that always seems like a trick but is not: that when the difference between world and thought is invoked as part of an argument to assert thought's essential limitedness, it is always *thought itself that thinks this difference*, and so the assertion is canceled at the very moment it is made.[45] In comprehending its own limits, thought overcomes those limits (although only negatively); thus in knowing its failure, it does not entirely fail. It thinks the very otherness it claims it cannot think and so shows it not to be so other after all. Adorno is of course acquainted with this argument, but for him it is only another delicious paradox, feeding his bittersweet pessimism by revealing the perpetual tendency toward hubris and illusion built into thought from the start. It leads him to talk of a "thought thinking against itself," a quasi-mystical *Besinnung* that somehow would heroically grasp both incompatible poles, but he never really suggests how such a thing might be accomplished.

As we saw earlier, Horkheimer and Adorno do not distinguish between *Besinnung* and *Reflexion*; but the theory of reification would clearly prefer the latter quintessentially Hegelian term over the former one with its connotations leading back to intuitionism and *Lebensphilosophie*.[46] A "reflexive" thought in the Hegelian sense is a thought that recognizes its own involvement in that which it thinks, and in so doing comes to recognize that "otherness" is always a *thought* otherness and hence not really a realm of the "nonidentical" after all, at least not if the latter term is given Adorno's strongly materialist meaning. This is the sense in which the Hegelian argument is *immanent*: acknowledging the apparent paradox in a thought that can think its own limitation and can recognize its own active involvement in the world it knows, it draws its epistemological conclusions about the "relation" of "subject" to "object" *from this recognition alone*, without that is the introduction of any additional (and epistemologically unjustifiable) assumptions about what the latter "is" or what the former somehow always "misses."

Thus although both views present an epistemologically grounded social critique, they differ on that in the name of which their critique is offered. The theory of nonidentity sees "domination" in any view that does not acknowledge the otherness and nonidentity of the world over and against the human and "conceptual"; as I have suggested it is thus finally a critique *in the name of nature*, in the name, that is, of nonidentity as such. But here it runs up against the Hegelian paradox, since the critique itself is part of the conceptual realm, and hence by its own admission is unable fully to grasp the nature or the nonidentical in whose name it wants to speak: "nature," too, and even "nonidentity" after all are themselves just concepts. The subject, the conceptual, "domination" of otherness are not so easy to give up; the critique finds itself enmeshed in the very difficulty it wants to criticize from the start. The theory of reification, more consistently, avoids these logical problems by offering its critique *in the name of the mediating subject*—the very subject the other critique vainly tried to overcome—and hence bases itself on a self-reflection, not a call to some mystical *Besinnung* that could somehow bridge the gap to a realm by definition unreachable by it. It is the dream of such a realm—of a cognition that could throw off the burden of being cognition, of humans who could somehow be other than human—that the theory of reification criticizes: not the hubris of natural subjects who fail to notice the otherness of the world, but the alienation of active subjects whose practices help to produce that world and yet who persist in seeing it as radically other.

3. NATURE AND NONIDENTITY

I mean by these last remarks to explain why nature appears as a problem for Horkheimer and Adorno, and why it remains one in Adorno's late work. Lacking the immanence I have suggested is crucial to the theory of reification's logical success, the "materialist" argument needs to appeal on the one hand to something external to the argument itself—calling it "nature" or, in the later form, the "nonidentical"—while admitting on the other hand that no access to this externality is ever really possible. It is not possible because the only external world to which we have access is always already the product of our mediating acts, which is why the appeal to the nonidentical must always take the paradoxical form of an appeal to something we can never pretend to know. Nature turns out to be both absolutely necessary to the critique and yet on the critique's own terms also absolutely unknowable. This dilemma is a familiar one: we saw it in Lukács, too, who struggled to reconcile the assertion that nature was a social category on the one hand with the materialist insistence on the objectivity of nature (and of scientific knowledge of it) on the other.[47] It is, I am arguing, the central dilemma of the Western Marxist tradition, which wants to combine a Hegelian epistemology emphasizing the social character of knowledge with a materialist faith in the otherness and priority of nature over the human—an impossible combination that only generates the antinomies about nature the tradition constantly confronts.

This offers a clue to understanding the curious ambiguity about nature's status in the dialectic of enlightenment we examined earlier.[48] Nature appeared there to represent the poignant possibility of the freedom that Horkheimer and Adorno discerned in the very indominability of the organic and its ability to escape even the most horrifying attempts to suppress it, but at the same time nature also seemed to reveal itself *in* the very violence applied to the victim of such attempts, as the terror of a repressed inner nature that comes ultimately to dominate human beings themselves. Nature seemed to be both *promesse de bonheur* but also that which was most to be feared, that which is dominated by enlightenment but also that which returns to take its terrible revenge when domination (as it always must) ultimately fails. This ambiguity is built into the argument, we can now see: for *only* as promise, as something deferred to an unachievable future (or remembered from an enigmatic past) can nature legitimately represent the nonidentical, that which escapes domination. As "present," as actually experienced, it is no longer the nonidentical at all, and turns instead into an emblem of the very domination it promised to overcome, appearing thus as terror. Here, in the inverse of reification, the danger arises when we think we finally "have" nature in our grasp, not when we believe it to be alien.

Thus nature can only *stand for* the nonidentical and ought never to be taken as itself identical to it. "Nature itself is neither good," Horkheimer and Adorno write in an important passage at the end of *Dialectic of Enlightenment*, "nor noble. . . . As a model and goal it stands for opposition [*Widergeist*], deceit, and bestiality. . . . The prevailing practice of domination [*herrschenden Praxis*] and its inescapable alternatives are not threatened by nature, which much more coincides with them, but by the fact that nature is remembered." Nature must be correctly understood: "only when known for what it is [*erkannte*] does nature become existence's craving for its peace, that consciousness which from the very beginning has inspired an unshakeable resistance to *Führer* and collective alike."[49] That nature must be "remembered" means that only as a conceptual memory of the nonconceptual can it serve as a positive impetus to social critique; it must not be misunderstood as some existing and graspable model for the construction of a social order. This is the mistake of Nazi ideology and other forms of right-wing "nature worship," which fail to see the inevitably social and historical character of the "nature" they take as such a model.

In Adorno's later work this theme becomes a major concern; he wants to avoid the error we saw him criticizing in Heidegger, of turning the nonconceptual into yet another concept and speaking as if the nonidentical could somehow itself be known, and he sees the danger of believing that in nature we somehow encounter the very immediacy he knows in fact can never be encountered. In the late *Aesthetic Theory*, he calls nature the *vermittelte Statthalter von Unmittelbarkeit*, the "mediated proxy of immediacy."[50] Here the mediated and social character of what we take as nature is acknowledged, while a special role is still assigned to the concept "nature": it *stands for* immediacy as a kind of surrogate or placeholder. "Nature" points at immediacy, hints at it, represents it perhaps in some mode of representation that is different than the ordinary one, showing what cannot be said instead of vainly trying despite everything to say it. Yet what this mode really is—just like what exactly is "remembered" in the passage just quoted from *Dialectic of Enlightenment*—remains obscure.

Adorno struggles with this problem throughout the *Aesthetic Theory*. Nature plays an important role in that work, particularly in the chapter on "Beauty in Nature," *das Naturschöne*, where Adorno complains about the disappearance from post-Kantian aesthetic theory of discussions of natural beauty (a disappearance he associates with idealism's denigration of nature in favor of spirit, and connects with the move in ethics to a concern with the autonomy of the subject).[51] An aesthetic theory that has nothing to say about nature, he wants to argue, will be too easily tempted to think of beauty as entirely the result of human making and so to identify it with the human maker, the mediating subject. Kant avoids this tendency (although he also helps make it possible), revealing a Rousseauian preference for natural over artificial beauty and an admirable sense of "the fallibility of that which is made [*das Gemachte*]," Adorno writes.[52]

Yet Adorno recognizes that ultimately nature too—only the *mediated* proxy of immediacy—is itself something "made," the social and historical consequence (as I have argued earlier) of human transformative acts. "Natural beauty is an ideological notion," he writes, "when it offers mediatedness in the guise of immediacy."[53] Indeed the very possibility of taking up an "aesthetic relation" to nature, or of viewing nature as a realm opposed to and independent of the historical, itself depends upon a distinct set of historical and social presuppositions.[54] Yet he still tries to find some special character in natural beauty that points to the immediacy he must admit it cannot itself ever really be. "The image of nature survives," he writes, "because its complete negation by artefacts would blind itself to what would be beyond bourgeois society, beyond labor and commodities. Despite its mediation by the social, beauty in nature remains an allegory of that beyond."[55] As this "allegory of the beyond," he adds, it "points to the primacy of the object [*Vorrang des Objekts*] in subjective experience."[56] It is "the anamnesis of something that is more than just for-other"[57]; it is the "cipher of the not-yet [*des noch nicht Seienden*], of the possible";[58] it is "the trace of non-identity in things under the spell of universal identity."[59]

In all of these evocative formulations, Adorno attempts to express the ineffable—something promised by, remembered in, made possible by, exhibited through our experience of natural beauty although not in any sense present as *part* of that experience. In a moving passage, he offers a reinterpretation of traditional notions of the sublime in nature, seeing in the sublime rather the suggestion of a freedom significantly different from that of the autonomous ego:

> Spirit confronted with nature becomes less aware of its own superiority, as Kant would have it, than of its own naturalness [*Naturhaftigkeit*]. This moment moves the subject to tears before the sublime. Awareness of nature cancels the subject's defiant self-positing. . . . With that the ego, as spirit, steps out of its imprisonment in itself. A glimpse of freedom arises which philosophy is guilty of falsely attributing to its opposite, the arrogance [*Selbstherrlichkeit*] of the subject. . . . Because the beautiful will not be subordinated to that natural causality which the subject imposes upon phenomena, its realm is one of possible freedom.[60]

But natural beauty as proxy of immediacy, as trace of nonidentity, as anamnesis of an in-itself prior to human mediation, as promise of a utopian "*noch nicht*," as allegory for something beyond labor and commodities, even as "glimpse of freedom"—finally these are just rhetorical moves, marvelous ones no doubt, but still ultimately bald assertions about what nature "is" not backed up (nor capable of being backed up) by argument or evidence. Anamnesis, of course, has been epistemologically suspect since the time of Plato, and even Adorno admits that that which is remembered in it is more like a dream, and never really did exist.[61] The idea of a *noch nicht*, of a nature that is not yet what it wants to be, is even more problematic, depending as it seems to on some mystical access to nature's (desired!) future form as something entirely independent of its present one. Similarly, the "primacy of the object"—which is to say, Adorno's materialism—is simply assumed here, since no experience of nature, essentially historical as such experiences by Adorno's own admission always are, could ever prove it or offer evidence for it. He is left with nothing more than a kind of pious hope for an ineffable something toward which nature points; the insight that our experiences of nature have a historical content is always supplemented by an undefended "yes, but" that simply asserts there to be a fundamental otherness supposedly showing itself in the center of such experiences.

A significant passage in the *Aesthetic Theory* on *Kulturlandschaft*—romantic "culturescapes" of castles, medieval cottages, ruins, and so forth—as a source of aesthetic pleasure is instructive here. Of course such landscapes are not "natural," nor do they give us access to any "immediacy"; they, too, like modern industrial landscapes, are the consequences of specific social processes (in this case feudal ones), and so offer no respite from mediation. Yet they appeal to a nostalgia easily derided as sentimental delusion. For Adorno, however, this nostalgia has its justification nonetheless: as representatives of a lost past, *Kulturlandschaften* remind us of days before the contemporary total domination of landscapes by human "making," and so in that sense may be *relatively* more "immediate" than modern cityscapes. Adorno knows the arguments against such nostalgia—that those landscapes too reveal a social order, and that it was not a just or happy one for most of those who inhabited it; that such nostalgia is easily co-opted and made part of the bourgeois market in tourism and the picturesque; that historically it has been associated with reactionary tendencies. Yet he doesn't care, writing:

> As long as the face of the earth keeps being ravished by utilitarian pseudo-progress, it will turn out to be impossible to disabuse human intelligence of the notion that, despite all the evidence to the contrary, the pre-modern world was better and more humane. . . . The universality of mediation has yet to generate a livable life. In this situation the traces of an old immediacy, no matter how outdated and questionable, acquire a certain corrective right.[62]

This is a kind of metaphor for what Adorno wants to say about nature in general. Nature is *not* ever a realm of immediacy, and yet the contrast between the natural and the social remains a meaningful one, in which the former can teach us something about the later. The "immediacy" of what we take as natural is always relative; each step in modernity (in "enlightenment," in the construction and reconstruction of the world through modern industry) involves a further mediation, and so previous stages, mediated though they themselves were, can still appear as immediate by comparison to later ones. "Natural" really just means "earlier"; to criticize what has been made by contrasting it to the natural is thus in truth simply a way to point us toward the transformative mediating processes that are going on today without necessarily positing an absolute immediacy as ever having really existed in the past. Indeed, only in the context of an administered social world that appears increasingly overcomplex and "overmediated" to individuals can nature come to have the meaning of something to which we dream of escaping. "The subject's helplessness in a society petrified into second nature prompts it to seek refuge in what is supposedly [*vermeintlich*] the first one," Adorno writes.[63]

Thus the nostalgia for some more "natural" time—as if feudalism were such a thing—is a clue, not to the character of feudalism, nor really even of nature, but of the social world inhabited by those who feel that nostalgia so strongly. What we see in nature, Adorno argues—and here he is at his best—similarly says something more about the social than about any (unknowable) nature in itself. "In every experience of nature," he writes (much as Lukács might have), "there is actually present the whole of society. The latter not only provides the schemata of perception in general, but also establishes ahead of time through contrast and similarity what will count as nature. Thus the experience of nature is constituted by means of determinate negation."[64] In this argument the mediated character of "nature" is taken quite seriously: we use our experience of (necessarily mediated) nature to learn something about *mediation*, which is to say about the social, not about immediacy or about nature in itself.

When correctly understood, the implications of this insight would I believe actually lead Adorno in the direction of the theory of reification; but he does not follow them through consistently. He wants more when he talks of nature, as the almost mystical appeals to nonidentity reveal—more, I think, than his own argument can support. He grasps the social origin and social meaning of the nostalgia for a lost (and nonexistent) immediacy; but he clearly shares that nostalgia, too, and in a way that suggests he has not entirely seen through it. The talk in Adorno about the historically mediated transformations both of nature and of our experience of it often regresses into a complaint about such transformations (and hence about mediation) as such. The critique is then not of what the contemporary appearance of nature reveals about the social but about nature itself—about what has been done "to" it.

When Adorno writes of the impossibility of attaining an immediate relation to the natural, his tone is thus often one of sorrow—not at the objectivistic illusion that fails to see the trace of human activity in what appears as other to it, but precisely at the loss of immediacy itself. Thus although he is generally careful to assert that "what is needed is an authentic mode of experience that in no way resorts to a lost immediacy," he explains this in a way that reveals how much he laments its necessity; it is the fact, for instance, that "a person who takes a walk in a forest, unless prepared to travel far away, has to put up with airplane noise" that makes the dream of an immediate relation to nature an impossible one.[65] The nostalgia for lost immediacy is evident in the resentful tone, which suggests that bourgeois society's greatest crime is that its industry and technology have destroyed immediacy. "Even when an experience presents itself of something natural, an unimpaired individuality somehow immune to the administration of society," Adorno bitterly writes, "chances are it is a deception. In an age of total mediatedness the beautiful in nature turns into a caricature of itself."[66]

Adorno wants to have it both ways: to assert the inevitability of mediation while criticizing it for distorting the very access to immediacy he knows does not exist. His delight in paradoxical formulations, like his and Horkheimer's injunction to "laugh at logic when it runs counter to humans," looks to me like a rhetorical cover for this unresolvable, and not particularly dialectical, contradiction. Even the appeal to *Kulturlandschaft*, finally, despite its highly self-conscious form as a nostalgia fully aware that that for which it pines was never really so wonderful nor so immediate, is finally an appeal to bad faith, to illusion, and to a kind of noble lie. Marx knew better than to appeal to the good old days of feudalism, recognizing that the enemy of my enemy—the feudal aristocracy—is only my friend to a crudely nondialectical thinking. The discovery of the unavoidably historical character of what we take to be nature—and of the social horrors that can be read in what we think about nature today—should not call us back to some imaginary immediacy that we know we cannot reach (and that was characterized by its own horrors) but rather *forward*—to *better* mediations, mediations that we know and plan and no longer mistake for the immediate. This is what the theory of reification would call for; but Adorno does not.

I have argued that Adorno attempts to resolve the difficulties about the status of nature in *Dialectic of Enlightenment* by moving to a more sophisticated account that maintains the materialist moment in the theory by an appeal not to nature but to a nonidentity that can never be conceptually grasped or "present." Yet finally that move, too, I have been suggesting, is a failure:

nonidentity in the last analysis must again appear as a deus ex machina that must at least be imagined as present in order to get the argument off the ground. The result is an antinomy at the heart of the account, since it gets its (substantial, and undoubted) emotional impact from the very kind of nostalgic appeal to a lost immediacy to which its own argument knows it has no right. We're yearning for something that the theory itself shows isn't there, and couldn't be known if it were, and no amount of paradox-mongering can erase that contradiction. What was true of nature in *Dialectic of Enlightenment* is true of nonidentity here: it both has to be and yet cannot be the foundation for the critique. The result here as in the earlier work is a cul-de-sac, a dialectic of the dialectics of enlightenment when they are carried out in the name of a nature or nonidentity or immediacy underlying human action but also inaccessible to it.

This dilemma cannot be resolved within the context of a materialism based on a theory of nonidentity. The real resolution, as I have tried to suggest, would lie rather in the direction pointed out by the theory of reification, and hinted at but not developed in some of the remarks about nature just discussed. The move would be to look directly at the objects in the world that surrounds us, recognizing them as "social hieroglyphics" bearing traces not of some nonidentity wholly other than us but rather precisely of us ourselves— our practices, our social structures, our capacity to organize our lives in accordance with our needs as well as our failure to do so. It would be to pay attention to the very things around us that appear as "immediate" and to uncover the ways in which they never really are—to "deconstruct" them in the sense I have used this word in Chapter 2. This would require a fundamental shift in the critique from the form it took in Horkheimer and Adorno: contemporary society would be criticized not for destroying immediacy, or "dominating nature," but for believing itself surrounded by it, for thinking and acting (that is) as if the environment it inhabits were a "natural" one, immutably given from eternity and independent of human action. Not the increasing sociality of nature (the wood desecrated by the sound of airplanes) but the illusory "naturalness" of the social (its appearance as unchangeable, and our resulting inability to decide how we wish it to be organized) would now become the target of the critique.

4. THE PARADOXES OF ART

Of course in the *Aesthetic Theory* art, not nature, is the center of the discussion. The account of the *Naturschöne* is really only preparatory for an account of the *Kunstschöne*. In art, the paradox implicit at the heart of Adorno's discussion of nature takes on an explicit and self-conscious form: the apparent immediacy of the artwork is belied by the complex and detailed mediations engaged in by the artist in order to produce it. Yet for this very reason, Adorno thinks, it is precisely in the realm of art that nonidentity, inexpressible as it is, actually comes closest to being expressed. Art *is* mediation and knows itself as such, but only in art can what Adorno calls the *"Münchhausenkunststück"* of "identifying the nonidentical" take place.[67] It is an expression in human terms of what can be only obscurely expressed in the language of nature.[68] That which the *Naturschöne* indicates (but cannot *be*)—nonidentity, otherness, the materiality of the subject—form for Adorno the central characteristics of beauty in art. "Art imitates neither nature nor particular beautiful things in nature," he writes, "but rather natural beauty as such [*das Naturschöne an sich*]. This is the paradox not just of natural beauty but of aesthetics in general."[69]

Art then is for Adorno the fundamental mode of appearance of the non-identical, the one in which this paradoxical nonconcept is experienced in its most adequate (which is to say its most inadequate) form. Art "expresses" the nonidentical above all through the inevitability of its *failure*: its ambition to unity and homogeneity is always thwarted—by the resistance of material, by the contingencies of performance, by the inevitable upsurge of "extraneous" matter (psychological, social, accidental) into the supposedly autonomous work. The result is a set of fractures and fissures that give the lie to the pretension to perfection implicit in every artwork and thus reveal most directly the irreducible remnant of nonidentity within every claim to identity. Great works of art are those that refuse to hide those fractures and fissures, subsisting instead within the tension thus produced. "Art cannot live up to its concept," Adorno writes. "Therefore each and every one of its works, including the most elevated, is smitten with imperfection, thus disavowing the ideal of perfection that all works of art must hanker after. . . . This dilemma must not be done away with. . . . It is only because literally no art work can succeed that the powers of art are set free; and it is here that art is akin to reconciliation."[70] In this way art is clearly associated with the negative dialectics that Adorno had defined as a "thinking against thought": "art is rationality criticizing itself," he continues, "without being able to overcome itself."[71]

The work of art always possesses a surplus, what Adorno calls a "more" or *Mehr*; like nature, it expresses or indicates something that it itself is not.[72] This "more" is not the "whole" of holism that goes beyond the parts, he writes, but rather something like the Benjaminian aura: not a totality or an identity but precisely that which escapes totality or identity. Thus the "more" is something utterly separate from the work and yet at the same time paradoxically something that appears within it: "the artistic moments in their connection [*Zusammenhang*] intimate what falls outside of that connection."[73] This fact, that "by becoming appearance artworks are more than they are," is what Adorno calls the element of *Geist* or "spirit" in the work of art.[74] Artworks are more than mere matter, and yet it is only through their materiality, he argues, that this "more" comes to appear. Nothing other than things, they yet become more than things through a process of reification (literally "thingification").[75] Duchamp's *In Advance of the Broken Arm* might be the paradigm here: to view a snow shovel in an aesthetic setting is to have its very materiality or thingliness thrust upon one, and yet the effect is to reveal something in the object that mysteriously suggests there is *more* to it than being a "mere thing."

Yet despite the provocative use of a Hegelian term like spirit, this remains a resolutely materialist theory. The "more" or "spirit" of the artwork refers for Adorno to the moment of failure and lack of unity in it, and thus in particular to the moment of matter (of resistance, of contingency): it is that which escapes the artist's intention or "idea." Adorno rejects any kind of subjectivism in aesthetics, including that characteristic of expressivist theories of the Hegelian sort. The aesthetic interest in the artwork lies precisely in its own *non*identity with that which was "intended" in it by the artist. Understanding a work of art, then, cannot be reduced to understanding the conditions of its creation, just as the *Eroica* symphony is not finally elucidated by recalling the story of its dedication.[76] "In art the distinction between the made object and its genesis, the act of making, is emphasized: artworks are made things which became more than merely made," Adorno writes. This suggests to him a distinction between a work of art (*Kunstwerk*) and an artifact (*Artefakt*): not all artifacts or made objects are works of art (some are *merely* made and possess no "more" or surplus), although of course all works of art are also artifacts.[77]

But here we are returned to the same paradox we have been tracing throughout this chapter. For it is only as an object that is made—the result, that is to say, of mediating acts by the artist—that the artwork comes, according to Adorno, to express that which is beyond making, the surplus or more. "All making in art is one long struggle to say what the made object can never be and what art itself can never know: that is spirit," Adorno writes. "The most profound of all the paradoxes in art is probably this: that it can attain to the non-made . . . only through making, by constructing particular and specifically organized individual works, and not through immediacy."[78] Again I would argue that this "profound paradox" is rather an antinomy, and one that shows the incoherence of what Adorno is trying to accomplish: to achieve immediacy through the elaboration of the most complex and sophisticated mediations. For it is not immediacy, or the "nonmade," that is thereby achieved at all, despite what he says.

The real conclusion ought to be a different one: that the "more" in artifacts, that which makes them more than mere things, is nothing other than the process of *Verdinglichung*, or more correctly of mediation, itself. It is the fact that the objects that surround us are always, and despite their appearance, the products of human processes: *this* is the surplus pointed to by works of art. To put the snow shovel in the museum reminds us that it too is an "aesthetic" object, but that does not (only) mean an object whose beauty we can contemplate. It means also that it is an object of human design and human use, a *made* object produced for human purposes and not just a tool sitting around ready-to-hand. Thus the "made" character of artworks—and here the distinction between artworks and other artifacts begins to collapse—reminds us precisely of the making and of the makers: of the practices of mediation and those who engage in them. What it does not do is in any sense point toward some "nonidentity" or immediacy other than those practices.

Adorno wants to resolve the paradox of works of art as made things that point beyond themselves very differently. Thus for instance he argues that, although all logic has a coercive character and is therefore associated with domination, still the fact that art has its own unique (and rigorous) logic allows it to play a subversive function with respect to the dominant one. In the precise and extensive "domination" over materials required in a work of art, a domination directed however by art's "purposeless purposefulness" and not by the instrumental rationality of the prevailing domination over nature, Adorno sees an implicit critique of that latter domination. This, he thinks, is how the "made" can yet indicate a realm other than making: the idea is that by positing a *different* mode of mediation, and following it through with seriousness and care but without accepting any of the instrumentalist assumptions of the prevailing modes of mediation ("purposefulness without purpose"), the arbitrariness of those prevailing modes can be revealed and hence criticized.[79] "When a piece of music compresses time," Adorno writes, "when a picture folds spaces together, the possibility becomes concrete that things could also be different [*es könnte auch anders sein*]."[80]

This is the standard strategy of a deconstruction that lacks a theory of reification and so lacks the directionality I spoke of in Chapter 2.[81] It wants to reveal the arbitrariness and historical contingency of our mediating acts, and does so by showing the possibility of engaging in very different ones. This is fine as far as it goes, but it still threatens to end up in relativism: all mediations turn out to be arbitrary, so why should we choose "aesthetic" ones over those that dominate nature? The problem is that this strategy thinks of itself as somehow breaking a spell and so pointing out to us a path *out of* the "circle" of our mediations. But it cannot. Adorno's *es könnte auch anders sein* is moving and powerful as a slogan, yet more closely considered it becomes clear that he is absolutely unable to give it any content: what *is* this "other" way things could be? How *ought* they to be?[82]

The real conclusion entailed by the discovery that "other" mediations are possible besides the ones that prevail today would go in a different direction, as I have already suggested: toward a concern not with that which is beyond the circle of mediations but rather with those mediations themselves. Then it would be discovered that—again, immanently to the argument—there *is* a criterion that allows us to distinguish "better" from "worse" mediations: those that know themselves as mediations and do not pretend to a "naturalness" and immediacy they cannot achieve are preferable to those still ignorant of their own character. This by itself does not offer any content for such "good" mediations either, but it suggests the only way such content could ever be achieved: through the self-reflective choices and acts of the community whose mediations they are and not through the appeal to a "nonidentity" over and against that community.[83]

Adorno's insistence on the distinction between "artwork" and "artifact" marks him as more of an idealist (and more of a Hegelian) than one might at first imagine, with an aesthete's disdain for mundane things built by ordinary labor: art, he writes, is in fact "a mode of practice beyond labor."[84] The use of the word *Geist* is the tipoff, serving in the usual mystical-idealist Hegelian fashion as the magical element distinguishing "higher" from "mere" objects. The irony with which one would expect the word *spirit* to be employed is remarkably missing in the *Aesthetic Theory*, and instead one gets formulations such as the following: "As the negation of the spirit that dominates nature, the spirit of art does not emerge as spirit at all, but rather is kindled in its very opposite, in materiality. . . . Art's redemptive character lies in the act through which spirit discards itself."[85] *Geist* turning into its opposite, *Geist* discarding itself: this is the language of idealism, of a thought that finds the "material" utterly foreign and torments itself by worrying how "spirit" could ever find a home there. Rather than seeing ordinary human practice—the practice of the artist and the labor of the worker both—as the real resolution to the problems posed by the impossible abstraction "spirit," Adorno like a disappointed Hegelian is driven to pose these sorts of desperate paradoxes of a spirit that must "discard itself" or "emerge in its opposite" in some magical moment of self-renunciation toward the nonidentical—toward, that is, the *real* material world that this sort of idealism never knows how to attain and finds itself constantly both tempted and amazed by.

Adorno finally hates practice, which is to say he hates labor, associated as it is for him with domination. Art's practice is itself a critique of practice, he says; and he is explicit that it is not merely a critique of contemporary (capitalist, exploitative, dehumanizing) practice that is involved here but rather a critique of practice *as such*. "Art is not only the proxy [*Statthalter*] for a better practice than the one that has ruled [*herrschenden*] until now, but is just as much a critique of practice as the rule [*Herrschaft*] of brutal self-preservation in the midst of that which exists,"[86] Adorno writes, adding elsewhere that "practice tends by sheer virtue of its form towards that which logically it ought to abolish: violence, which is inherent in it and maintains itself in its sublimations."[87] Here we are at the key point, where materialism turns into idealism. In its desire to assert the reality and "otherness" of the world, this position ends by rejecting any *real* human attempt to interact with that world, worrying that all interaction is a transformation and so inevitably betrays the egoism of domination, the violence of "brutal self-preservation." But if real interaction is ruled out, all that is left is thought or spirit—or "art," identified now as a mode of interaction that somehow is not interaction, as a making that does not make. It is the failure to appreciate the epistemological role of practice, I want next to argue, that ultimately accounts for Adorno's problems, and by extension those we found as well in *Dialectic of Enlightenment*.

5. THE ROAD NOT TAKEN

The nonidentity thesis (like its more recent formulation as a thesis about *différance*) no doubt has something important and right about it. Against an idealism and a foundationalism that still believe in the possibility of deducing a priori a system that could grasp and explain everything there is in the world, it insists rather on the simple realness of the world, on its hardness and resistance to us, and on the limitations of our knowledge and the fallibility of our acts. But its real objection, it seems to me, is to what might be called the *theoreticism* of such an idealism, and it misunderstands itself when it thinks there is more to its critique. To say that the world cannot be grasped as a whole, or cannot be grasped by pure thought, is not to say that it is not graspable at all but rather simply that "grasping" is primarily a matter of practice and not of theory. In our practices, by which I mean first of all our laboring practices, we *do* grasp the world. We do so not by getting some correct "view" of it into our "minds" but by transforming it—a transformation, to be sure, that is never complete, never infallible, and certainly never easy.

Adorno in *Negative Dialectics* praises classical German idealism for identifying spirit with activity, and then correctly points out that this identification leads to the *Aufhebung* of idealism itself, since activity necessarily involves a moment of resistance that is essentially extramental.[88] Similarly he praises Marx for his clear-headed rejection of utopianism and his emphasis instead on the importance of the moment of planning (and hence mediation), thereby preserving what Adorno calls "the alien thing [*das dinghaft Fremde*]"—which is to say, a moment of resistance and difficulty against the idealist dream of a perfect knowledge that would automatically generate a perfect world.[89] But he interprets these examples only negatively, as pointing to the existence of some substrate or realm of the nonidentical underlying or beyond human practice, and this does not follow from the argument. To say that our activity in the world must be real and not just theoretical activity, and that it therefore is

difficult, involves planning, and sometimes fails, does not by itself show the
world to be "ontologically independent of the subject" unless the subject is
taken to be merely a *thinking* subject—which is exactly the mistake of traditional idealism. German idealism's arguments, from Kant on, against the notion
of a "substrate" "upon" which activity works continue to be valid ones; what
considerations like those introduced by Adorno show is that this activity cannot be thought of as the mysterious act of a disembodied *Geist* but rather as
the real concrete practices of living human beings.

What I am suggesting is that, correctly understood, *practice already
contains within itself the moment of what Adorno calls nonidentity*. Indeed,
it is just this that distinguishes it from "theory": unlike thinking about the
world, changing the world is difficult, is fallible, encounters resistance, requires planning, and so on. This is not because "thought never fully compre-
hends its object" or "concepts do not correspond with things" (although both
those statements are true), since real practice is in fact not a matter of
"thought" or "concepts" being "applied" to some external reality independent of it. And it is also not because the world is "other" than us, unless the
"us" referred to is the pure (mental) subject of classical idealist metaphysics.
We are always already in the world, which means that we are also always
already acting upon it and changing it in our practices. It is in this sense *not*
other than us, but always already formed and transformed by us. The world
we live in is the world we have created, and are creating, through our practices—which is not to deny that it is a world that sometimes looks quite
different from the one we "thought" we were creating or from one where
our practices never fail.

My claim, then, is that the concept of practice—rather than that of
nature or the nonidentical—allows one to reject the theoreticism and idealism that Adorno quite rightly wants to overcome and that he sees as associated with the catastrophe of enlightenment, without having to accept the
materialism, naive or sophisticated, whose *aporia* I have tried to outline
earlier. One can say, as I just have, that part of what it is to be a practice is
to be difficult, fallible, to encounter resistance, and so forth, without having
necessarily at the same time to posit a static "nature" independent of us that
produces the difficulty, that causes the failures, that does the resisting. The
unquestioned metaphysical assumptions that prevent us from seeing that,
leading us to believe that practice requires some "substrate" that is other
than us and upon which we must act, are precisely the contemplative ones
identified by Lukács and associated by him with a world marked by reification.
This by itself is not a decisive argument that those assumptions are false, of
course, but it does suggest that they are neither so self-evident nor so trivial
as they might at first appear. To think of practice as some sort of "relation"
"between" two distinct realms (like thought and world) is already to make a

set of substantive ontological decisions—and given the difficulties to which those decisions seem always to lead, one might be tempted to try to make them differently.

The crucial distinction, I am arguing, is between thought and action, not between thought and world (or subject and object, or concept and thing). The theory-practice distinction *cuts across* these others, emphasizing not the subject but what the subject *does*: thus in particular it is not parallel to the distinction between "idealism" and "materialism." Adorno, as we have seen, wants to be a materialist, asserting the *Vorrang des Objekts* and insisting on the supposedly fundamental asymmetry that, although objects can exist that are not subjects, every subject is also an object.[90] But this is simply false, depending as it does on a curious Cartesian hyperdualism that fails sufficiently to recognize that subjects and objects are always related: objects *do* always have something of the subjective about them. Adorno says that without objectivity the subject "would literally be nothing," but although he denies it, the opposite is really true as well. This is so first of all because although we can, as Adorno says, doubtless think of objects "independently of subjects," such objects are obviously still nonetheless *thought* ones.[91] But (more important in this context) it is also true because most of the objects we encounter in the world are quite literally the result of some subjects' action: they are *made* objects. The critique of reification suggests that when we see them as "mere" objects, as "independent" of the subjects who built them, we are missing what they really are. This was the central point of the kind of "philosophy of practice" toward which we earlier saw Lukács's arguments as tending.

And note that the point here is not simply a compromise whereby Adorno's materialist asymmetry is replaced by a symmetry in which the mutual interpenetration of subject and object is prudently asserted, a nice "dialectic" that evenhandedly claims that even though every subject is also objective, so too every object is also subjective. Rather there is still an asymmetry to be pointed out here, but quite a different one, leading to quite a different primacy or *Vorrang*: for subjects "are" objects only in a passive and static sense, whereas to say that objects have something subjective about them (where this is meant in terms of practice and not thought) is to point to subjects as *active*, as world-changers. The one side thus returns again to reification, to Lukács's "contemplative attitude," viewing humans as passive, acted upon, "objects," while the other represents the critique of reification, calling humans to recognize their own activity and explicitly assert it. This is what is wrong with traditional materialism, as Marx had already pointed out in his first thesis on Feuerbach—that it views humans as the passive product of something extrahuman and hence cannot conceptualize the "active side," the side that idealism (theoreticism) grasps but only mythologically, as some mysterious power of spirit. A practice-oriented account would agree with materialism that humans are "natural" but would understand this to mean that they are *active in nature*, the subjects of an activity that constructs and reconstructs nature as it works.

For Adorno, as we have seen, the "active side" appears rather as negative, and as associated with domination; this kind of view is common nowadays in environmentalist critiques of science and technology employing Frankfurt School themes. But it forgets the crucial role in what Adorno calls "domination" of the moment of *List*, of cunning, of Odysseus's "renunciation" and "sober estimation of forces": such domination cheats the natural powers *by passively accepting them as given*, which is to say by approaching them with Lukács's contemplative attitude.[92] Thus it is not the "active side" at all that is involved here but rather precisely the passivity of a naturalistic materialism. To emphasize the active side, on the contrary, would be to speak of a humanity aware that the environment and its powers are not "given" but rather themselves the consequence of our choices and our acts; we do not dominate it but rather recognize that what "it" *is* (and what "we" are, too) is determined nowhere other than in the practices we engage in.

Rather finally it is Adorno who in his paradox-mongering looks to me like Odysseus. He is the *listige* one, appealing to a beauty, both in nature and in art, that he knows full well is always mediated, as if he might nonetheless somehow find in it the magical access to an immediacy otherwise forbidden to mortals. Bound at the mast by mediations, he yet still secretly dreams that he might, if he listened hard enough and perhaps stopped struggling, hear that sweet song of immediacy, of a nature in itself that offers a promise of future reconciliation or a reminder of past happiness. But it will not work—not because, as *Dialectic of Enlightenment* says, the renunciation and domination implicit in his bondage changes the Sirens' song forever, but because there were never any Sirens at all, nor any song without a human singer.[93] It was all a dream—Circe and the Sirens and the Cyclops, too: there was never anything other than Odysseus and his weary sailors, plowing through uncharted waters, and wondering which route would take them home.

I have been arguing, it will be clear, for a return to something like a philosophy of practice along the lines of Lukács's theory of reification. This seems to me to represent the road not taken in the later history of Western Marxism. Even in *History and Class Consciousness* we saw a tension between a critique based on the Hegelian notion of a dialectic of reification and self-recognition on the one hand, and a critique oriented toward neo-Kantian and *Lebensphilosophische* themes on the other—between a critique in the name of a mediating activity become conscious of itself and one in the name of a "nature" that mediating reason will always fail to grasp. Horkheimer and Adorno's work, and especially Adorno's development of it after the war, involve a sophisticated and intellectually impressive elucidation of the latter set of themes; to have taken the other route, however, might have avoided some of the antinomies in which the Frankfurt School position found itself entangled. But thinkers such as Marcuse and Habermas did not take that route, which left them vulnerable to the same sorts of problems. It is to their work that I shall now turn.

CHAPTER 5

Marcuse, Habermas, and the Retreat to Nature

1. MARCUSE AND THE NEW SCIENCE

Despite his reputation as a sharp critic of technology and "technological reason," Marcuse in truth held views of technology that were considerably more ambiguous than those expressed by Horkheimer and Adorno. The implacable pessimism we have seen the latter two express in the 1940s about the connections among science, technology, and domination, and their wholesale rejection of the traditional orthodox Marxist faith in science as allied with social progress, do not harmonize well with Marcuse's self-consciously utopian speculations. At least in the 1950s, technology appeared to him to provide, if not a guarantee of human freedom, then at least a necessary condition for it.

In *Eros and Civilization* he argued that the development of automation had finally made it possible to reduce the labor time necessary for the satisfaction of human needs to a bare minimum, and in so doing had opened up the possibility of an end to the repression that work demands. His vision of a new society hence depended essentially on the virtual abolition of labor (and scarcity) by technology.[1] Freedom in such a vision is identified, as in the earlier Frankfurt School, with the liberation of a repressed "inner nature," but this is now seen as being made possible precisely by the completion of technological development, which Marcuse provocatively describes not as the abolition but the consummation of labor's alienation: "The more complete the alienation of labor, the greater the potential of freedom: total alienation would be the optimum. It is the sphere outside labor which defines freedom and fulfillment."[2] Hence, although labor on this view is inevitably a realm of unfreedom, automation allows us to minimize it and so opens up a sphere of play, of polymorphous perversity, *external* to labor—the only sphere in which freedom is possible.

Influenced on this point more by Freud than by Hegel, Marcuse here insists on the pain and difficulty of labor, of labor as *toil* rather than as means of self-expression or self-development. The break with traditional Marxism's celebration of labor here is apparent, although in another sense this view is quite continuous with Marxism's faith that development of the "forces of production" will provide the preconditions for human liberation. Marcuse is the great hedonist among Western Marxists, the eloquent spokesperson for the instincts and the body; he is without a doubt the *sexiest* of the critical theorists. The utopian ideal for which critical social theory speaks, he constantly reminds us, ought to be nothing more or less than the ideal of human somatic happiness, a life of pleasure and instinctual satisfaction marred by as little necessary labor as possible. Freud may be right that a certain quantity of instinctual repression is necessary for society to be possible at all, Marcuse concedes, but then it is the responsibility of a critical theory to identify the quantity of *surplus*-repression that a particular social order demands of its citizens and show how that extra repression can be jettisoned. The development of modern technologies has on the one hand helped to increase the quantity of surplus-repression required of us, he argues, but it has also at the same time in principle made possible a decrease in necessary labor time of a sort unimaginable to any previous generation.

Yet the dualisms asserted here—between "basic" and "surplus" repression, between "toil" and "play"—are too simplistic in their assumption that the realm of painful necessity could be kept distinct from the realm of pleasure and liberation it somehow makes possible (and too reminiscent of the bourgeois distinction between "work" and "leisure" that Marcuse wants to reject). The utopian dream of an entirely automated world that chugs along while silently propping up the realm of freedom but leaving it otherwise unaffected is impossible for Marcuse to maintain very long. And the themes from Lukács and Weber of suspicion about science and technology's negative social role that were so important to Horkheimer and Adorno's critique are too significant to his own worldview as well. In the realm of freedom, even "toil" would have to be different, even the character of "basic" repression would have to change. Marcuse's recognition of this accounts for the ambiguity in the treatment of technology in *Eros and Civilization*.[3] He is consistently driven towards a claim that the framework of that book cannot easily handle: that the liberation of human powers a nonrepressive society would make possible would necessarily transform the very character of labor, and of technology, in themselves.[4] Both realms, that is to say, that of work as well as that of play, need liberation; or, rather, it is the very distinction between the two that must be abolished.[5]

This means first of all that the easy optimism about contemporary technology's ability to overcome scarcity and produce a realm of freedom has to be rejected; to the extent that the technological project as currently organized is in itself inimical to liberation, it cannot serve as a foundation for it. "The machine is *not neutral*," writes Marcuse in 1965; "technology is always a historical-social *project*: in it is projected what a society and its ruling interests intend to do with men and things."[6] But it means secondly as well that our concept of a liberated society must be expanded to include a "liberated technology": a technology that could found human liberation would have to be a "new" technology, one that viewed its own project and the nature it engaged with in a new way. These two positions emerged in the 1960s at the center of Marcuse's discussions of science and technology.[7]

Thus in *One-Dimensional Man*, one finds a critique of "technological rationality" that sees contemporary science and technology as by their very nature yoked to capitalism and domination. Technology's very "neutrality," its apparent indifference to the political or social purposes to which it is put, serves at a deeper level, Marcuse argues, to tie it to a society in which substantive critical discourse about values is systematically blocked.[8] By treating the external world as merely matter for instrumental manipulation and as subject only to formal mathematical laws, science and technology deny the reality of ethical, aesthetic, or political values, leaving only the value of control as unquestionable.[9]

Marx's faith that a technology freed of capitalist fetters could by itself make human freedom possible has to be tempered, Marcuse now argues, because technology turns out itself to function as a medium of social control and domination. Automation now appears to Marcuse at least questionable in its implications: by reducing the worker's contribution to a set of automatic motions stupefying in their repetitiveness and boredom, it produces a kind of "mechanized enslavement" in which the worker is "incorporated into the technological community of the administered population."[10] But rather than ending in a pessimistic distrust of all technology as such in the manner of Horkheimer and Adorno, Marcuse takes this conclusion to suggest the need for a "new" technology, different from the old not merely in terms of the values and interests that guide it but in its intrinsic structure.[11] A liberated society would require its own technology, not just a commitment to apply existing technology in the interests of human freedom.

But, because science and technology are fundamentally linked, standing behind such a new technology would have to be something like a "new science" with a new conception of scientific method as well. It is this possibility that Marcuse raises in certain celebrated, and highly utopian, passages in *One-Dimensional Man*:

> Science, *by virtue of its own method* and concepts, has projected and promoted a universe in which the domination of nature has remained linked to the domination of man—a link which tends to be fatal to

this universe as a whole. . . . If this is the case, then the change in the
direction of progress, which might sever this fatal link, would also
affect the very structure of science—the scientific project. Its hypotheses, without losing their rational character, would develop in an
essentially different experimental context (that of a pacified world);
consequently, science would arrive at essentially different concepts
of nature and establish essentially different facts.[12]

Here a position only hinted at in *Eros and Civilization* is explicitly asserted: that science and technology are not simply the material foundation of
the liberation called for by Marcuse's utopianism but rather must themselves
be transformed by that liberation, to the extent of radically changing their very
methods and even results. The liberation of inner nature is linked to a liberation of outer nature, too, and so a nondominative society would require a
nondominative approach to nature, and a new sort of science and technology
guided by that approach. *One-Dimensional Man* does not say much about
what such a new science would look like; the book is still marked by a pessimism about the possibility of alternative social forces arising that might counter
the loss of the "second" or critical dimension Marcuse laments in contemporary mass society. But as the 1960s went on his pessimism began to lift, as he
started to discern in third-world revolutionary movements, in the emerging
counterculture, and then above all in the burgeoning of feminism the concrete
development of a new sensibility that might indeed serve as the foundation for
a new approach to nature.[13]

Thus in later works such as *An Essay on Liberation* and *Counterrevolution and Revolt* he allowed himself to speculate a bit about what this new
sensibility might involve. No longer treating nature as a mere object to be
controlled and manipulated, the new sensibility would now treat it, he says,
"as a *subject* in its own right—a subject with which to live in a common
human universe."[14] Not only humans but nature thus deserve liberation:
"nature, too," Marcuse writes, "awaits the revolution!"[15] "In sharp contrast to
the capitalist exploitation of nature," he asserts, the new approach "would be
nonviolent, nondestructive: oriented on the life-enhancing, sensuous, aesthetic qualities inherent in nature."[16] The result would be "the reconstruction of reality," a transformation of the world by "a science and technology
released from their service to destruction and exploitation" that would explicitly see their task as part of a "collective *practice of creating an
environment* . . . in which the nonaggressive, erotic, receptive faculties of
man, in harmony with the consciousness of freedom, strive for the pacifica-
tion of man and nature."[17]

The notion of "reconstructing reality" is an important one (and one to
which I will return): Marcuse emphasizes that his position is not a Luddite

rejection of technology so much as a call for a new technology that does not leave nature as it is, but rather transforms it in the interest of liberation—ours *and* nature's own.[18] "No longer condemned to compulsive aggressiveness and repression in the struggle for existence," he writes, "individuals would be able to create a technical and natural environment which would no longer perpetuate violence, ugliness, ignorance, and brutality."[19] Such a transformation would distinguish itself from what in *One-Dimensional Man* Marcuse called the "repressive mastery" of nature characteristic of contemporary technology, turning rather to a "liberating mastery"[20] that paradoxically frees nature in its very transformation of it, thereby allowing nature (in a phrase of Adorno's Marcuse quotes) "on the poor earth to become what perhaps it would like to be."[21]

This idea had already arisen in *Eros and Civilization*—that an "aesthetic" or "erotic" attitude towards nature transforms the things of nature in such a way as to allow them to realize their own inherent telos: "The things of nature become free to be what they are. But to be what they are they *depend* on the erotic attitude: they receive their *telos* only in it."[22] "Released from the bondage to exploitation," Marcuse writes in *An Essay on Liberation*, "the imagination, sustained by the achievements of science, could turn its productive power to the radical reconstruction of experience and the universe of experience"; "the rational transformation of the world could then lead to a reality formed by the aesthetic sensibility of man."[23]

This talk of "transforming the world" and "creating an environment" is ambiguous, of course, in a sense that we have seen before. On one level, Marcuse may simply mean that the technologies of a liberated society, socially guided by an interest in human happiness and not by corporate profits, would produce different products: windmills and not nuclear power plants, people's parks and not shopping malls. But the clear implication of his language goes further. His point is not just that a new society would apply technological skills in different and more humane ways; it is that such a society would have a new *kind* of technology, eschewing the "domination" of nature in favor of a "liberating mastery" of it and driven by a new science whose very epistemological foundations would be different from those of the natural science we know.[24]

Taken seriously, of course, such claims are strong indeed. Underlying them is the unmistakable intention on Marcuse's part to relativize science and technology to the social order and in a way which seems to have an ontological import. To say that a nondominative science would "establish different facts" and that with its associated technology it would "reconstruct reality" is to return to Lukács's thesis that "nature is a social category" with a vengeance: a liberated society would not merely have a new technology and a new science, it seems that it would literally inhabit a new world. Nature itself would change.[25] It is this conclusion above all, with its apparent fall into an out-and-out idealism, that Habermas in the 1960s was so concerned to challenge.

2. HABERMAS ON KNOWLEDGE AND INTEREST

Habermas's critique derived directly from the theory of "knowledge-constitutive interests" that was central to the epistemological position he elaborated during this period, in particular in his *Knowledge and Human Interests*.[26] With this theory Habermas reintroduced a methodological distinction between natural science and social theory into Western Marxism not unlike the one we saw Lukács trying to formulate, and with a similar intention—to develop, against "positivism," an account of the sociality of knowledge that nonetheless avoids the antirealist implications that follow if that account is permitted to extend its reach to include knowledge of nature. From Habermas's point of view, the Frankfurt School had been too willing to include natural science and technology as part of its critique of "enlightenment"; its reluctance to acknowledge in any but an ironical way the great intellectual and practical successes that science and technology had made possible, and the epistemological significance of the scientific method and worldview, left its position seeming increasingly irrelevant, a cranky throwback to old and discredited notions from the counter-Enlightenment. Yet its insight that the triumph of science was connected to the crises of modernity was one that Habermas did not want to discard. Like Lukács, then, he wanted to find a way reject *scientism* without rejecting *science*—to assert the epistemological independence of a critical social theory without limiting the validity of natural science when applied within its own legitimate realm—by proposing his own version of what I have called the misapplication thesis.[27] But unlike Lukács, he recognized that such a thesis demands a new and independent epistemological account of natural science, since the standard positivist ones are simply not compatible with the sort of methodological dualism it requires.

The difficulty in Lukács's position, as we have seen in Chapter 1, derived from an apparent contradiction between (1) his thoroughgoing (and convincing) critique of objectivism or the "contemplative attitude" and (2) his assertion that nonetheless science is valid when applied to nature. Although Marcuse might be read as taking this as a reason to deny (2), condemning contemporary natural science itself as ideological and suggesting a "new science" that would avoid the critique of objectivism, Habermas notices that the contradiction depends on the suppressed premise (3) that contemporary natural science can only be accounted for on objectivistic grounds, and then goes on to deny this premise. The critique of reification only shows that *objectivism* is ideological, not natural science. If a nonobjectivist account of the "old" natural science were possible which at the same time maintained the epistemological independence of social theory, then that science could be saved without falling into the contradictions of Lukács or the romantic speculations of Marcuse or the earlier Frankfurt School.

This is Habermas's project in *Knowledge and Human Interests.* His critique of objectivism is straightforward, and reminiscent of Lukács's critique of "contemplation," employing as it does themes familiar from German idealism. The trouble with objectivism is that it "renounces inquiry into the knowing subject" and so "loses sight of the constitution of the objects of possible experience," Habermas writes. "In Kantian terms, [it] ignore[s] the synthetic achievements of the knowing subject. . . . In this way the naive idea that knowledge describes reality becomes prevalent. This is accompanied by the copy theory of truth."[28] Habermas's immanent critique of theories of science from Comte and Mach to Peirce and Dilthey makes up much of the book; its point is to dissolve what he calls the "objectivist illusion" by indicating the irreducible contribution of the knowing subject to the constitution of the objects of knowledge.[29]

His theory of *knowledge-constitutive interests* asserts the existence of certain fundamental modes of human action each of which is associated with a particular human "interest" bound in turn to a specific form of knowledge. The two central ones Habermas calls *work* and *interaction*: as *homo sapiens*, he argues, we are necessarily characterized from the beginning by the dual projects of finding ways to provide ourselves with the physical necessities of life on the one hand (work) and of interacting with our fellow creatures in the communicative practices that make up the social order on the other (interaction). In work, we use tools to change the world around us to satisfy our needs; in interaction, we use language to interpret our actions, our fellow beings, and ourselves. To each of these modes is linked an "interest" and a form of knowledge. On the one hand, work or "instrumental action" is tied to the fundamental human interest in prediction and control of the external environment, and out of that interest arises what Habermas calls "empirical-analytical" knowledge, the knowledge of the natural sciences. On the other hand, communicative interaction is tied to the fundamental interest in the achievement of mutual understanding, and this interest serves as the basis of "historical-hermeneutic" knowledge, the kind produced by the *Geisteswissenschaften*.[30]

Built into the very structure of the species itself, the two interests and hence the two forms of action are mutually irreducible and "equiprimordial," Habermas writes. They function as what he calls "quasi-transcendental" conditions of the objectivity of knowledge, meaning that they

> have a transcendental function but arise from actual structures of human life: from structures of a species that reproduces its life both through learning processes of socially organized labor and processes of mutual understanding in interactions mediated in ordinary language. These basic conditions of life have an interest structure. The meaning of the validity of statements derivable within the quasi-

transcendental systems of reference of processes of inquiry in the natural and cultural sciences [*Geisteswissenschaften*] is determined in relation to this structure.[31]

With this elegant move, Habermas seems to succeed where Lukács failed. The theory of knowledge-constitutive interests represents an improvement on Lukács in several ways. First, it grounds the dualism between social theory and natural science that Lukács wanted to assert in a manner that leaves the status and realm of applicability of natural science considerably less ambiguous and hence leaves the misapplication thesis more plausible. The distinction between labor and interaction as "equiprimordial" and "quasi-transcendental" frameworks of action justifies the claim for the epistemological uniqueness of the *Geisteswissenschaften* over against the sciences of nature, while simultaneously conceding and explaining the validity of the methods of the latter within their own realm. Natural science is no longer left epistemologically hanging. Yet at the same time positivist accounts of natural science are ruled out: Habermas blocks the move to objectivism by employing the notion of a knowledge-constitutive *interest*. The natural sciences, on his view, do not investigate "reality as such," but rather that segment of the world constituted by the human interest in prediction and control of the environment—just as the *Geisteswissenschaften*, marked not by empirical methods but by hermeneutic ones, investigate a different segment, constituted by the human interest in achieving mutual understanding.[32]

Thus it is not natural science but its own "scientistic self-misunderstanding" that Habermas criticizes: its belief that the nature it investigates is ontologically independent of us and that the methods it employs are value-free ones unconnected to any human interest. But if this conclusion is effective against scientism, it functions at the same time conversely to cast doubt on Marcuse's arguments as well. We do not need a "new science," Habermas is suggesting, so much as we need to understand the old science in a new way. Marcuse's call for a liberation of nature based on a radically new science and technology appears in this context as misguided, based on a misunderstanding of the connection between science and interest. For science and technology, "interested" though they may be, still turn out on Habermas's view not to be connected to any particular social project but rather to a project of the species *as a whole*: to a transsocial "species-interest" in the prediction and control of nature.[33] Science is not, on this view, the ideological reflection of a social order based on domination but rather simply the most recent form of a practice and a knowledge that have been characteristic of all human societies from the start and that have their roots in the very structure of work itself. Hence no alternative, "liberatory," science is possible. Habermas writes:

Technological development . . . follows a logic that corresponds to the structure of purposive-rational action regulated by its own results, which is in fact the structure of *work*. Realizing this, it is impossible to envisage how, as long as the organization of human nature does not change and as long therefore as we have to achieve self-preservation through social labor and with the aid of means that substitute for work, we could renounce technology, more particularly *our* technology, in favor of a qualitatively different one.[34]

This idea is key to Habermas's critique not just of Marcuse but of Horkheimer and Adorno as well, and despite various revisions of terminology he holds to it throughout his work. It is not natural science as such that needs to be criticized, he repeatedly argues, for in fact natural science and its associated technology are unavoidable and irreversible achievements of modernity. It is rather the illicit application of the methods of that science to realms where they do not belong that must be rejected. The methods of empirical observation, hypothesis formation, and experimental test are perfectly appropriate ones, Habermas believes, for the investigation of the realm of experience constituted by the human interest in prediction and control associated with labor; the trouble is not with those methods but rather with the attempt to employ them in a different realm, the social one constituted by the human interest in mutual understanding associated with communicative interaction. (This, of course, is the misapplication thesis.)

In the 1968 essay criticizing Marcuse, Habermas presents an account of the dilemmas of modern society that already presages in its broad outlines the more detailed and sophisticated one he will offer years later in *The Theory of Communicative Action*. In a move that parallels the distinction between communicative interaction and work he distinguishes between the overall structure (or "institutional framework") of a social order and what he calls the "subsystems of purposive-rational action" embedded within that structure.[35] The institutional structure finds its normative basis in communicative processes: in premodern societies these are the traditions, myths, religious worldviews that serve to legitimate the form of social organization, while in modern ones they begin to take on a more "rationalized" form, involving the notion of justification in terms of ideals of fairness or universality or human rights. In either case, legitimation of an element of the structure involves the application of "consensual norms" in which it is the normative rightness of the particular element that is put in question and in which it is the potential agreement of all affected parties that serves as the criterion of such rightness. The subsystems of purposive-rational action, on the other hand, represent spheres of activity in which the logic of work predominates. Here normative rightness is not an appropriate criterion but rather whether the proposed course of action is "successful"—whether, that is, a predicted effect is actually observed.

The trouble with contemporary society, Habermas argues, is that these subsystems—he mentions specifically those not just of science and technology but also of the economy and the state bureaucracy—are no longer subordinated to an overall structure guided by communicative norms. Instead the logic of the subsystems themselves has come to take over, leading to the phenomenon of a "scientization" of politics.[36] Processes that ought to be guided by normative social considerations instead appear themselves as the model for social institutions and social decision making in general. Thus questions that are essentially political and ethical, and hence ought to be decided by affected citizens on the basis of communicatively determined norms, are treated today as though they were technical ones, to be decided by experts on the basis of the technical norms of "efficiency" and "success." Habermas writes that "technocratic consciousness reflects not the sundering of an ethical situation but the repression of 'ethics' as such as a category of life. . . . The reified models of the sciences migrate into the sociocultural life-world and gain objective power over the latter's self-understanding. The ideological nucleus of this consciousness is *the elimination of the distinction between the practical and the technical.*"[37]

This is the phenomenon that Horkheimer and Adorno were attempting to explain with their notion of a dialectic of enlightenment, and that Marcuse has in mind in his critique of instrumental rationality. But the umbrella concept "enlightenment," Habermas thinks, is simply not differentiated enough to capture the complexity of the real historical process. It hides within itself two quite different notions—that of a *scientific* enlightenment, employing purposive-rational action and aiming at the achievement of technical control over the external environment, and that of a *political* enlightenment, employing discourse about norms and aiming at the sort of mutual understanding characteristic of a society of free and autonomous individuals. Habermas's predecessors in the Frankfurt School had assimilated both of these to a concept of instrumental reason in which the technical predominated, thereby being led to see a fatal dialectic within the very concept of enlightenment itself. But the solution to the contemporary crisis, he contends, lies not in giving up either of these goals but rather in asserting and holding to the distinction between them and resisting any attempt at conflation.

This way of putting the problem, Habermas asserts, exposes Marcuse's theoretical error: the latter conceptualizes the utopia of a "new" scientific approach to nature on the model of *political* enlightenment (for example, with his talk of "liberating" an "oppressed" nature), thus confusing the two distinct realms. Indeed, Marcuse's error looks like the mirror image of the one Habermas criticizes in contemporary scientism. If the "one-dimensionality" Marcuse laments is really the consequence of the misapplication of categories appropriate to technical inquiry in a realm that is fundamentally discursive and political, Marcuse looks to Habermas to be guilty of exactly the opposite mistake: to speak of nature as another subject, as a possible (communicative) partner in the creation of a "common universe," as we have seen Marcuse doing, is to use the language of interaction in a realm constituted by work.[38] Nature cannot be "dominated" and cannot be "liberated" either because concepts such as "domination" and "liberation" are applicable only to relations between subjects—to the communicative realm—and the nature that is the object of science and technology is not a subject. The intrinsic link between the structure of science and the structure of work means that science is from the start essentially oriented toward the prediction and control of nature, not to an oxymoronic "liberating mastery" of it based on a quasi-communicative relation in which it is somehow freed "to become what it would like to be."[39]

The "New Science" thus stands revealed as a romantic dream: to have a technology that is somehow not a technology, to satisfy human needs without controlling nature. It is the dream of a nature with whom we could speak, a nature that is itself a moral agent and with whom a reciprocal moral relation is a possibility. Like all romanticism, it correctly rejects the claims of science to intellectual hegemony, but incorrectly thinks it can do this only by rejecting science's validity as such. Habermas sees the real situation as more complex, and one in which the success of science and technology (not as a prop for domination, but as a way of satisfying real human needs) cannot and need not be denied. The contemporary social phenomena that the earlier Frankfurt School condemned, and that they correctly saw as bound up with the increasing scientization and technologization of the social world, can in fact be criticized, Habermas suggests, without repudiating science and technology as such. These phenomena derive rather from *boundary violations*—that is, from the conflation of the technical with the communicative interest—and are not the inevitable result of a technical rationality oriented in its very core toward "domination."

3. TWO PROBLEMS

With the notions of quasi-transcendental interests in the first place and the dualism of labor and interaction in the second, Habermas seems neatly to resolve the problems with Lukács's early Western Marxist position while avoiding the cul-de-sacs of pessimism (Adorno) or utopianism (Marcuse) that seemed to follow from the Frankfurt School's critique of instrumental reason. By taking the basically neo-Kantian approach of distinguishing value spheres rather than the Hegelian approach with its emphasis on self-reflection (and its reluctance to distinguish the natural from the social), Habermas seems to place the misapplication thesis on a firmer footing, thereby avoiding the (supposed) danger of a "socialized nature." Yet systematic difficulties arise with respect to his strategies that raise questions as to whether he has really overcome the tension between materialism and an "activist" view of knowledge that I have suggested generated severe difficulties both for Lukács's version of the misapplication thesis and for the earlier Frankfurt School as well.

Indeed, a problem arises with each of these notions—that of quasi-transcendental interests and that of the distinction between labor and interaction. I want to examine each in turn. They certainly have not gone unnoticed by commentators[40] or by Habermas himself, who has been a model of intellectual integrity in terms of his willingness to respond to criticism, to engage in self-critiques, and to abandon views when he has been persuaded of their inadequacy. It is indeed at least in part in response to these difficulties that Habermas recast his project in the course of the 1970s, dropping the theory of knowledge-constitutive interests in favor of a new paradigm based on a theory of communicative action.[41] Yet I think it is worthwhile to look again at his earlier view and re-examine these problems, because there is still something to be learned from them: they share a common source. There is, I believe, a deep structure to Habermas's view of nature, one which in fact has not changed significantly since *Knowledge and Human Interests* was published and which reveals him not to have escaped the basic problem about nature that I have been arguing has been endemic to Western Marxism from the beginning. When taken seriously, furthermore, these two problems seem considerably to weaken his argument against the possibility of a "new science," at least if the latter is suitably reinterpreted along not-quite-Marcusean lines. (It will paradoxically turn out, however, that *Marcuse's* own vision of a "new science" has more in common, in terms of its underlying difficulties, with Habermas's view than might at first be apparent.) I shall return to this point in Section 6.

1) The first problem has to do with the ambiguous status of nature within a theory of "quasi-transcendental" interests.[42] On the one hand, as the object of natural scientific inquiry, nature for Habermas must be a *constituted* realm—constituted in the context of the technical interest in prediction and control of the environment. This is the Kantian moment in Habermas's "quasi-transcendentalism": the nature of natural science has no existence independent of human interest. Yet on the other hand nature must simultaneously also play another role in the theory of interests, one that for any full-blooded Kantianism will necessarily appear incompatible with the first. For Habermas wants his theory to be a materialist one, meaning that nature must also appear as somehow the *source* of the interests he describes. It is the contingent "natural" structure of the human species, after all, that gives rise to the interests indi-

cated by work and interaction. Hence the "behavioral framework of instrumental action," on Habermas's account, is itself simply a natural characteristic of *homo sapiens,* and presumably developed in accordance with ordinary evolutionary processes. Therefore nature appears not only as constituted *by* the interests, but also as the independent physical realm that *generates* them and so underlies the possibility of the act of constitution. Habermas asserts both:

> The conditions of instrumental action arose contingently in the natural evolution of the human species. At the same time, however, with transcendental necessity, they bind our knowledge of nature to the interest of possible technical control over natural processes. . . . The objectivity of the possible objects of experience is thus grounded in the identity of a natural substratum, namely that of the bodily organization of man, which is oriented toward action, and not in an original unity of apperception.[43]

This is why the interests are only *quasi*-transcendental.

> Since it is posited with the behavioral system of instrumental action, this framework [i.e., the conditions under which nature is constituted] cannot be conceived as the determination of a transcendental consciousness as such. Rather, it is dependent on the organic constitution of a species that is compelled to reproduce its life through purposive-rational action. Hence the framework that establishes a priori the meaning of the validity of empirical statements is contingent *as such*.[44]

The Kantian solution to this problem, of course, is to distinguish phenomena from noumena; and Habermas, too, seems forced to posit a distinction between "nature in itself," the nature preceding human history and giving rise to the systems of action that underlie the interests, and "nature for us," the nature disclosed to us via the medium of the behavioral system of instrumental action.[45] But whereas Kant keeps the two realms rigorously apart, Habermas cannot. The trouble is that the quasi-transcendentalism here will only allow quasi-noumena: Kant's unknowable things in themselves here become a "natural evolution" and an "organic constitution of the species," that are explicitly the objects of human knowledge. The "contingent framework" that binds our knowledge of nature "with transcendental necessity" is something *we learn about* from sciences such as paleontology, evolutionary biology, anatomy, and so on, not to speak of "social sciences" such as anthropology, sociology, linguistics, and so forth as well.

To call the interests quasi-transcendental seems only to name the problem, not to solve it: how could an interest that grounds our knowledge of the empirical itself be known to have an empirical origin?[46] A circle apparently arises: we need to *know* something about nature as it is independently of the "knowledge-constitutive interests" to ground the theory's assertions about the "interested" structure of cognition, but if these assertions are true it is just this sort of knowledge that turns out to be impossible. The issue is not, as Habermas sometimes suggests, whether "sciences of origin" such as the theory of evolution might involve some species interest *other* than the instrumental one, but rather whether they can coherently be thought of as operating subject to *any interest at all.*[47] For if they do so operate, then the "nature" they disclose is not nature in itself but rather nature as constituted subject to some interest; whereas if they do not so operate and are somehow "interest-free," then the claim that all knowledge is intimately bound with interest is vitiated.[48] In the first case, "nature," including the nature we believe preceded us, turns out to be a human (social) product; in the second case, "objectivism" turns out to be justified.

The trouble here is that Habermas wants to have his cake and eat it too—to assert, against positivism, the "interested" contribution of a species-subject to the nature investigated by natural science on the one hand, while maintaining a naturalistic belief in the origin of this subject through purely natural processes on the other. The dilemma thus engendered is another form of the one we have been tracing throughout. To say that nature, including the nature preceding human history, is somehow constituted by humans in their activity would be to risk idealism, apparently putting into question our scientific certainty that nature gave rise to us and not vice-versa. Habermas thinks he can avoid this danger only by arbitrarily excluding our knowledge of prehuman nature or of the fundamental structures of human action from the theory of knowledge-constitutive interests, just as Lukács avoided it by excluding natural science as a whole from the critique of objectivism.

The real function of the notion of "nature in itself" in Habermas's epistemology is thus to save materialism, by insuring that the theory conforms to our (and natural science's) prephilosophical intuitions that nature is independent of us and antedates us. But these intuitions are ones that the rest of the epistemology simply contradicts. The problem is the same one Lukács faced: the difficulty of combining a theory of knowledge as the act of a world-constituting subject with a materialism in which nature must retain ontological priority. The antinomical status of nature in Habermas's quasi-transcendentalism is the first hint that his attempt at synthesis does not succeed.

2) The second problem with Habermas's account has to do with the methodological distinction it draws between natural science and the *Geisteswissenschaften.* Although as I have suggested Habermas's position represents an advance over Lukács in recognizing the need to offer a nonobjectivist, nonpositivist justification of natural science's claim to *validity*, nonetheless on the level of *method* Habermas in his early works remained incongruously

beholden to an outmoded positivism. Habermas himself in later years conceded as much, writing for instance in the 1982 "Reply to My Critics" that "in the light of the debate set off by Kuhn and Feyerabend, I see that I did in fact place too much confidence in the empiricist theory of science in *Knowledge and Human Interests*."[49] Yet I am not sure that even then Habermas recognized the full significance of his failure to examine that debate. Indeed, I want to argue, the deeper implications of the postempiricist critiques help to point out some major difficulties in Habermas's epistemological position as a whole—difficulties, further, that continue to haunt even his later work, in which the problems of *Knowledge and Human Interests* have supposedly been resolved.

Natural science, according to the scheme of *Knowledge and Human Interests,* is fundamentally *monological:* the scientist is confronted with a world of objects he or she is concerned to control, not a world of other subjects with whom he or she needs to communicate. "Purposive-rational action . . . is in principle solitary," Habermas writes.[50] It is based on the possibility (quasi-transcendentally guaranteed) of the replicability of experiment: "every *individual* experiment assures us of a *universal* relation, which, under exactly similar conditions, must also be confirmed in all future repetitions of the same experiment."[51] It is *erfolgskontrolliert,* concerned with the success or failure of technical operations. It is marked above all by *progress*—indeed, Habermas writes, this is "the exemplary feature" that distinguishes it from other forms of knowledge.[52]

It is clear in hindsight how much Habermas's account of natural science's method depended in the 1960s on the very positivism he thought he was criticizing. In his 1965 inaugural address at Frankfurt, for instance, he asserted that the framework of the natural sciences "establishes rules both for the construction of theories and for their critical testing. Theories comprise hypothetico-deductive connections of propositions, which permit the deduction of lawlike hypotheses with empirical content. . . . In controlled observation, which often takes the form of an experiment, we generate initial conditions and measure the results of operations carried out under these conditions."[53] And in *Knowledge and Human Interests* he wrote that

> Theories in the empirical sciences are required strictly to separate [theoretical] propositions from facts. The empirical accuracy of their . . . inferences is subsequently checked [*kontrolliert*] by means of empirical propositions expressing the result of systematic observations independent of the theory. To the extent that they have empirical reference, "pure" languages [i.e., those employed by empirical science] demand in principle a separation between understanding logical connections and observing empirical matters of fact.[54]

The language sounds terribly old-fashioned today. Habermas uncritically repeats the very dogma of a split between theory and observation, between language and "data" (and between analytic and synthetic), that postempiricist philosophy of science placed decisively into question. Not even contemporary scientific realists would put matters in anything like this form. Of course Habermas in truth is less concerned with methodological questions about natural science than he is with similar questions about the *Geisteswissenschaften*; his real point is to show that the latter are *not* marked by these splits and indeed to use that difference to support his critique of positivist attempts to assimilate social science to natural science.[55] But he is fighting a straw man. He attacks mainstream epistemology for defending the applicability of positivist methods to social material without noticing that among mainstream epistemologists by the late 1960s faith in the applicability of those methods *anywhere* was rapidly dying.[56]

The truth, as Mary Hesse was one of the first to point out, is that the picture of natural science painted by Kuhn and the postempiricists looks remarkably similar to Habermas's picture of a *hermeneutic* science.[57] Natural sciences as well as social sciences, in that picture, are marked by an unavoidable, and nonvicious, circularity in the relation between interpretive scheme (theory) and data, by a constitutive role for discourse among investigators, by the lack of any formalizable neutral framework for obtaining "truth." What postempiricism did, in fact, was to discern the element of discursive (as opposed to formal) rationality so important to hermeneutics within the natural sciences themselves, thereby shattering the positivist dream of a formalizable method for science uncorrupted by the messiness of ordinary language.[58] This seems to put into question not only Habermas's strong emphasis on the monologic character of natural scientific investigation, but also his sharp dualism between "empirical" natural science and "hermeneutic" social science.[59]

This point can be pushed too far, though. It would be a mistake to accuse Habermas in *Knowledge and Human Interests* of having failed to recognize a fundamentally discursive aspect to the work of natural scientists. Indeed, on the contrary, pointing to this aspect is central to his antipositivist argument that the methods of the natural sciences are not the only route to knowledge. Habermas criticizes Mach and Comte for ignoring the constitutive role played by the actual processes of scientific investigation, which crucially include discourse, in constituting the world "disclosed" by natural science.[60] Peirce's advance over early positivism, Habermas argues, lay precisely in his recognition that the pragmatic conditions that make scientific inquiry possible must play a role in the theory of science, and that those conditions have ontological implications that render "copy theories" untenable. "If the only propositions that count as *true* are those about which an uncompelled and permanent consensus can be generated by means of scientific method, then *reality* means nothing but the sum of those states of fact about which we can obtain final opinions";[61] and if this is so, then the process by which such opinions are formed becomes pivotal. Peirce recognizes, writes Habermas, that "the cognitive process is discursive at every stage"[62]—opinions are not formed monologically but through discussion. "The logical analysis of inquiry, therefore, is concerned not with the activities of a transcendental consciousness as such but with those of a subject that sustains the process of inquiry as a whole, that is with the community of investigators, who endeavor to perform their common task communicatively."[63]

A communicative element to natural science is thus admitted by Habermas from the beginning. In the *Positivismusstreit* of the early 1960s Habermas had already argued in a similar manner, with respect not to Peirce but to Popper. The latter had exposed, in *The Logic of Scientific Discovery*, a basic circularity in the positivist account of the relation of theory to observation. Universal theoretical statements, early positivism held, had to be "verified" by appealing to singular statements ("basic statements," "protocol sentences") expressing the results of empirical observation. But these basic statements themselves, Popper pointed out, could not be formulated without employing universal terms, in essence committing the utterer to theoretical claims, especially dispositional ones. Hence the process of testing a theory "has no natural end": it is not a matter of stopping at indubitable protocol-sentences but of *deciding*, Popper argued, which basic statements we wish (tentatively) to accept.[64] This decision is inevitably a social one, made by the community of investigators, and reveals itself as sedimented in the very language scientists speak. Science thus depends upon the possibility of this sort of social agreement; its absence, Popper writes, would mean the "failure of language as a means of universal communication. . . . In this new Babel, the soaring edifice of science would soon lie in ruins."[65] Popper's work, Habermas argues, thus reveals scientific research to be irreducibly social, because essentially tied to discursive agreement from the very start, just as Peirce's does.[66]

In fact Habermas criticizes both Popper and Peirce for failing to take this insight far enough. Neither figure adequately recognizes that the discovery of an irreducibly communicative element at the heart of natural science's theorizing explodes the empiricist identification of natural scientific knowledge with knowledge *tout court*: it now turns out, Habermas argues, that there must be another form of knowledge, a hermeneutic one, to account for the possibility of communicative action among investigators. If Popper had taken his position further, he would have seen that a hermeneutic social theory, employing methods and "values" quite distinct from those of the natural sciences, is thus not only possible but even necessary in order to ground natural science's own claim to validity and remove the arbitrary, decisionistic element he finds there.[67] The same is true of Peirce, Habermas writes:

> Had Peirce taken seriously the communication of investigators as a transcendental subject forming itself under empirical conditions, pragmatism would have been compelled to a self-reflection that overstepped its own boundaries. In continuing his analysis, Peirce would have had to come upon the fact that the *ground of intersubjectivity* in which investigators are always already situated when they attempt to bring about consensus about metatheoretical problems is not the ground of purposive-rational action, which is in principle solitary. . . . The communication of investigators requires a use of language that is not confined to the limits of technical control over objectified natural processes. It arises from symbolic interaction between societal subjects who reciprocally know and recognize each other as distinct individuals. This *communicative action* is a system of reference that cannot be reduced to the framework of *instrumental action*.[68]

But something is puzzling in this argument. The recognition of an unavoidable communicative element to natural scientific inquiry would seem to entail that such inquiry cannot be understood on the model of monologic instrumental action at all; it is curious that Habermas interprets it instead as simply meaning that there must be *another* form of inquiry, the hermeneutic one. He accepts Peirce's account of natural science, that is, but then wants to complement it with a different account of the *Geisteswissenschaften* as tied not to "labor" but to "communication." It isn't clear, though, why the recognition of the discursive character of natural science doesn't vitiate just the dualism Habermas is trying to establish. If natural scientific theorizing isn't monologic, then the sharp break between "empirical" and "hermeneutic" sciences Habermas asserts no longer seems plausible. Instrumental action alone turns out to be no more the sole foundation for natural science than it is for the sciences of society, which is exactly what postempiricism leads one to expect.

Habermas's argument in the *Positivismusstreit* perhaps makes his position—and what is wrong with it—clearer. He convincingly criticizes Popper for a residual positivism in still believing that the potentially falsifying "facts" that are compared with theoretical predictions in an empirical test of a theory can themselves be identified as such in a theory-independent way, and shows indeed that the impossibility of conceptualizing a falsifying fact separately from a theoretical context really follows from Popper's own account of the "basis-problem."[69] It turns out, however, that what Habermas means by the "theoretical context" in which the facts of science are constituted is simply the technical project of science as instrumental action *as a whole*—the facts are constituted, that is, by the "technical interest."[70] He doesn't see what Kuhn, making a similar critique of Popper, saw: that there is not *one* "theoretical context" in which scientific facts are constituted but rather potentially many such competing contexts. Habermas could in a sense be said to anticipate postempiricism here in that he insists on the theory-ladenness of facts in science; but the only "theory" he really finds them laden with is the single one implicitly posited by the universal and evolutionarily determined behavioral system of instrumental action. He doesn't recognize, as postempiricism does, that "theory-ladenness" means that facts may be laden with *particular* scientific theories, and thus may change over historical time.

Kuhn's insight suggested that scientific facts might be constituted in a *social* context, not merely in the anthropological one suggested by the notion of "knowledge-constitutive interests," and this is what Habermas cannot accept. Although he is concerned to emphasize the social and hermeneutic element to scientific theorizing (and uses this as we have seen as the basis of his argument for a dualism between social and natural science), Habermas still wants sharply to separate it from, and indeed in the last analysis to subordinate it to, a nonsocial, nonlinguistic framework of "action" that is the source of the "data" scientists discuss. For Habermas, discursive justification is thus a *part* of science, but only a part; the normative principles (the "values") that guide it, such as successful prediction and control, come from elsewhere—from an independent realm of monologic purposive-rational action where hermeneutic categories do not apply.[71] Again, the Kuhnian and post-Kuhnian insight is more radical: it is that something like discourse, and the hermeneutic categories and logic it entails, are central to the *actions* and the *norms* of scientists too, affecting what they see, what they do, what standards they employ, what counts as successful prediction or control for them, and so on.

Habermas criticizes Popper for the latter's faith in theory-independent falsifiers, but the former seems equally criticizable, in the postempiricist context, for his own faith in discourse-independent action. In the last analysis, Habermas turns out to be operating with a relatively minimal notion of the contribution of discourse to natural science, according to which the only role it plays is in theory choice; "data collection," "experimentation," and so on, are still taken as essentially monologic, and tied to the framework of instrumental action. That the state of the discussion about theories might in turn affect the "observed data," a commonplace of postempiricism, seems not to be seriously considered by Habermas; to recognize it would be to see the inadequacy of his dualism. The "instrumental framework" is simply never encountered independently of the communicative one; his attempt to separate the two seems indicative of the extent to which Habermas himself remains in thrall to positivist assumptions.[72]

4. INTERESTS AND "INTERESTS"

I want to suggest that a deep structure connects the two problems we have just examined—that of a quasi-transcendentalism that falls into difficulties about "nature in itself" on the one hand, and of a dualism embarrassed by the discovery of social and hermeneutic elements in the natural sciences on the other. A significant remark Habermas makes in a relatively early text offers a useful entry point.

In his 1965 Frankfurt inaugural lecture, reprinted in English as the appendix to *Knowledge and Human Interests,* Habermas argued eloquently against what he called the "illusion of pure theory"—common, he said, to positivism and Husserlian phenomenology—for failing to see the unbreakable connection between knowledge and interest. Positivism's power, in particular, depended on its unjustifiable claim that science describes reality "as it is" independently of any human interest; this "objectivist illusion . . . deludes the sciences with the image of a reality-in-itself consisting of facts structured in a law like manner; it conceals the constitution of these facts, and thereby prevents the interlocking of knowledge with interests from the lifeworld from coming to consciousness."[73] It is not science's "interested" character, its rootedness in the lifeworld, that Habermas wants to criticize, but rather the delusion that the connection between knowledge and interest could be, or in science has been, overcome. Positivism's failure lies in its lack of self-reflection.[74] Once a philosophical self-reflection on the methodology of science recognized the role of interest in the a priori constitution of the objects of knowledge, the false claims of scientism to possess the only possible method for achieving objective truth about "reality in itself" would be unmasked; this was to be the project of *Knowledge and Human Interests.*

Yet on closer analysis Habermas's own commitment to the connection between knowledge and interest, and to the importance of self-reflection, turns out to be ambiguous. Toward the end of the inaugural lecture he writes:

> The glory of the sciences is their unswerving application of their methods without reflecting on knowledge-constitutive interests. From knowing not what they do methodologically, they are that much surer of their discipline, that is of methodical progress within an unproblematic framework. False consciousness has a protective function. For the sciences lack the means of dealing with the risks that appear once the connection of knowledge and human interest has been comprehended on the level of self-reflection. It was possible for fascism to give birth to the freak of a national physics and Stalinism to that of a Soviet Marxist genetics . . . only because the illusion of objectivism was lacking. It would have been able to provide

immunity against the more dangerous bewitchments of misguided reflection.[75]

This is a remarkable, and revealing, passage. In the context of a lecture otherwise extolling the virtues of self-reflection about the connection between knowledge and interest, it is astonishing to find Habermas suddenly asserting that in certain cases ignorance is bliss. The seemingly evenhanded dualism that says natural science's methods are valid "in their own sphere" turns out to have a patronizing core: it's best, apparently, for scientists not to know too much—not to know the limits their methods really have, nor the reasons for these limits. Only "we," on the other side of the divide, may safely be entrusted with the esoteric knowledge that objectivism is wrong. A methodologically self-aware science, easily seducible by the "bewitchments of misguided reflection," would present "risks," so a noble lie must be told—the lie that "pure theory" *is* possible and is exemplified by scientific method.

The "risk" is that methodologically self-aware scientists would take the connection of knowledge and interest too seriously, asserting just that social character to scientific knowledge Habermas is insistently unwilling to accept. Positivism, it turns out, is not the only enemy against which his account is directed: Lysenkoism, which is to say the "politicization" of science, must be defeated as well. He is fighting on two fronts—not only against the positivist assimilation of social theory to natural science, but also against any hint of a relativization of science to society (à la Marcuse). The result is a complex double game, in which Habermas must simultaneously reject objectivist accounts of science (to save the autonomy of social theory) while also maintaining, on a new epistemological basis, the usual claims for natural science's value-freedom (to save its rootedness in nonsocial reality). He needs, in a word, to assert the "interested" character of natural scientific knowledge while denying it any *social* character.

He can do this only by employing an ambiguous notion of "interest." The assertion of a "connection of knowledge and interest" central to his early work cannot be understood in the sense of the sociology of knowledge or even of *Ideologiekritik*. Habermas is quite explicit, as we have seen, that the knowledge-constitutive interests he discusses are not the interests of any *particular* social group or social order, but rather are universal and presocial interests built into the very structure of the species itself. "The concept of 'interest' is not meant to imply a naturalistic reduction of transcendental-logical properties to empirical ones," he writes. "Indeed, it is meant to prevent just such a reduction."[76] By founding science on *this* kind of interest, the move to a "Lysenkoist" socialization of science is blocked.

Thus against objectivism's faith that science investigates an independent, external "reality," Habermas asserts that objectivity is constituted by interests;

to save himself from "relativism," however, he has to push these interests, and the activity of constitution, back into the mists of presocial, prehistorical time. Just like Lukács, he both wants to say that the nature of natural science is a human construct, constituted by humans in their practice, and yet also fears the apparently idealist implications of this. The result is a mythical conception of "constitution," and of the humans who engage in it, based on an entirely ahistorical notion of "interests."

In the last analysis it is "objectivity" itself that Habermas, the arch antiobjectivist, wants to defend—the objectivity of nature despite the interests involved in our knowledge of it and the objectivity of natural science despite its irreducible discourse- or paradigm-boundedness. It turns out to require a *double* protection: first, in the concept of "nature in itself" guaranteeing that the "quasi-transcendental" interests underlying knowledge are not socially variable ones, and then second, in the distinction between empirical and hermeneutic science further guaranteeing an additional degree of asociality to our knowledge even of "nature for us."

But neither of these strategies work, as I have argued: the two problems with Habermas's account outlined in the previous section arise at precisely the junctures where he attempts to immunize the objectivity of nature against the "subjectivist" implications of his own theory of interests. Indeed, the two problems turn out to be connected. The problem raised for Habermas's dualism by the postempiricist critique of monological theories of science, I argued, is at bottom a problem about the social character of knowledge. We can now see that the problem of the ambiguous status of nature in his quasi-transcendentalism has the same source. Indeed, *the antinomies to which Habermas's quasi-transcendentalism gives rise are simply the result of the projection onto a mythical past of the problem of the social character of scientific knowledge.* The "Lysenkoist" dangers of a knowledge subject to particular social interests are not avoided by seeing these interests as "natural," built into the species as such: they are simply shifted to a different level, where they reappear as the problem of "nature in itself." The relativist's dilemma as to how science could be both "socially interested" *and* true turns into the quasi-transcendentalist's dilemma as to how the species could both constitute nature *and* evolve out of it; from the frying pan of the sociology of knowledge, Habermas falls into the fire of a quasi-transcendental Kantianism.

There is an irony here. Habermas's fundamental critique of positivism in *Knowledge and Human Interests,* as we have noted, is that it fails to see the constitutive role of the human subject in knowledge; his project is to present instead an epistemological theory in which that role is explicitly thematized. Yet his desire to defend the "objectivity" of natural science over and against the social blocks him from carrying that project through. He wants to reintroduce the subject, but his fear of relativism is such that it can't be any *real* socially and historically situated subject that is introduced: it must be "the human as such," a universal species–subject defined by contingent species characteristics, and itself "constituted" (somehow) by nature in itself. And— just as he demonstrates in the cases of Mach, Comte, Peirce, and the others— it is precisely the unavoidable return of the repressed subject that marks the location of the most serious problems in his own theory. The quasi-transcendentalism finds itself unable to account for the (apparently natural) origin of the constituting species-subject, and the dualism has trouble assimilating the role of the communicative community of scientific investigators into its picture of formal, monologic, *erfolgskontrolliert* (and endlessly "progressive") objective natural science.

This means that Habermas's self-confessed failure adequately to consider Kuhn's and Feyerabend's critique of empiricism is more than an unfortunate omission. At first glance the Kuhnian attack on science's pretensions to objectivity might seem quite congenial to Habermas's project of combating objectivism, but in fact the real implications of the postempiricist critique are inimical to Habermas's position. They threaten the dualism central to his account and in a way that reveals what turns out to be a residual "objectivism" in Habermas himself—his commitment to natural science's "objectivity" and its independence from the social, along with a deep reluctance to admit the Lukácsian "nature is a social category" because of its apparently relativist consequences. Habermas's dualism, we discovered, allowed him to assert an independent and epistemologically justified role for the *Geisteswissenschaften* while at the same time insisting on natural science's validity in its own sphere. But postempiricism, I think, persuasively shows this dualism to be untenable.

We are returned here to the same dilemma we have been tracing throughout—the one between a view of nature as social (and of knowledge of nature as socially produced or "interested") and materialism. The antinomical structure of Habermas's account of nature and natural science is yet another indication that these two views simply cannot be rendered compatible. Nature cannot be both constituted by us and independent of us, not both produced by interests and the origin of those interests; one or the other claim has to be given up. I have already indicated that I think it ought to be the latter; this seems to me to be the lesson to be learned from the trajectory of Western Marxist thought on nature as a whole from Lukács to Habermas. There is no "nature in itself," or at least none we can say anything about or that it does the slightest good for our epistemology to assume. The nature we "encounter" has no noumenal status nor even any noumenal correlate: it is something we constitute—in our actions, our theories, our poetry, our metaphysics and religion, our social institutions—and so it changes as we do.[77] Lukács was right the first time: nature *is* a social category. And Habermas was right, too: it is constituted subject to interests. But these interests are real social interests, which arise historically and also pass away. Thus nature turns out to be social from the very beginning.[78]

It is this conclusion that Habermas wants to avoid, clinging to his own remnant of objectivism. He avoids it by asserting the dualism between work and interaction, and by the astonishing preference we have seen him expressing for a natural science kept ignorant about its own epistemological foundations. But these strategies cannot work, and inevitably issue in antinomies. Rather, his own better instincts are right. Science—natural science—is "interested," which means it is historical, it is social, it is connected not only to prediscursive, monologic labor but also to communicative interaction. Fascist physics or Stalinist genetics are undoubtedly risks—but so, after all, are fascism and Stalinism; the former can only be avoided in the same way as the latter, by the continual and self-conscious struggle for human autonomy, for enlightened reason, for the ideals "unequivocally expressed [by] our first sentence."[79] To call explicitly for "false consciousness" among scientists is a denial of the very Enlightenment ideals Habermas wants to uphold; such is the perverse cul-de-sac into which his objectivism has forced him.

The real defense against the dangers of Lysenkoism would lie in the opposite direction—in the careful and principled reflection by methodologically self-aware scientists about science's true epistemological status.[80] The consequences of such self-reflection cannot help but include the recognition that science and society, and hence also science and human values, are inextricably intertwined. This does not mean that science must follow the lead of whatever social forces are currently in power, but rather that scientists too must see their work as part of a broader public discourse about social issues—one in which both Lysenkoism or fascist physics and the social relations of domination that underlie them could and should be shown to be illegitimate; "empirical" questions and "normative" ones are not so easily separable as Habermas's dualism assumes.[81] But the reflexivity of this discourse would then also mean that it would not leave science "as it is." With that, we are returned finally to Marcuse's notion of a "new science" with a new relation to nature. For a natural science that knew itself to be social might well become such a new science, for the first time explicitly and consciously oriented towards real, discursively determined, "human interests," and hence more consonant in its methods and even maybe in its results with the goals of a truly human society.[82] But before we ask whether this is really the sort of "liberatory" science Marcuse had in mind, we need to follow Habermas's development somewhat further.

5. SCIENCE, DISCOURSE, AND DUALISM

In Habermas's work of the 1970s on theories of science, beginning with his self-critical "A Postscript to Knowledge and Human Interests," he attempted to overcome the predicaments we have examined by clarifying the role of discourse in natural scientific method.[83] The problematic notion of knowledge-constitutive interests is now abandoned; and instead of trying to found the distinction between natural science and the *Geisteswissenschaften* on that between instrumental action within a world of objects and communication within a social world of subjects, Habermas now explicitly admits that both kinds of action play a role within natural science. His new theory of universal pragmatics asserts a constitutive role for discourse in the genesis of all validity claims, including those in the natural sciences. The truth of a statement cannot be explicated independently of an account of the process of argumentation in which consensus on that truth is achieved; hence scientific theories, to the extent they are correctly called "true," cannot be viewed as tied only to a monologic framework of purposive-rational action.

Indeed, *discourse* now becomes a technical term, reserved by Habermas for a specific sort of communication, of which the paradigm case is precisely scientific argumentation. Whereas under ordinary conditions of communication actors simply tacitly assume the validity of the claims being raised in speech acts, in discourse these naive assumptions are "problematized" and explicitly move to the center of attention:

> Discourses serve to test the validity-claims of opinions (and norms) that have become problematic. In discourses, the only permissible force is the force of the better argument; the only permissible motive is the cooperative search for truth. Because of their communicative structure, discourses are freed from the requirements of action; they do not accommodate processes in which information is *acquired;* they are purged of action and experience. Information serves as the input to discourse; the output consists in the acceptance or rejection of problematic validity-claims. Nothing is produced in the discursive process except arguments. . . . The strange suspension [*Virtualisierung*] that makes hypothetical thinking possible extends to validity-claims that in the practical realms of communicative and instrumental action are normally naively accepted.[84]

Scientific and normative discourse follow similar patterns. Instead of focusing, as ordinary communication does, on our experiences in the world—and simply taking for granted the validity of the truth claims implicit in them—discourse focuses on the truth claims themselves and tries through argument to determine whether they are justified.[85]

In discourse, where "the only permissible force is the force of the better argument," *everything* is potentially up for debate—not only the particular truth claim whose validity has become problematic, but the theory employed to justify it and even the correct language for the description of the observed phenomenon and the method for its observation. "The formal properties of discourse," Habermas writes, "must . . . be constituted in such a way that the level of discourse can be shifted at any moment, and that whenever necessary an initially chosen linguistic and conceptual system can be recognized as inappropriate and subjected to revision: progress in knowledge takes place in the form of a substantial critique of language."[86] Habermas presents an account of theoretical discourse as moving through a series of stages marked by increasing reflexivity, as first individual assertions, then theories, then languages are rendered problematic. Ultimately the very process itself by which alternate languages are proposed becomes the explicit topic of debate, which leads to what Habermas calls "a normative concept of knowledge in general." As discourse becomes increasingly self-reflexive, that is, it is inevitably driven to epistemology.[87]

Here Habermas not only accepts the Kuhnian point that satisfactory explanation of "anomalies" may require high-level shifts in theoretical frameworks ("paradigms") but also helps resolve some of its problems. Kuhn saw the constitutive role of something like discourse among scientists in the development and justification of an individual theory—a role that could not be trivialized as relevant only to the "context of discovery" or reduced to some (in principle monologic) "hypothetico-deductive method"—but the lack of any neutral language or other metatheoretical framework for choosing *between* alternative theories led him to view such choices as irrational (thereby betraying his own unconscious positivism). Habermas sees, on the other hand, that the appeal to discourse works here as well: although the correctness of a paradigm or a proposed paradigm shift cannot be deductively (i.e., monologically) proven, it can be discursively argued for—on the basis, naturally, of principles that themselves also require discursive justification. The circle here is not vicious but hermeneutic; and Habermas's account interestingly suggests that once the discourse becomes self-reflexive, engendering discussion about its own status and structure, substantive epistemological conclusions can be expected to arise, for instance about the untenability of positivist notions of method or rationality, or of "objectivism" in general.

I shall argue in the next chapter that with this notion of discourse and its connection to truth Habermas has made a powerful contribution to resolving the problems about the status of nature that I am claiming have bedeviled Western Marxism from the beginning—one that helps both to elucidate and defend the only apparently paradoxical idea that "nature is a social category." Yet in his work of the 1970s and after, Habermas continues to maintain a stubborn commitment to a dualism that insists on distinguishing nature from the social and natural science from the *Geisteswissenschaften* and that thus stands in significant conflict with such an idea. He may give up certain forms of this dualism, like the one posited in the 1960s between work and interaction, but the underlying intention itself remains untouched; indeed, Habermas's instinct for dualism seems so deep seated as to be absolutely unshakable. But as in the similar case of Lukács, the result is a weakness at the heart of the position that shows itself in a series of troubling inconsistencies.

One form Habermas's dualism took in the 1970s involved the distinction between discourse and experience. We have seen him assert that the very language employed by science must be open for discursive revision and is not "determined" by some neutral "data"; in the postempiricist context this kind of assertion typically leads to the denial of any theory- or language-independent framework of *experiences* that scientific theories are about. "The scientist with a new paradigm," Kuhn writes, "sees differently from the way he had seen before."[88] But *this* conclusion is one Habermas cannot accept:

> The *a priori* of experience (which lays down the structure of the objects of possible experience) is independent of the *a priori* of argumentative reasoning (which lays down the conditions of possible discourses). . . . Theories can only be constructed, and progressively reconstructed . . . in a theoretical language whose fundamental predicates are always related to the independently constituted objects of possible experience. The theory languages . . . can *interpret* the structures of an object domain not yet penetrated by science. They can also to a certain extent reformulate them. But . . . these languages cannot *transform* the structures themselves into conditions of *another* object domain. It is always the experience of identical objects of *our* world which is being interpreted differently according to the state of scientific progress we happen to have reached. The identity of experiences in the manifold of interpretations we produce of them is assured because of the conditions of possible objectivation.[89]

There is no argument here, simply an assertion, and one in which the instinct for dualism is clear. The extent to which linguistic changes can react back onto descriptions of observations is carefully limited by Habermas to the realm of discourse and explicitly separated from that of "action." Habermas appeals here to the commonsense view that the objects of experience are what they are independently of us, and hence that changes in our theories cannot really produce changes in *them*; but in fact such an argument is not open to him, because in his account the objects of experience are not independent but are rather themselves constituted objects (as the Kantian language, with its reference to an a priori that "lays down the structure of objects of possible experience," indicates). He is thus left simply to suggest that they are constituted independently of discourse, in a special prediscursive framework somehow exempted from the requirement of discursive justification and thereby immunized against critique. Once it is admitted, though, that "objects of experience" are not independent of us, the increasing reflexivity of the critique of knowledge Habermas mentions would seem to require that the framework in which they are constituted be brought into the light of discourse as well; his attempt arbitrarily to limit this reflexivity by asserting that it does not extend to "the conditions of possible objectivation" seems unjustifiable on his own terms. The same problem, that is, arises as appeared with respect to *Knowledge and Human Interests*'s appeal to naturally evolved "behavioral frameworks" underlying the interests: if all knowledge must be discursively redeemable, how could the prediscursive "a priori of experience" he mentions ever come to be known?[90]

This notion of scientific theory-choice as involving "different interpretations" of an unchanging domain of "experience" whose stability is assured (transcendentally?) by the "conditions of possible objectivation" is just the one that postempiricism has radically questioned. If scientists see the world differently after a paradigm shift, then the very conditions of objectivation themselves would seem to have changed. More recent work in the sociology of science by Latour and others has suggested just how problematic the assertion that scientific theorizing can only "reinterpret" but not "transform" experience turns out to be.[91] Indeed, science and technology *do* transform our experience, not only by changing our perceptions of the objects around us but by *making new objects*, a process that takes place not in some rarefied realm of discourse but also (indeed, chiefly) in the realm of ordinary action as well. Kuhnian "paradigm shifts" do change the world and quite literally: the germ theory of disease leads to a world where techniques of sterilization and inoculation are commonplace, just as the break from Newtonian physics leads to a world of nuclear power and weaponry and the biological revolution of the 1950s leads to a world of genetically altered foods and genetically certified babies. The "identical objects of *our* world" to which Habermas appeals—a world which as I examine it includes computers, electric lights, automobiles, plastics, sidewalks, and so on—would be almost entirely unrecognizable to most human beings who have ever lived: to what, then, does he think they are identical?[92]

Only what is essentially a piece of sleight-of-hand allows Habermas to accept the postempiricist relativization of truth to particular theories while still asserting the existence of a theory-independent realm of "objective experience" constituted by action. "Truth," he argues, arises as a meaningful concept only within discourse, not ordinary communicative action. Only when the tacit validity claims implicitly assumed in ordinary speech acts are problematized and become the explicit focus of discursive argument does the question of truth arise. Habermas distinguishes between the "objectivity" of experiences that occur in ordinary action and the "truth" of statements decided upon in discourse:

experiences arise with a claim to *objectivity*, but that is not identical to the truth of the corresponding *statement*. . . . The objectivity of a determinate experience is proven by the verifiable success [*kontrollierbaren Erfolg*] of actions based on these experiences. Truth, i.e., the justification of the validity claim implicitly put forward by assertions, shows itself on the other hand not in successful feedback from action [*erfolgskontrollierten Handlungen*], but rather in successful argumentation [*erfolgreichen Argumentationen*], through which the validity claim can be discursively *redeemed*.[93]

Here the distinction between objectivity and truth does the same dualist job as the earlier distinction between work and interaction. Since at the prediscursive (and hence presocial) level of action, truth is not an issue, neither are the problems of relativism or of the theory-ladenness of observation introduced by postempiricism. In this way the problem of the social character of our experience of the world is sidestepped: sociality is said to affect "truth" but not "objectivity." The advantage of this formulation over that of *Knowledge and Human Interests* is that now natural science is explicitly associated with discourse and hence with the social; Habermas has here given up the untenable positivist account of its method as "monologic." But a corresponding disadvantage emerges in its stead, for the dualism can now be maintained only at the cost of a rupture between (discursive) science and the realm of ordinary prescientific "experience."

This is particularly problematic because prescientific experience of course involves communication too, expressed in ordinary speech acts with propositional content. Habermas is thus forced to draw a rather unconvincing distinction between "statements" about "facts" whose truth is justified in discourse and the "information" about "objects of experience" communicated in ordinary action.[94] Only previously problematized statements, he has to assert, can really be called "true" or "false," and then only in the context of discourse; the mundane pieces of information we trade with each other—"it rained last night," "he's mad at his boss," "TWA no longer flies nonstop to Boston"—are only "objective" or "subjective."[95] Such a distinction seems a questionable contortion at best and at worst makes it impossible to account for the obvious connection between the sentences of scientific discourse and those we ordinarily utter in communicative action.

Mary Hesse has criticized Habermas particularly persuasively on this score. On the one hand, if one admits (as Habermas does) that the truth of ordinary empirical remarks such as "this ball is red" is in some sense "grounded" in the objectivity of the experience of dealing with the ball (in the framework of action), it is hard to see why more complex statements of science are not so grounded as well.[96] To deny "this ball is red" any even "proto-scientific" status would seem to regress behind the insight of *Knowledge and Human Interests* into the connection between science and action. On the other hand, if as we have seen the very language employed by science is subject to discursive justification and hence possible revision, it is hard to see why the language of the lifeworld in which ordinary communicative action takes place is itself somehow immune to such revision.[97] (This is especially so once it is acknowledged that science plays a concrete role in literally transforming the lifeworld itself, as suggested previously.) From both points of view, as Hesse points out elsewhere, the sharp dichotomy posited by Habermas looks much more like a continuum.[98]

The impulse to dualism drives Habermas into other contortions as well. He repeatedly finds himself compelled to draw a distinction between a scientific experiment, which in his account is part of scientific discourse, and what he calls "the structurally analogous experience I would gain in the context of life-praxis" or ordinary action.[99] "Structurally analogous" here seems to be a euphemism for "identical": at what point in the course of his experiences did Galileo move from the "life-praxis" of looking at clocks to the "scientific discourse" of observing pendulums? Despite Habermas's suggestion, what scientists do in the laboratory, as ethnographic works like Latour and Woolgar's *Laboratory Life* have made clear, is in fact continuous with the working practices of automobile mechanics, childcare providers, supermarket shoppers, accountants, and so on.[100] They all engage in "life-praxis"—what else could they be doing?—using tools and language to get around within a context they know well and against a background of unarticulated assumptions and tacit knowhow that makes those practices possible.

Habermas is imagining the scientist as engaging in some strange kind of practice which is scarcely practice at all, a "discourse" in which experimentation takes on an otherworldly purity and bears little or no connection to the practices of ordinary people under ordinary circumstances or to the objects with which they interact. But the objects scientists use in the laboratory are not some ontologically special kind of "theoretical" objects: they are gauges and bottles and computers and labels and so forth, and the experience of working with them is no different from that of any other kind of worker with any other kind of tool.[101] And although the sort of language use that Habermas calls "discourse" certainly plays an important role in laboratory work, it occurs in no special hallowed realm but is rather continuous with other kinds of language use, as laboratory workers jump back and forth between defending truth claims, examining instruments for breakdown, reporting on readouts from recording devices, criticizing (ad hominem) competitors, and so forth.[102]

In *The Theory of Communicative Action* Habermas restates his methodological dualism, attempting to reformulate the kind of distinction between natural science and social science that postempiricism had threatened to undermine by appealing to the notion (due originally to Anthony Giddens) of a "double hermeneutic."[103] Habermas now concedes an irreducible hermeneutic element to natural scientific method, having to do with the theory-ladenness of the observation language, but insists that nonetheless social scientific inquiry presupposes an additional and *prior* layer of interpretation as well, because the *objects* of such inquiry are themselves already prestructured in accordance with social meanings. Thus he writes that in the social sciences

> there is already a problem of understanding below the threshold of theory construction, namely in *obtaining* data and not first in *theoretically describing* them. . . . It is not only that the observation language is dependent on the theory language; *prior* to choosing any theory-dependency, the social-scientific 'observer,' as a participant in the processes of reaching understanding through which alone he can gain access to his data, has to make use of the language encountered in the object domain.[104]

But there is *nothing* "prior" to theory-dependency, which is in any case not something that is "chosen": the hermeneutic situation here is one in which we are *always already*. The "language encountered in the object domain" is itself encountered only through the language already spoken by the interpreter; "obtaining" the social scientific data or "gaining access" to them takes place against the background of the interpreter's own expectations, "paradigms," practices, and so forth—which is to say, in a hermeneutic situation not fundamentally different from the one that arises when a natural scientific observer "obtains" data about subatomic particles by examining tracks in a bubble chamber.

Habermas and Giddens are, of course, right to point out that the "objects" examined by social scientists are themselves already meaningful ones, symbolically prestructured in the lifeworld of the "natives," but this just means that there are more possible interlocutors with whom the investigator can develop her interpretation (i.e., her sense of what the data "say"). Hence the community whose practices and interpretations form the background against which the data are what they are includes not just other scientists but "natives" too. This may *enrich* the hermeneutic situation of science, but it does not impose an additional "prior" one; the investigator does not first "participate" in the native lifeworld and only then interpret it scientifically—one reason for this being of course that "natives" and "scientists" are not always that easy to distinguish.

And in any case the objects examined by natural scientists are meaningful and symbolically prestructured, too. That Habermas does not see this follows from his attempt to distinguish the "experience" of objects from "discourse" about them. Even in *The Theory of Communicative Action* he still describes natural scientific observation as monologic, just as he had in *Knowledge and*

Human Interests: "Observations are made each for himself, and the observation statements of another observer are checked once again by each for himself. . . . By contrast, intersubjective understanding [of the sort necessary for social science], because it is a communicative experience, cannot be carried out in a solipsistic manner."[105] But it is simply false that observations are ever made "solipsistically": the scientist in her laboratory, like the bus driver on her route, operates in a lifeworld that is always already socially prestructured. The paradigms she implicitly accepts, the theories she explicitly believes, the questions she thinks are important or irrelevant, but also the practices she engages in and even the very instruments with which she is surrounded are all social through and through, the product of communication and of communicatively mediated practices—and it is only against the background of these that the objects she "experiences" come to be what they are for her. Not only that: the objects *themselves* are almost always built ones, constructed in highly complex procedures that are the product of much prior social negotiation and possess a high degree of social meaning.[106]

Objects in the world, as I have already argued, do not magically fall into one of two distinct categories, social ones that are "symbolically prestructured" and natural ones that can be monologically observed.[107] Objects can come to be "observed" as "natural" only in the context of certain sorts of (typically, scientific) *practices,* and nothing can be a practice except in a social (and thus communicative) context. Habermas's instinct for dualism leads him to separate discourse from practice, which is doubly mistaken. There are no practices that are not socially mediated, not even those that involve interactions with "things of nature"; and conversely there are no discourses that are not directly related to concrete practices.

Indeed, part of the point is that *discourse and practice cannot be separated,* and so neither can theory and experience or truth and objectivity.[108] Natural science is a difficult case for Habermas because it has its feet in both worlds, the world of the social and discursive and the world of practice and the "objectivity of experience." The trouble is that these turn out actually to be only one world after all, which is exactly what Habermas wants to deny. He returns repeatedly in his later work to a trope according to which human beings inhabit three distinct worlds: "the world" of nature and physical processes, "our world" of the social, and "my world" of an individual's personal experiences.[109] But of course it is just this distinction that I have been questioning here; the world we take for granted as "natural," I have been arguing, is itself always the result of a set of social constructions. I want to return to this notion of three worlds later;[110] here I will just point out that in the context of Lukács's notion of reification Habermas's view might seem to do little more than beg the question. No one denies that to members of *this* social order, "the world" and "our world" appear to be distinct; but it is just this (reified) appearance of the "real" world as independent of the social processes that produce it which Lukács would identify as characteristic of "the antimonies of bourgeois thought." The difficulties I have been tracing in Habermas's attempt to maintain his dualisms at any cost might then appear as themselves symptoms of such antimonies.

With these considerations we are returned to the same conclusion we reached with respect to Habermas's position in *Knowledge and Human Interests*. Although the discursive (and hence social) element in science is recognized by Habermas, the significance of this recognition is explicitly limited by a dualism that tries to separate theory from action, asserting the existence of a prediscursive realm of "instrumental action" or "objectivity of experience" that is independent of language and hence (in Kuhn's terms) paradigm-neutral. The purpose of the dualism, early and late, is clear: it blocks the apparently relativistic and potentially "Lysenkoist" implications of the postempiricist discovery of the theory-ladenness of observation—and hence of the socially constituted nature of experience—by materialistically insisting on an unchanging and nonsocial "reality" that both grounds natural science and is ultimately what that science is concerned to know.

The original dualism between labor and interaction, and between natural and hermeneutic science, then, has not really disappeared, only returned in a different form. In either form, it is an attempt sharply to distinguish between the observational, monologic, "third-person" stance one takes up with respect to objects and the participatory, social, dialogic stance one takes up with respect to other subjects—between *the* world" and "*our* world." But postempiricism, of both the Kuhnian and the more recent constructivist sort, seems precisely to indicate that this attempt must fail: what counts as "*the* world" can be defined (or is built) only by "us," and the plaintive cry that after all we must assume some one world underlying what "we" see, commonsensical though it seems, turns out to be either empty or incoherent—as empty or incoherent as the Kantian assertion of the existence of things in themselves. Habermas offers no argument to show that postempiricism is wrong about this—he simply doesn't like it, because it seems to threaten not only the independence of natural science from social science but also even that of nature from society.

Taking the postempiricist critique seriously would have led to the conclusion that such a strategy is untenable. It would have suggested that not only natural science, but all our interactions with nature, indeed everything Habermas calls instrumental action as such, are intrinsically bound up from the very beginning with the communicative, with the social, with our relations to each other. It would have meant recognizing a fundamentally and irreducibly hermeneutic and indeed normative aspect to our relations to and knowledge of nature (and a fortiori to natural science); it would have meant, once again, that nature is a social category.

6. SCIENCE AND SELF-REFLECTION

The social character of our knowledge of nature and the connection between discourse and practice show the limitations of Habermas's dualisms. But this has significant implications for his critique of Marcuse. His argument that no alternative or "new" science was possible depended (in *Knowledge and Human Interests*) on an account of natural science as connected to a presocial "interest" built into the structure of the species and distinct from the one grounding the *Geisteswissenschaften*; but it is just this kind of account that I have suggested causes the difficulties about nature that seriously flaw that work, difficulties that the more sophisticated but still essentially dualist account of natural science as discursive he developed in the 1970s was still not able to resolve. Habermas, we might say, was right to assert the interested character of knowledge, but wrong to deny that this means that all knowledge, including natural scientific knowledge, is intrinsically connected to the social—that "the world" is always part of "our world."

In this sense it may well be Marcuse who gets the best of the argument. Science *is* always a historical project and *does* "project a universe," which is why it may indeed make sense to talk of the connection between the "value-free" universe projected by contemporary science and the alienating social order in which that science is embedded, and to raise the possibility of an alternative science that might "arrive at essentially different concepts of nature and establish essentially different facts." A new society based on a new sensibility could in this sense plausibly be expected to bring along with it a new science and a new technology—and, yes, a new nature as well. "Nature is a historical entity," Marcuse writes; I have argued repeatedly in the preceding pages that this sort of claim must be taken literally.[111] The "nature" we currently inhabit—the urbanized and constructed world that surrounds most of us most of the time; the landscapes (urban, suburban, or rural) that form the constant background of our experience; the parks in which we play and the wilderness we protect; the objects with which we have most primarily to do; the substance or "matter" of which we believe these all to be made—all of these are historical entities, produced not in accordance with some universal and ahistorical "quasi-transcendental" framework but by particular and historically varying sets of social practices.[112]

Hence a change in these practices would mean a change in the world. This is the point we saw Marcuse making earlier in his talk of a "new sensibility" that, if successful, would "literally transform . . . reality," and of the task of the "new science" as the "reconstruction of reality" or "the transformation of nature."[113] It is precisely because "nature is a historical entity" that Habermas is wrong to deny out of hand the possibility of an alternative natural science that might discover essentially different facts. But of course it is just this conclusion, with its implications of a politicized science and technology, that worries him. His quasi-transcendentalist strategies, we have seen, are an attempt to hold on to the constituted character of nature without admitting its historical character; but they only issue in antinomies. It is finally the active, historical, *social* character of our relation to nature that Habermas cannot acknowledge, and that Marcuse seems to assert. If a new social order would produce for itself a new worldview, this also means that it would inhabit a new world.

And yet to recognize this, which I think is the key to understanding the sense in which Marcuse is right about the "new science," is also to see the sense in which he is quite wrong as well. For he remains committed to the same strategy—and hence is caught in the same dilemma—as his colleagues Horkheimer and Adorno, the one analyzed in Chapter 3. He wants to found his social critique (and his critique of science) on a theory of nature and indeed to carry out that critique *in nature's name* ("nature, too, awaits the revolution!"): but the characteristic problems of such a strategy, indebted more to romanticism and *Lebensphilosphie* than to the Hegelian notion of self-reflection emphasized by Lukács, ought by now to be familiar.[114] Less pessimistic than Horkheimer and Adorno, Marcuse introduces the important idea of a "new science" into the discussion, proposing the possibility of a real alternative to the science he wants to reject instead of depending on vague appeals to mimesis or the ineffability of the aesthetic; yet his conception of what that new science would be and even why it is needed remain trapped in the naturalism that led Horkheimer and Adorno into the dead end we have already examined.

In his talk about what the new approach to nature instantiated by a "new science" and "new technology" would involve, Marcuse constantly speaks of something like a noumenal nature, a nature in itself that previous technology has repressed and that a new technology will somehow free. In *Counterrevolution and Revolt,* he writes that dominative technology "offends against certain objective *qualities* of nature.... The emancipation of man involves the recognition of ... truth in things, in nature."[115] Like Adorno, he associates the new sensibility with anamnesis: the new science would be a form of "*recollection:* ... the rediscovery of the true *Forms* of things, distorted and denied in the established reality."[116] The liberation of nature would mean that "nature's *own* gratifying forces and qualities are recovered and released,"[117] thus allowing nature for the first time to "exist '*for its own sake*'."[118] But what is the "it" being discussed here?

Once again we find a contradiction between an acknowledgment of the social character of nature and a desire nonetheless to assert for it a special status as the presocial material and even normative foundation of historical change. The contradiction is quite evident in *Counterrevolution and Revolt's* chapter on nature. On the one hand, as we have seen, Marcuse says that "nature is a historical entity" and eloquently insists that the role of a new science and a new technology is to rebuild the world; but on the other hand he constantly writes as though the model for this rebuilt world is to be found somehow in a noumenal nature's "own" "objective" or "inherent" qualities. In an insightful analysis of Marx's *Paris Manuscripts*, Marcuse emphasizes the active character of sensibility and the world-constituting role of human practice and human knowledge; but (as I have argued repeatedly) if knowledge is active and world creating, then it is not clear how we could ever know anything about what nature "in itself" is like or what talk about its "objective" qualities would mean.

In fact the reference to Marx turns out to be, in the context of Marcuse's account of the "new sensibility"'s *content*, really a red herring.[119] For it is not the active character of knowledge that the new science is supposed to emphasize but rather (and quite inconsistently) its *receptive* character: "the faculty of being 'receptive,' 'passive,' " he writes, "is a precondition of freedom: it is the ability to see things in their own right."[120] Earlier he had described the central characteristics of a "non-exploitative" relation to nature as "surrender, 'letting-be,' acceptance."[121] The Heideggerean language is evocative, but is simply inconsistent with the thrust of the argument, which must emphasize that the human relation to nature is fundamentally active and transformative, thereby entailing that no truly "receptive" (and ahistorical) acceptance of "nature in itself" can be coherently imagined.

The theme of a call for such "receptivity" runs deep in Marcuse's work.[122] In *Eros and Civilization*, "productiveness" is explicitly associated with toil, and with the performance principle that his utopianism wants to overcome. It is "receptiveness" that is connected with "joy," with "play," with the "absence of repression," and so with the pleasure principle that the advance of civilization was forced to renounce but that the development of technology makes it possible once again to satisfy.[123] Activity almost always appears in that work as negative, as "domination"; freedom is associated with fulfillment, with completion, with an end to striving.[124] Rejecting the image of Prometheus ("the culture-hero of toil, productivity, and progress through repression"[125]) in favor of those of Orpheus and Narcissus, Marcuse writes that the latter

> reconcile Eros and Thanatos. They recall the experience of a world that is not to be mastered and controlled but to be liberated—a freedom that will release the powers of Eros now bound in the repressed and petrified forms of man and nature. These powers are conceived not as destruction but as peace, not as terror but as beauty. It is sufficient to enumerate the assembled images in order to circumscribe the dimension to which they are committed: the redemp-

tion of pleasure, the halt of time, the absorption of death; silence, sleep, night, paradise . . .

and ends by quoting Baudelaire's "ordre et beauté, / Luxe, calme, et volupté."[126] Such talk—linking Eros and Nirvana, pleasure and death, in a way Freud would have found unrecognizable—reveals a deep ambiguity in Marcuse's position, in which the emphasis on the active, transformative role of humans in nature clashes with a romantic yearning for passivity, for "silence" and "sleep," for delicious surrender to the powers of nature.[127] Nature here is not to be transformed but rather "let be"—the "powers of Eros" are inherent in a nature-in-itself that existed prior to human action but that human action has repressed. All we need to do is cease our dominative struggle, and a liberated nature will liberate us.

When he does speak in *Eros and Civilization* of transformation, it takes a highly paradoxical form. The erotic and aesthetic attitude toward nature symbolized by Orpheus and Narcissus "awakens and liberates potentialities" in nature, he writes; "these potentialities circumscribe the *telos* inherent in [natural objects] as: 'just to be what they are,' 'being-there,' existing. . . . In being spoken to, loved, and cared for, flowers and springs and animals appear as what they are—beautiful."[128] But this is an odd sort of transformation indeed and one that aims at an odd sort of telos: "just to be what they are"? Marcuse is sometimes just Adorno in a good mood: the same paradoxes through which the latter expressed his pessimism about the power of thought to capture nonidentity here underlie instead a utopian optimism about the possibility of a human "eroticization of nature" whose ultimate task, remarkably, is to let nature become . . . what it already is.

Behind the paradoxical (incoherent?) formulation no doubt lies a more familiar metaphysics, according to which what is now true of nature only implicitly or *an sich* will become explicit and overt after humans take up a new attitude towards it. "Nature [today] is a world of oppression, cruelty, and pain," Marcuse writes; but "the [liberating] song of Orpheus pacifies the animal world, reconciles the lion with the lamb and the lion with man. . . . [It] breaks the petrification, moves the forests and the rocks—but moves them to partake in joy."[129] Even if we ignore the wild utopianism here—letting nature be what it already is apparently involves an end to predation, and some large-scale geological changes as well—still there is no serious role for human agency in this account. Rather it depends on a pre-established harmony between inner and outer nature in which the expression of erotic impulses in the former coaxes forth the hidden erotic potentials of the latter.[130] This is not nature as a *historical* entity, but rather one unfolding according to an immanent logic based on a romantic metaphysics in which human action serves only as catalyst.

Real activity, real practice, involves negation, as Hegel taught us: it is not a matter of merely releasing potentialities that are already there but rather of producing substantial change in the object upon which one acts. This is why it is historical. To serve merely as a catalyst in which a pre-existing telos in nature is allowed to express itself is not to engage in (historical) transformative activity at all, but rather precisely in "contemplation"—the very word of Schiller's that Marcuse quotes but that in the context of Lukács's critique of reification has quite a different connotation.[131] Marcuse wants to assert an active role for humans in the liberatory transformation of nature, but can only do this by imagining an activity that does not really act and instead leaves everything as it was. The truth is that, like Adorno, he is deeply suspicious of activity *as such*: it is too closely bound up for him with "productivity," "the performance principle," and hence domination.[132]

As we have seen, Marcuse like Adorno appeals to anamnesis as a source of our knowledge of what nature *an sich* is supposed to be; the role of memory in the argument is instructive. In *Eros and Civilization* a chapter on "Phantasy and Utopia" asserts on a Freudian basis that phantasy preserves the memory of an archaic or "subhistorical" time (phylogenetic or ontogenetic?) before the reality principle split off from a pleasure principle henceforth to be subordinated to it, and so before the ego itself separated from a primal unity with the genus and with the world; phantasy thus comes to have, Marcuse writes, "a truth value of its own . . . envision[ing] the reconciliation of the individual with the whole, of desire with realization, of happiness with reason."[133] Phantasy is explicitly connected here with the aesthetic; art is the conscious working up of the contents of phantasy, and thus "behind the aesthetic form lies the repressed harmony of sensuousness and reason—the eternal protest against the organization of life by the logic of domination, the critique of the performance principle."[134] Phantasy "aims at an 'erotic reality' where the life instincts would come to rest in fulfillment without repression," Marcuse adds; in this memory of an archaic past before the formation of ego he finds both the source and the justification for the utopian thinking upon whose necessity he insists.[135]

The thought-form here is a familiar romantic one: art and imagination are valued for reminding us of a lost unity—between pleasure and reality, sensuousness and reason, individual and group—that has been dirempted but to which we could somehow return.[136] "The Orphic-Narcissistic images are those of the Great Refusal," Marcuse writes: "refusal to accept separation from the libidinous object (or subject). The refusal aims at liberation—at the reunion of what has become separated."[137] He tries valiantly to deny that this is really a call for a regression into the past, arguing that "the truth value of imagination relates not only to the past but also to the future. . . . In its refusal to accept as final the limitations imposed upon freedom and happiness by the reality principle, in its refusal to forget what *can be*, lies the critical function of phantasy."[138] But this is entirely unconvincing; the idea that a memory of what "once was" can offer a clue as to what "can be" makes sense only in the magical world of the unconscious where past and future are systematically confused. In truth, superseded moments are just that—superseded, and unrecoverable. Although often presented in the language of a Hegelian *Aufhebung* of the dirempted unity where the division is preserved while also being rationally comprehended and overcome, in fact Marcuse's vision here is merely the romantic nostalgia for that unity itself, unchanged and uncomprehended—not the negation of the negation, but simply a longing for the positive.[139]

A real *Aufhebung* would take a different form, and would involve an appeal to concrete human practice. But there is no room for such practice in Marcuse's utopian vision, because to engage in transformative activity upon the world requires the division between self and other already to have been drawn. The deep "subhistorical" past he yearns for is one that precedes human action. His dream is of a world without difference or change; it is the dream of Nirvana, in Freud's sense—a world without time or effort or self. It is the dream of the womb, of a world that is no world at all. *This* is why real human practice always appears in Marcuse's work as "toil" and why he repeatedly returns to the daydream of a totally automated world where labor would be unnecessary.[140] But real practice, as I have argued earlier, in fact crucially involves the moment of resistance and otherness in the world; that is what separates it not just from theory but from "phantasy."[141] Real labor in the world is hard, and not guaranteed to succeed; this is not to deny that it can be a source of sensuous pleasure, of course, but only to point out that it is at bottom ontologically incompatible with the undifferentiated unity Marcuse identifies with the pleasure principle.[142]

"Nature is a historical entity," I have been arguing, because the nature we inhabit is through and through the product of human practice; to say this however is not to deny but rather to *assert* the otherness and resistance of the world to us. We do not think the world, or imagine it, but rather build and rebuild it through concrete action that is difficult and sometimes fails. Adorno at least understands and incorporates this moment of resistance into his account of art, despite his own ambivalence about practice. But Marcuse dreams of a world where practice ("toil") is unnecessary because resistance has disappeared, flattened out in an oceanic pan-eroticization where reality turns back to pleasure and the phantasy is equivalent to the deed, and where all that is needed to make something beautiful is to sing to it. Marcuse's view hates the world, the real world that is, although that hate is hidden behind a utopianizing metaphysics that claims to discern behind the real world a secret erotic one where lion and lamb no longer quarrel. It is he who wishes to "dominate" nature, thoroughly and totally, so that all traces of the resistance that otherness poses to practice evaporate. The dream of total automation that never lies far below his words is the symptom of a wish that the real world would go away, so that humans could spend all of their time in that other phantasy one.[143]

Thus if Habermas fails to see that the active character of our relations with nature is inseparable from their social and historical character, Marcuse can be faulted for failing to see the opposite—that a historical entity is always already the product of human action and hence that "passivity" or "receptivity" or "surrender" to it is not even an option. Instead he constantly tries to appeal to a noumenal (and thus *a*historical) nature independent of human action as the foundation for social critique, and without Adorno's sophisticated appreciation of the paradoxes such an appeal engenders. This explains the curious tendency toward biologism that marks Marcuse's work. The project of *Eros and Civilization* is explicitly to ground critical theory in the instincts—in the memory of the instinctual gratification repressed by civilization but preserved in the realm of the unconscious and of imagination. The same theme recurs in *An Essay on Liberation*, where Marcuse writes of "a biological foundation for socialism."[144] The assumption seems to be that only a social critique founded in biology (and hence in nature) can claim validity for itself.

To be sure, in Marcuse's works of the 1960s and 1970s his biologism is also often expressed in a quite different and more surprising claim—that revolutionary change requires the production of *new* instincts, even of a new biology for humans, so as to produce "new needs."[145] Contemporary society has generated needs for consumption, competition, and waste, Marcuse writes, that have "sunk down" into the organic dimension.[146] A liberated society would thus have to replace those needs with new ones—"for peace, . . . for calm, . . . for the beautiful."[147] The idea would be to produce "men who have developed an instinctual barrier against cruelty, brutality, ugliness."[148] Here the "historical" character of internal nature is certainly asserted, but only in such a way as to betray the depths of Marcuse's biologism and naturalism—as if the only manner in which revolutionary action could be justified would be if it became a matter of natural impulse.[149] Nature continues here to be the foundation of social change, but perversely we are now supposed to change nature first in order to make it possible for it in turn to change us.

But if nature really is historical, then "changing nature" is not so much a precondition for social change as an effect of it; building a new society doesn't require humans changing their own instincts but rather changing their own minds. This illuminates what is absolutely right about Habermas's critique: like the Marxist scientism earlier Western Marxists had rejected, Marcuse wants to make social revolution a requirement of nature, thereby taking what are essentially ethical questions and trying to turn them into biological ones.[150] The result is to remove social critique from the communicative realm and hence from the requirement of discursive justification. For the young rebels Marcuse supports, he says, the struggle "is not a question of choice; the protest and refusal are parts of their metabolism."[151] The rhetoric is impressive but misguided: where there is no choice, there can be no liberation either.[152] The mistake is to try to ground social theory in nature, which is to say in the extrasocial—a move that always ends up making humans subservient to things, and that Marx had criticized as fetishism and Lukács as reification.[153]

But we can see Marcuse's motivation: where else could social theory be grounded? He too fears relativism, just as Habermas does. Without an appeal to some ahistorical nature independent of human will and choice, it does not seem possible to justify criticism of a social order that admittedly "delivers the goods" and apparently satisfies most people's needs, or even to give a content to the critique. The solution seems to be to posit a nature (-in-itself) whose *own* "needs" are being violated by such a system and then to make the revolution in its name.[154] Yet if "nature is a historical entity" no such nature-in-itself really exists; it is always already the consequence of historical practice and so a product of social construction. And as we have seen to try to speak of "constructing" nature in such a way as to "let it be," of allowing it to exist "for its own sake" or to realize its inherent telos, will not work: for again there is no "it" there, no model for the "natural" separate from what we *do*.

But then Marcuse's problem turns out to be identical to Habermas's, and to stem from the same source. Both writers follow lines of thought that lead to the conclusion that the external world of nature is actively constituted through social practices; both try to avoid the apparently relativist implications of this conclusion by attempting to ground those practices (from the beginning of the species, for Habermas; "after the revolution," for Marcuse) in a nature in itself prior to any constitution. But neither is able to explain how we can have access to this noumenal nature, given the original assertions about the active character of our relation to nature. Once again the problem is the fundamental one we have been tracing—how to reconcile an account of knowledge as active and social on the one hand with the "materialist" commitment to a nature independent of the human on the other.

But if the recognition of the active character of knowledge and the constituted character of nature reveals the shortcomings of both sides of the dispute between Habermas and Marcuse about technology, at the same time it shows there to be something right about each side as well. Habermas's emphasis on the role of human interest in our knowledge of nature shows that nature is *not* itself a subject but rather instead is the object of our constitutive acts. We cannot have a communicative relation to it: it has no "rights," it cannot be "liberated," it does not "speak to us" or "await the revolution." It is a historical product, the result of human action. But for just this reason something like Marcuse's "new science" *is* possible: a new social order would mean a new mode of action and would bring with it a new world.

Yet the meaning of this "new science" would have to be very different from the one Marcuse proposes for it. Not the Orphic dream of passive contemplation of an eroticized nature-in-itself magically released from any connection to the human and no longer offering resistance to human practice, it would rather be the self-conscious act of humans who know their own responsibility for the world they inhabit and thus know that world as historical and social through and through. This call for self-reflection, as I have argued in the previous chapter, is what distinguishes a Hegelian critique of science based on the theory of reification from one based on what are finally romantic and irrationalist themes. Habermas, we saw, fears the relativist consequences of a self-reflective science, one that knows its own interested character; but just this, it seems to me, is the best candidate for the "new science." Marcuse, fearing relativism too, thinks he can argue for the superiority of *his* science over the old "dominative" one only by showing it to be founded on the instincts—either old ones that have been hidden under years of surplus-repression or new ones that a revolution would create; but this kind of attempt to avoid relativism, as I have already argued, only plunges the theory into the antinomies of an appeal to nature-in-itself. Rather, as suggested earlier, the new science's superiority would come from its foundation in self-reflection.

What would a science be like that had given up what Habermas calls the "illusion of objectivism" and no longer believed itself to be discovering timeless truths about a world independent of the social? What would happen if scientists saw themselves as participants in a broader social process of transformation in which their practices served not merely to describe but also to shape the world they inhabit, both "social" and "natural," and if society as a whole too saw science in this light? Habermas worries about the consequences of a "politicized science" and points to Lysenkoism and fascist physics as dangers; but those seem to me rather examples of sciences still oriented toward discovering the eternal truths of nature-in-itself while claiming to derive their validity from the privileged insights of a particular class or race into the "real" structure of the universe. A self-reflective science that knew its own rootedness in the social would be *less,* not more, likely to make such a mistake.

To speak of a new science that would know its own sociality and would no longer believe in the discovery of nonsocial truths is not to speak of a science magically free to "discover" anything it wanted. Lysenko's claims about how to grow wheat were false; the agricultural practices they led to failed. A self-reflective practice of science would acknowledge such failures but would not see them as fundamentally different from other types of failure, social "side effects" that today are treated as unfortunate but extrascientific, like those that followed the supposedly nonpolitical agricultural practices of the "Green Revolution" for instance.[155] Such a science would know that what counts as a failure is always a *social* question, to be decided by citizens in open discourse. The social "consequences" of science and technology would no longer be thought of as external to that science and technology themselves but rather as intrinsic. (And note that a self-reflective science would also know how subtly the concept of "consequence" must be understood; consequences flow not merely from applications of discoveries but from laboratory techniques, from language and metaphors, from paradigm shifts themselves.) The move from theory to practice is crucial here, not least in answering the Habermasian challenge. For the question a self-reflective science and technology would pose for society would not be "what theories do we wish to be true?"—which does suggest a wild idealism of the sort Habermas fears, if "truth" is taken to mean "correspondence with a nonsocial world"—but rather "what practices do we wish to engage in?" And *that* question can only be answered in the communicative realm. (It is Habermas himself, of course, who has insisted above all on the centrality of that realm to social theory and social critique; I will argue in the next chapter that his notion of a "discourse ethics" is enormously fruitful in elucidating the idea of a self-reflective "new" science, despite his own resistance to that idea.)

Underlying my own argument here, of course, is the critique of reification. What is wrong with the society we live in is precisely that in it human beings' own responsibility for the environment they inhabit (the "social" environment, in the first place, but the so-called "natural" one as well) is systematically hidden from them: this is the phenomenon Marx called alienation. A nonalienated society would be one where that illusion is punctured, and humans consciously and explicitly assert their responsibility for the world, transforming it on the basis of needs that are discursively expressed and social decisions that are democratically made. The science and the technology *that* society would have would doubtless be radically different from the one we know today. No longer in thrall to objectivist myths about the possibility of a pure description of external reality (myths that themselves simply reflect the prevailing reification), such a science would finally know itself to be social, to be historical, to be "interested," and hence would know its own connection to the world it helps create. It is that very knowledge that breaks the link between science and domination Western Marxism has always feared. Without the seductive faith in its own "neutrality," science would know itself as an instrument of liberation—not silent nature's, but our own.

CHAPTER 6

Towards a Communicative Theory of Nature

1. ETHICS AND COMMUNICATION

The key methodological insight introduced in Habermas's sprawling but magisterial *Theory of Communicative Action,* an insight which forms the core of the research program he and his associates have been developing ever since, lies in the call for critical theory to undertake a "paradigm shift" from the "philosophy of consciousness" to one based on communication. By this Habermas means that rather than taking the model of an *individual subject confronting an object* in the world as theoretically central, philosophy should concentrate instead on the *linguistically mediated relations among subjects.* Once that shift is made, he writes, "the phenomena in need of explication are no longer, in and of themselves, the knowledge and mastery of an objective nature, but the intersubjectivity of possible understanding and agreement. . . . The focus of investigation thereby shifts from cognitive-instrumental rationality to communicative rationality."[1] Instead of emphasizing a subject's manipulation of objects, and defining rationality in terms of the success or failure of that manipulation, the new view focuses on the specifically linguistic phenomena through which social relations are produced and reproduced, and defines rationality in terms of concepts such as validity and consensus.[2]

This important idea allows Habermas to come to terms with his predecessors in the Frankfurt School, developing and extending the kinds of critiques we saw him offering in the 1960s and early 1970s.[3] His more recent discussions of Horkheimer and Adorno—which have clearly influenced my own critique above—reformulate his old objections.[4] On his new account it is their commitment to the "philosophy of consciousness" that leaves them unable to conceptualize any kind of rationality other than the instrumental (subject-object) one they reject. This places them in an impossible position, because the sorts of categories they need for the critique—which is to say, the very ethical ones they decry instrumental reason for having abandoned—then have, by their own admission, no defensible rational status. Having "submitted subjective reason to an unrelenting critique from the ironically distanced perspective of an objective reason that had fallen irredeemably into ruin," as Habermas puts it, Horkheimer and Adorno inevitably fall prey to the problem of normative grounding: how can they justify their own critique?[5] They can solve it only by appeal to "a reason that is before reason": to nature, to mimesis, to a "speechless 'mindfulness.' " But of course they can offer no *theory* of this ineffable otherness, because to do so would entangle them in the usual circle, and hence they are left with nothing but the exquisitely paradoxical attempts to say the unsayable while denying that one is saying it that we have examined earlier.[6]

But there was another turn they could have taken, Habermas suggests: the communicative one he is proposing. Their conception of reason is insufficiently differentiated; they suffer from a "cramped optics" which fails to see that instrumental reason does not exhaust the concept of reason as such.[7] Concepts such as freedom, domination, and reconciliation—the very concepts Horkheimer and Adorno must be able to justify to ground their own critique—derive *not* from the instrumental relations of a subject to the world of objects but precisely from the communicative relations obtaining among subjects who interact through language. In communicative action, Habermas believes, Horkheimer and Adorno could have found the normative foundation whose absence had rendered their own critical stance so paradoxical as to cancel itself.

This line of argument should be familiar from the earlier criticisms we have considered. On one level, of course, what we have here is yet another Habermasian dualism—another form of the distinction between work and interaction. I will not repeat the reasons I would have for objecting to that dualism and in particular to the way it ignores the social character of our interactions with objects by treating them as "merely" instrumental and monologic and hence lacking in normative significance. Instead I want to consider the account of the *social* realm involved here. For in fact I think that there is something extraordinarily important in the "communicative turn" Habermas is proposing, and in the communicative solution he offers to the problems of normative grounding which he rightly sees as having doomed the earlier Frankfurt School project. By emphasizing the connection between normativity and language, Habermas makes a significant contribution not just to ethics and social theory, I want to argue, but also to the (social) theory of nature as well.

He develops the idea of what he has come to call *discourse ethics* in a number of places, beginning with the "Wahrheitstheorien" essay and others of the 1970s, continuing with a more detailed discussion in *The Theory of Communicative Action*, and most recently in a series of essays collected in English in *Moral Consciousness and Communicative Action* and *Justification and Application*.[8] The argument varies to some degree, but the central strategy (due also to Karl-Otto Apel) is to ground ethics *self-reflexively* via an account of the structure of the kind of discursive argumentation in which moral claims are made and justified.[9] Moral scepticism is countered by pointing out that the sceptic cannot present her view in argument without falling into a "performative contradiction," since to engage in argumentation at all is already to presuppose the validity of certain moral principles.

Building on Austinian and Searlian speech-act theory, Habermas argues that every utterance can be analyzed as implicitly making various "validity claims": the speaker claims that what she says is *true*, that the normative relation her speech act is supposed to bring about is *right*, and that the expression she is giving of her own intentions and emotions is *truthful* or sincere. This supports a rough tripartite classification of utterances, depending on which validity claim is most directly thematized—the claim to truth in "constative" speech acts, that to rightness in "regulative" ones, that to sincerity in "expressive" ones.[10] To make a validity claim of one of these sorts is furthermore implicitly to take up the responsibility to "redeem" it in argumentation—to explain, if challenged, *why* what is said is true, is right, is sincere. Willingness to enter into argumentation (or "discourse," in Habermas's technical sense[11]) is therefore a presupposition required by any language use whatsoever.[12]

The existence of something like normative "rightness," according to this account, is thus as much built into the pragmatics of language use as is the more familiar notion of "truth." The two kinds of validity claims—that such-and-such is true and that such-and-such is right—are to be understood as analogous, Habermas asserts.[13] "Rightness" is not a nonnatural property nor is it merely an expression of an emotion or personal belief, but rather, like "truth," involves a tacit claim about the course of a possible process of argumentation; to say that an act is right is implicitly to say that its rightness could be defended discursively by the giving of reasons.[14] Both "It is right to do X" and "It is true that X" are therefore to be analyzed in terms of argumentation and grounding; and for each case Habermas (again, much like Apel) defends something like an ideal consensus theory. When I say "X is right," just as when I say "X is true," what I *mean*, on this analysis, is that I could in principle give sufficiently good reasons for accepting X that any and all interlocutors would be convinced.

But if this account is correct, it means that to raise a validity claim to the rightness of an action—that is, a moral claim—is implicitly to appeal to the (counterfactual) possibility of a universal discourse in which all potentially affected persons could take part and in which "the only permissible force is the force of the better argument." Moral argumentation, then, presupposes a commitment to something like a universalism of the Kantian sort; to engage in such argumentation is to have always already assumed that an act is moral only if it could receive the approval of all those whom it would affect. To say "this action is right" while also conceding that certain persons who are affected by it would never accept it is simply to fail to see what the concept of rightness entails.[15] This is why the moral sceptic is caught in a performative contradiction, at least as long as she engages in any communicative action at all (and how could she not?): to speak at all is to raise validity claims, which in turn is implicitly to be willing to give reasons for them, which then further implicitly commits one to an argumentative process in which universalism is necessarily presupposed.

Such, very schematically presented, is the line of reasoning that leads Habermas to the formulation of his "principle D" of discourse ethics, which asserts that "only those norms can claim to be valid that meet (or could meet) with the approval of all affected in their capacity as participants in a practical discourse."[16] Note that it has the structure of a transcendental argument, although as Habermas repeatedly insists (correctly, I think) this has to be understood in a considerably weaker and more fallibilist sense than was intended by Kant.[17] It is an empirical hypothesis, proposed as a rational reconstruction of the competences for communicative action we already possess; what it claims to demonstrate is that in order that there be such action certain presuppositions must already have been made by speakers and hearers, and that therefore to take part in communication while attempting to deny those presuppositions is to enter into a performative contradiction.

Even if transcendentalism is abandoned here, the Kantian flavor is of course still very strong. It is evident as well in the strongly *deontological* and *proceduralist* character of the moral theory Habermas presents. Discourse ethics prescribes an ideal *procedure* for the justification of rightness claims: subjecting them to the scrutiny of a public discourse in which all affected are equally able to speak. It does not prescribe any particular *substantive* ethical theses, however, and indeed as should be clear cannot do so without violating its own tenets. The validity of normative claims can only be evaluated from the point of view of such a discourse; any substantive normative claims that an ethical theory wished to proffer could only be understood as contributions to that discourse, offering up validity claims that could be redeemed only in discussion with others. There can be no a priori moral claims, where "a priori" means prior to intersubjective discussion and the giving of reasons, and so discourse ethics must abjure the attempt to determine the specific sorts of acts justice requires or forbids.[18] Instead what it offers is a formal characterization of justice or the moral point of view: acts are just if all affected parties would be able to agree to them following an open discourse.

The reference to justice indicates the *deontological* character of the theory. Discourse ethics limits its ambition; it can speak of justice, Habermas says, but not about "the good life." He draws a sharp distinction, particularly in the 1980s and later, between "moral questions" about norms and "evaluative questions" about values.[19] Only norms, which are the rules that regulate interactions among subjects, are amenable to rational justification via discourse, because in the very idea of such regulation the ideal of universality is already contained. "Values" or conceptions of the good, on the other hand, are in principle multifarious; what counts as a good for me (or for us in a particular community) is relative to who I am (or who we are) and who I or we want to be. Habermas, especially recently, is too impressed by hermeneutic considerations about the internal relation between conceptions of the good and the specific historical traditions in which they arise to believe any longer that they admit of universal consensus. Now he distinguishes between the "moral" and the "ethical" uses of practical reason: in the ethical use one answers for oneself a set of existential questions about who one wants to be and what is good for one, whereas only in the moral use do universalistic considerations arise following the recognition that there are others who do *not* share my values or my sense of the good.[20] But Habermas, always the rationalist, does not by this mean to suggest that what he calls "ethical-political discourse" is impossible or irrational, and explicitly asserts that such discourses, in which individuals or communities engage in processes of self-clarification, have an important role to play as well.[21]

These arguments allow Habermas to elucidate and begin to resolve the problems of normative grounding that shipwrecked the earlier Frankfurt School, from *Dialectic of Enlightenment* to *Counterrevolution and Revolt*. Not only do they make it possible for him to avoid the naturalism into which his predecessors were constantly being forced, they also help to clarify why such a naturalism is untenable as a foundation for a critical social theory. By pointing out the internal relations linking critique and normativity to *language*, Habermas shows why the sorts of claims the earlier theorists wished to make could only be justified within the social realm itself—or more precisely, within a discourse—and not through any utopian appeal to "what the poor earth would like to be." Critical concepts like "domination," "liberation," and "reconciliation" have a normative content that ties them uniquely to relations between members of a potential communicative community, and so attempting to derive them from, or apply them to, the natural world simply involves a category mistake.

But to say this is already to reveal a problem, for nature now threatens to drop out of the sphere of the normative entirely. There is a crucial ambiguity in Habermas's proposal for a paradigm shift to a communicative philosophy, fruitful and important though that proposal is. His objection to the "philosophy of consciousness," as we have seen, is that it takes subject-object relations as its primary model while subject-subject relations are treated as secondary and assimilated to the former. The paradigm shift is supposed to reverse matters so that linguistically mediated relations among subjects form the standard model. But now subject-*object* relations become problematic: how are *they* to be understood? Do the old analyses continue to hold for them, or do they simply fall by the wayside, treated as insignificant and subject to some derivative analysis? Or does the paradigm shift affect them, too, so that we need now to speak of a "communicative theory of nature"?

I think the answer to the last question is yes, and so understand Habermas's view as suggesting that a shift to a linguistic analysis can also usefully help elucidate the relations between humans and the world of nonhuman entities that earlier philosophy had taken as its exemplar. Such an elucidation might begin with the sorts of considerations raised in earlier chapters, asking specifically about the communicative processes that organize (or should organize) the practices by which we construct the objects of the environing world we inhabit. The world of objects, too, it might propose, is in a certain sense communicatively structured; our interactions with "things" do not take place independently of the linguistic processes by which we decide how to organize our relations with each other. And this is also true of our interactions with "nature." To this extent the intention of the earlier Frankfurt School would still have a place, although admittedly with a markedly transformed tone—the intention, that is, to include an account of nature, with an explicitly normative character, within a critical theory of society.

Yet as we have seen Habermas is deeply uneasy with that intention, an unease that does not lift but even grows in his later works. The result is that the status of nature is left significantly ambiguous in those works, and that the possibility of a communicative theory of nature is never seriously taken up. When he speaks of the shift in paradigms (as in the passage quoted earlier) he continues to assume that subject-object relations can be interpreted on the monologic model of a solitary subject "manipulating" an independent object under rules of purposive-rational action oriented toward "success" or "failure" "in reality." That such a subject is never solitary, that such manipulation is always mediated by language, that the object involved is typically already the product of earlier social labor, that success or failure is socially negotiated and socially defined, and that reality is something we help to construct through our practices—none of these points, all of which suggest something like a communicative theory of the world of objects, is conceded by him, consistently loyal as he is to his dualism.

It is remarkable, in fact, to note how small a role categories such as labor or practice play in the sociological analysis of *The Theory of Communicative Action*; references to nature and the human relation to it are almost as rare.

The interest in providing a systematic theory combining an account of both social *and* natural "realms" that so clearly animated *Knowledge and Human Interests* seems by the 1980s simply to have disappeared; one might be tempted to say that Habermas has now taken Lukács's claim that a theory of nature has no place in social theory to heart, to such an extent that nature is barely mentioned (a strategy that doubtless has the advantage of avoiding the contradictions in which Lukács found himself entangled). If in his early work Habermas criticized Marx and others for emphasizing labor and ignoring interaction, in his late work he seems guilty of precisely the opposite sin.[22]

Yet nature does not *entirely* drop out of Habermas's discussion. It returns, repeatedly, perhaps a bit like the repressed, as he responds on several occasions to objections from the point of view of something like environmental ethics. What, these objections ask, can discourse ethics tell us about our responsibilities *to* the environment or about nature's intrinsic value? A number of authors, including Joel Whitebook, Henning Ottmann, Thomas McCarthy, John Dryzek, and others, have raised versions of this question, expressing reservations about the anthropocentrism that seems to be at the core of Habermas's view and that appears to them to make an adequate conceptualization of the ethical dimension of contemporary environmental crises problematic.[23] Such objections clearly bother Habermas, which may explain why he returns to them several times. I want in what follows briefly to examine his responses, which reveal I think both the strengths and weaknesses in his position. The difficulties he finds himself in, I will argue, derive from his failure to acknowledge that "nature" and "objectivity" are socially constituted. Yet discourse ethics, I will also suggest, possesses important resources for defending a communicative theory of the environment that does not leave the latter ethically insignificant, while at the same time avoiding the naturalism and romanticism Habermas rightly wants to leave behind.

2. THE PROBLEM OF NATURE IN A DISCOURSE ETHICS

The accusation that discourse ethics leaves nature stripped of any moral qualities and is therefore incapable of conceptualizing anything like an ethical responsibility *to* nature certainly seems plausible at first glance.[24] The upshot of Habermas's dualism, early and late, does point in a direction whereby normativity is explicitly reserved to relations among humans. The speech-act analysis carefully distinguishes constative speech acts that raise validity claims to truth from regulative ones that raise claims to normative rightness. Nature is "the world," not "our world": it is the world to which one refers when speaking in the third-person, "objectivating" attitude—and as Habermas points out, to take up this attitude is precisely to leave the moral realm behind.[25]

Norms refer to and arise out of a situation in which subjects must coordinate their actions via language (and hence via validity claims); they therefore have no place in a realm such as the natural one where one party is in principle incapable of such coordination.

Both Ottmann and Whitebook (to varying degrees) objected already in the 1970s to the anthropocentrism they perceived in Habermas's account, and in particular to the apparent impossibility given such an argument of envisioning any intrinsic value *in* nature or even of acknowledging the possibility of an approach to nature that goes beyond the technical-instrumental one associated with pure descriptions of states of affairs. In "Reply to My Critics" (published in 1982) Habermas attempted to respond to this critique by presenting a more systematic account of the relation between nature and normativity; some of the same material appears in *The Theory of Communicative Action*.[26] He begins by admitting that it is certainly possible to relate to the natural world in something other than the technical-instrumental manner that he had earlier connected with labor, writing however that "while we can indeed adopt a performative attitude to external nature, enter into communicative relations with it, have aesthetic experience and feelings analogous to morality with respect to it, there is for *this* domain of reality only one *theoretically fruitful* attitude, namely the objectivating attitude of the natural-scientific, experimenting observer."[27] More specifically, he argues, only that attitude—the one that retains its independence from the normative—is capable of being developed into cumulative knowledge, and therefore of being subject to rationalization processes in the Weberian sense.

He elucidates this thesis by presenting a chart in which the three "formal world concepts" mentioned earlier (the world of external nature, the social world, and the world of inner nature) are paired with three possible "basic attitudes" (objectivating, norm-conformative, and expressive) deriving from the three kinds of speech acts and the associated validity claims.[28] This produces nine possible "formal-pragmatic relations" between subject and world; of these, however, Habermas argues, only a limited number can serve as possible areas for rationalization.[29] The "objectivating" attitude toward external nature, for instance, is exemplified by the instrumental relations associated with technical processes, whereas taking up the same attitude toward the social world generates the relations Habermas calls "strategic" (i.e., goal-oriented relations to others not bound by normative considerations or a commitment to discursive redemption of validity claims). Both are rationalizable, as shown by the development of science and technology on the one hand and (to some extent) of social engineering on the other. The "norm-conformative" attitude toward the social world similarly generates normatively regulated social behavior, whereas an "expressive" attitude toward external nature finds its articulation in aesthetic phenomena. These are subject to rationalization, too, as part of the differentiation processes Habermas views as central to modernity: moral-legal reasoning and aesthetic criticism each develop in the modern world according to their own internal logics.

But when it comes to norm-conformative attitudes toward nature, Habermas is dismissive, summarily suggesting that no significant examples are available: "The phenomena that are exemplary for a moral-practical, a 'fraternal,' relation to nature are most unclear," he writes, "if one does not want to have recourse here . . . to mystically inspired philosophies of nature, or to taboos (e.g., vegetarian restrictions), to anthropomorphising treatment of house pets, and the like."[30] The supercilious tone—not to speak of the glaring *petitio principii* involved in relegating vegetarianism without argument to the status of irrational taboo, or in trivializing concern for animals into sentimentality about pets—doubtless sets one's teeth on edge; Habermas seems blind to the serious kinds of concerns expressed by proponents of an ecological ethics. Yet then his attitude suddenly and surprisingly shifts, as he concedes that there are indeed occasions when

> our experiences of non-objectivated dealings with nature . . . have unmistakably moral qualities. The impulse to provide assistance to wounded and debased creatures, to have solidarity with them, the compassion for their torments, abhorrence of the naked instrumentalisation of nature for purposes that are ours but not its, in short the intuitions which ethics of compassion place with undeniable right in the foreground, cannot be anthropocentrically blended out.[31]

He develops this latter idea in connection with the concern, characteristic of the earlier Frankfurt School, about how a utopian "reconciled world" might redeem the sufferings of those (humans) who died in the past.[32] So too do the sufferings of animals require some sort of redemption. But the former problem is actually easier to solve within a discourse ethic than the latter, Habermas admits, because we can at least counterfactually imagine earlier generations of humans as potential members of the discourse community, whereas animals cannot seriously be so imagined even counterfactually. "Anamnetic solidarity" with those who suffered in the past, then, can be comprehended within a discourse ethic; but compassion for animals extends "beyond moral-practical insights." Such compassion, Habermas claims,

> would become accessible to moral consideration only if this ethic were extended beyond the domain of interpersonal relations to our relationship with creatures that cannot fulfil the conditions of responsible action. With these living creatures—who are indeed *affected* by the normatively regulated, morally relevant behaviour of humans, but who could not, even counterfactually, step out of the

position of those affected and take up the role of *participants* in practical discourses—nature-in-itself would come into view in a certain way, and not only the nature instrumentalised by us.[33]

But then he shakes himself free of this reverie; his real point is that although such an "ethics of compassion" is conceivable, it lies beyond the limits of what a rationally justifiable normative theory could ever hope to defend.[34] Although "our intuitions tell us that attempts to open up a *moral access* to nature-in-itself are by no means absurd," the project of doing so faces fundamental difficulties, Habermas says, analogous to those faced by the attempt to gain *theoretical* access to nature in itself as well.[35] He mentions three. An ethics of compassion for nonhuman creatures could only be grounded in a naturalism that would itself require the kind of substantive metaphysical foundation Habermas believes modernity (and especially modern ethical theories) are better off having jettisoned. Second, such an ethics would require a conception of the moral realm in which crucial notions such as equality and reciprocity could not easily find a place; animals are *different* from humans, and cognitively weaker, and so such an ethic would inevitably depend upon a form of paternalism inconsistent with modern conceptions of the moral point of view. And finally, Habermas points out, it is in any case entirely unclear towards *which* creatures we are supposed to feel compassion—mammals? insects? plants?—or what our duties are when such compassion comes into apparent conflict with fundamental human needs. Thus he concludes that "while in our dealings with external nature we can indeed have feelings analogous to moral feelings, the *norm-conformative attitude* to this domain of external nature does not yield any problems susceptible of being worked up cognitively, that is, problems that could be stylised to questions of justice from the standpoint of normative validity."[36]

Furthermore, he remarks, our concerns about the ecological damage produced by human interventions in nature can in any case be adequately formulated within the confines of the sort of anthropocentrism discourse ethics seems to entail.[37] Whitebook had developed this idea (which is the standard claim of a left-wing anthropocentrism), albeit very tentatively: a normatively good society, he suggested, one where the domination of humans over humans had come to an end, would arguably ipso facto be one where unnecessary environmental damage would have ended as well. No rationally organized society—and no rational discourse—could countenance technologies that threaten the very earth on which it stands.[38]

Habermas's whole discussion is notable above all for its palpable ambivalence. He vacillates, as we have seen, from a strong and even contemptuous rejection of the possibility of an ethics of nature to a more subdued (and eloquent) acknowledgment that we have moral intuitions in this area that his account has difficulties elucidating. His discomfort is clear, and may partially account for the somewhat rambling and disjointed character of his remarks.[39] The argument gets even more tortured in the later "Questions and Counterquestions," first published in 1984 as part of a symposium on Habermas in *Praxis International*.[40]

In his contribution to the symposium, Thomas McCarthy had raised some important objections to Habermas's claim that only a few of the nine possible "formal-pragmatic relations" between actors and worlds were amenable to rationalization.[41] Habermas, as we saw, argues that a norm-conformative attitude toward nature cannot be a candidate for rationalization on the grounds that it is not "theoretically fruitful" or suitable for the accumulation of knowledge; yet in what sense, McCarthy asks, does the "aesthetic" attitude—or for that matter the ethical (social) one—admit of an accumulation of knowledge either?[42] This and other difficulties seemed to indicate a serious problem in providing and justifying a consistent criterion for determining which attitudes were and which were not "rationalizable."

Habermas's response to these criticisms was to concede many of them and retreat, suggesting now that the chart of nine relations should be understood more as an attempt to reconstruct the logic of Weber's views than as an expression of his own.[43] The error had been to imagine the three worlds and the three attitudes as operating in free variation; but clearly there are internal rational connections binding specific attitudes to specific worlds—the objectivating attitude to the external one, the norm-conformative attitude to the social one, and the expressive attitude to the world of the self. Hence, Habermas now asserts, cells on the diagonal of the charts possess a priority, and the argument ought to have been made simply on the basis of that priority. Dangers arise when an attitude is applied to worlds other than the one to which it is internally connected: just as "objectivism" with regard to the social or internal world must be avoided, as must an inappropriate "aestheticism" with regard to the natural or social worlds, so, too, "moralism" ought not so quickly be extended from its appropriate place in the social into the world of internal or external nature.[44]

What McCarthy is really looking for, Habermas claims, is a way to continue to conceive of something like the unity of reason—a way to bring together the three modes of rationality (scientific, ethical, and expressive-aesthetic) whose differentiation Habermas, following Weber, thinks is a crucial and irrevocable step in modernity. In one sense such a unity exists already, Habermas says, within communicative action, where constitutive, regulative, and expressive validity claims all occur together; but when it comes to re-establishing such a unity at a *theoretical* level, especially along the lines of a "reconciliation with nature," he can only mildly express his "skepticism in the face of so many failed attempts to have one's cake and eat it too: to retain both Kant's insights and, at the same time, to return to the 'home' [*Behausung*] from which these same insights have driven us."[45] The earlier Frankfurt School dream of reconciliation must be abandoned.

In the 1985 essay "Morality and Ethical Life: Does Hegel's Critique of Kant Apply to Discourse Ethics?" Habermas returns to the topic of an ethical relation to nature, but now with a noticeably more modest tone.[46] At the end of a strong defense of his version of neo-Kantianism against Hegelian objections, he explicitly mentions "ecological ethics" as a problem for which discourse ethics has difficulty finding an answer: "How does discourse ethics, which is limited to subjects capable of speech and action, respond to the fact that mute creatures are also vulnerable? Compassion for tortured animals and the pain caused by the destruction of biotopes are surely manifestations of moral intuitions that cannot fully be satisfied by the collective narcissism of what in the final analysis is an anthropocentric way of looking at things."[47]

He goes on first to admit that discourse ethics has no response, but then suggests in an interesting remark that this need not be seen as a defect in the theory. Rather it may follow precisely from the theory's proceduralist insistence that substantive moral theses can derive only from discourse itself:

> What moral *theory* can do and should be trusted to do is to clarify the universal core of our moral intuitions and thereby to refute value skepticism. What it cannot do is make any kind of substantive contribution. By singling out a procedure of decision making, it seeks to make room for those involved, who must then find answers on their own to the moral-practical issues that come at them, or are imposed upon them, with objective historical force. Moral philosophy does not have privileged access to particular moral truths.[48]

The suggestion thus is that the question of what our relation to the natural world ought to be is the sort of substantive question that must be left up to the participants in the discourse itself; moral theory by itself cannot solve it. Yet even this idea is not unproblematic. For who exactly counts as a "participant"? If the underlying question really has to do with nature's intrinsic value, then to imagine it as answerable only in a discourse limited to humans seems unacceptably to prejudge the matter. The ones who should decide, Habermas says, are "those involved," but what (so to speak) is the universe of discourse here? Aren't animals "involved"? What about trees, or lakes, or ecosystems?

The difficulty is plain, and runs deep. The proceduralism of discourse ethics is not supposed to predecide any substantive questions, but its own assumptions cannot help but constrain the sorts of answers that are given. Once moral issues have been formulated in terms of a theory of language, it is no longer clear how it could ever be possible to offer arguments about intrinsic value in, or human responsibility to, creatures who are languageless. Habermas needs to say more; it is not sufficient to leave the question of the human relation to natural entities up to some future discourse without saying anything further about what that discourse might be like or who might be imagined as taking part in it.

Habermas attempts to give more content to his view in his most extended recent discussion of environmental questions, which comes at the end of a long essay entitled "Remarks on Discourse Ethics," first published in German in 1991.[49] Here he comments primarily on some arguments in which Günther Patzig attempted to develop an ecological ethic "within the limits of reason alone," which is to say in a "postmetaphysical" context where appeals to faith or intuition or general metaphysical worldviews are ruled out and where something like Kantian universalism (and anthropocentrism) is assumed.[50] Patzig proposes that humans do stand in a moral relationship to animals and in particular are under an obligation to prevent and mitigate animal pain and suffering. Each individual human knows in his or her own case, he argues, that pain and suffering are things to be avoided, and rationally expects other humans not to cause such suffering. If I expect you not to cause pain to me, however, then on universalistic grounds I must acknowledge that I may not cause pain to you; and so a general duty to refrain from hurting others is derived. But to the extent that animals clearly experience pain as well, it "would not be rational" to draw a radical distinction between them and humans as far as this duty is concerned, Patzig argues.[51]

Habermas interestingly does not find this argument, with its undertone of utilitarianism, to be strong enough. The dilemma of anthropocentrism is only papered over, not overcome: *why* do animals deserve the same respect for their interest in avoiding pain that humans do, given that they cannot be a party to the discourse in which universalization procedures are grounded? Patzig's talk of "duties," Habermas says, is misleading: we can have duties only to creatures with whom we can stand in reciprocal moral relations and who therefore also have duties to us. Patzig's argument is in truth not a deontological one but rather really teleological in form, oriented that is to a particular conception of the good life, Habermas claims—a life that ought to include compassion for animals. But such arguments belong to what Habermas now calls "ethics," not "morality," and as such sees as relative to particular traditions or communities. Against this, Habermas writes, with respect to animals

> our moral intuitions speak an unambiguous language. We have an unmistakable sense that the avoidance of cruelty toward all creatures capable of suffering is a moral duty and is not simply recommended by prudential considerations or even considerations of the good life. . . . We have a sense of being under categorical obligations to

animals. The horror inspired by the torment of animals is, at any rate, more closely related to outrage at the violation of moral demands than to the pitying or condescending attitude toward people who, as we are wont to say, have made nothing of their lives or are failures by their own standards of authenticity.[52]

Hence because "categorical obligations" can arise only within the sphere of the moral (which is to say, the discursive sphere where universal considerations obtain), Habermas must find a *moral* argument to defend a responsibility to animals—which means an argument based on discourse itself. It is not our knowledge of the similarity of animal *suffering* to our own that will be crucial, then, but rather an analogy involving the animal potential for something like *communication.* Animals can be seen, at least in certain typical situations, as virtual communication partners with us; we interact with them in a quasi-social, quasi-communicative manner. Our duties to animals arise within the social world, Habermas argues, where we do in fact to a certain extent "encounter [them] in the role (if not *completely* filled) of a second person, one whom we look upon as if it were an alter ego." We do not always relate to animals in what Habermas had earlier called the "objectivating" attitude, or at least we need not do so; we can encounter them in the "performative" attitude as well. Thus we can and often do "ascribe characteristics of agents to animals, among others the ability to initiate utterances and to address them to us." This is especially true, of course, of domesticated animals, which is why it is with respect to them that, as Habermas puts it, "our conscience is particularly insistent."[53]

Thus our relationship to animals is a "quasi-moral" one, Habermas says, and in it "we have duties that are *analogous* to our moral duties, because like the latter they are rooted in the presuppositions of communicative action."[54] But such duties arise only within the communicatively structured social world; the "rights" of animals in this sense are socially constituted, and do not extend beyond the boundaries of the social. We humans are always in that world, but animals are in it only so to speak to the extent that we allow them to be. "The limits of our quasi-moral responsibility toward animals," Habermas writes, "are reached once humans, in their role as members of·one species, confront animals as exemplars of another," thus explaining (he says) our intuitions that the duty to prevent animal suffering does not entail a duty to vegetarianism, or that medical experimentation on animals can under certain conditions be justified.[55]

Thus Habermas's strategy here is to bring at least some of the natural world into the realm of the moral, albeit only in a way marked by talk of "analogies" and "incompleteness" and "quasi-moral" relationships. But this solves the problem only by defining it away. The difficulty posed for discourse ethics (and Habermas's "communicative turn" in general) by anti-anthropocentric environmental philosophy, after all, is the problem of our ethical relation to entities *in the nonhuman world*, not to entities that have been redescribed as quasi-humans. Habermas in "Reply To My Critics" had suggested that our experience of compassion for animals brings us in touch with something like nature-in-itself; by the time of his response to Patzig, however, it clearly no longer does. Animals are now subjects of "morality" only through being (virtually) socialized, that is, turned into interlocutors; but then to that very extent we no more confront nonhuman "nature" in them than we do when we interact with each other. The specific subject matter of an "ethics of the environment" has here dissolved away.

And of course, this kind of strategy can hope to work in only a limited region anyway. In all his discussions Habermas is noticeably more interested in and comfortable with talking about responsibilities regarding individual animals than he is with the broader concerns raised by the bio- or ecocentrism of a more radical environmental thought often marked by an explicit holism.[56] With respect to *those* issues he simply throws up his hands: "human responsibility for plants and for the preservation of whole species cannot be derived from duties of interaction," he writes in the last paragraph of his discussion of Patzig, "and thus cannot be *morally* justified." Other sorts of justifications are of course possible—prudential ones, in the first place (we may need certain plants or species or ecosystems for our own survival, e.g.), but perhaps others as well. Only at the very close does Habermas write that he agrees with Patzig that there also may be

> good *ethical* reasons that speak in favor of the protection of plants and species, reasons that become apparent once we ask ourselves seriously how, as members of a civilized global society, we want to live on this planet and how, as members of our own species, we want to treat other species. In certain respects, *aesthetic reasons* have here even greater force than ethical, for in the aesthetic experience of nature, things withdraw into an unapproachable autonomy and inaccessibility; they then exhibit their fragile integrity so clearly that they strike us as inviolable in their own right and not merely as desirable elements of a preferred form of life.[57]

Yet it is not at all obvious how these sorts of considerations, vague as they are, escape anthropocentrism or involve a real confrontation with a "nature in itself": the "ethical" reasons suggested are explicitly relativized by Habermas to *our* conceptions of the good and of who we want to be, while it is not even clear how the "aesthetic" experience mentioned here could lead to anything like a "reason" at all. Nor, of course, does Habermas indicate how he proposes to overcome the deep paradoxes Adorno had so eloquently explored in any attempt to capture the nonidentical through the aesthetic experience of nature. Thus even this most recent attempt by Habermas to address problems of an "ethics of nature" remains unsatisfactory.

3. "CAN THEY TALK?": LANGUAGE AND ANTHROPOCENTRISM

But perhaps at this point we need to ask more questions about the view referred to by that loaded and ambiguous term *anthropocentrism*, including the question of why avoiding it is so important. The source of the problem that people like Whitebook and others see in Habermas's work, and that he struggles with in the passages we have just analyzed, is that something like anthropocentrism does doubtless seem built in to the discourse-ethical position from the very start. By grounding morality, and even "ethics," in discourse and specifically in what participants in a discourse would themselves agree to, Habermas limits the boundaries of his universalism to those who could potentially be such participants. To act morally is to take account of all those whose interests are potentially affected by the act, but the structure of the argument for this is such that those interests have to be *discursively communicable* in order to count, and so the "all" here refers only to humans. Animals (perhaps) and (certainly) plants, nonliving entities, ecosystems, etc., have no role in such a discourse, and so one does not universalize over *them*.

This does indeed at first appear to be a weakness in the position, and to be motivating Habermas's evident discomfort about human responsibility to animals. The critique of anthropocentrism, so familiar nowadays as to be almost taken for granted without argument, itself involves an appeal to universalism, of course. Why, after all, should only the interests of humans count? Why should animals and other natural entities be excluded from the charmed circle of those who possess rights? In what sense are *species* differences any more morally relevant than the status or racial or gender differences that earlier universalisms rejected as illegitimate grounds for differential treatment?[58]

Yet the fact is that discourse ethics has an answer to these questions. The morally relevant distinction between humans and animals (one that does *not* arise between races or genders or across other intra-human differences) has to do with *language*. The very arguments from speech-act theory with which Habermas defends the principle of discourse ethics provide considerable resources for a response to anti-anthropocentric challenges. Note that the argument is *not*, as some contractarians influenced by rational choice theory sometimes suggest, that there is nothing to be gained by humans in attempting to treat animals "morally" because on the one hand they cannot much hurt us (so we are not in a Hobbesian situation with them) and on the other they are in any case incapable of entering into agreements and so none can be broken when we harm them.[59] Nor is it that animals are incapable of conceiving of moral action, nor that moral praise and blame do not accrue to them. Rather the point is the central one animating Habermas's call for a paradigm shift from philosophy of consciousness to philosophy of communication: that *normativity is internally connected to language*. The upshot of Habermas's theory of universal pragmatics is that claims to rightness, like claims to truth, arise only *in* language; without communicative action there would be no such claims. To raise a normative validity claim, furthermore, is on his analysis implicitly to stand willing to defend it discursively against all who might themselves dispute it, and so is to presuppose the legitimacy of such a discourse in deciding the rightness of such a claim. Normative value itself then is tied up from the very start with language use and language users, and with the possibility of discursive justification through the giving of reasons.

If this is so, then it in turn follows that language users, those beings capable of raising normative validity claims and discursively justifying them, have a unique moral status. To say this, it is important to see, is not to say that they have a "higher" moral status or are more "worthy" than those beings who do not use language, nor is it to say that all value must be defined relative to human needs and interests. The point is not that language users have more value or even that only they have value, but rather that without them there would simply be no value at all. Nor would there by any valuelessness either: the very category would so to speak be absent. *Whatever* entities in the world do have value, that is to say, the fact *that* they have it refers implicitly to the possibility of discursive redemption of a validity claim, and hence to those language-using entities who can engage in discourse.

Language users in this sense are the "subjects" of morality: they are the ones whose ultimate consent is relevant to and indeed constitutive of normative rightness. In *this* sense we can say they are "ends in themselves," which means among other things that no one language user may act toward another one in a manner the reasons for which that other one could not accept. That no particular individual's interests and needs may morally outweigh the interests and needs of any other individual follows directly from the ability that other individual has to give reasons why he or she ought not to be disregarded. But animals are not capable of giving reasons in this way; they are therefore not the subjects of morality in this sense. They may still be the *objects* of morality, though, which is to say that they may indeed *have* value; but they do not *determine* value through their contributions to a normative discourse.

Every anti-anthropocentric essay about animal rights quotes Jeremy Bentham's famous remark that regarding our moral duties to animals "the question is not, Can they *reason*? nor, Can they *talk*? but, Can they *suffer*?"[60]

What I am suggesting, though, is that discourse ethics offers good reasons to believe that inability to talk *does* make a moral difference, precisely because value is determined in and through talking—which is not, of course, to say that the difference it makes is one that would permit cruelty to animals or rule out vegetarianism. When Bentham writes this, what he leaves out of account (and what those who quote him fail to notice) is that his own claim is itself formulated in and gets its undoubted strength from language, and is offered as a good reason directed not at animals but at other language users whom he wishes rationally to persuade. It is, in a word, a contribution to discourse. Bentham is caught in a performative contradiction: he wants to argue that there are no morally relevant differences between humans and animals, but in doing so he cannot help but presuppose *the moral relevance of the ability to engage in moral argumentation*, an ability that animals lack, thus exhibiting in his own argument the very sort of difference whose existence he denies.[61]

John Dryzek has proposed extending discourse ethics to include the natural world, arguing that we engage in communicative relations with entities in the biosphere as well.[62] But communication has to be understood in the specific sense that Habermas employs, and it is not at all clear (and certainly not in Dryzek's discussion) that in *this* sense animals or other natural entities communicate at all. Central to the argument for discourse ethics is the role of *validity claims;* to be a communicating "subject of morality" requires being able to raise such claims, which in turn means being able to express in one's utterances semantically meaningful propositions that make discursively appraisable claims about the world. Language use in this sense is not (merely) signaling, nor is it the kind of self-revelation that occurs through "body language" and other phenomena of gesture, bearing, facial expression, and so forth. And it is certainly not the product of feedback loops of the sort that arise when an ecosystem "responds" at a macrolevel to alterations at the microlevel.

One frequently hears claims that animals or nature in general "speaks" to us. This is in a certain unexceptional sense true, but the sense is a metaphorical one, and one must be careful not to confuse the metaphorical with the literal here. Dryzek himself seems mostly to argue for the possibility of a communicative relation with natural entities on the basis of the discovery of something like "subjectivity" or "agency" in nature; but this begs the question, since communicative ability is itself one of the criteria by which we decide to attribute subjectivity to something.[63] That natural entities act as though they have purposes is not sufficient to show that they are engaging in communicative action: to think so is precisely to confuse communicative rationality with *Zweckrationalität*, the ability to organize actions so as most efficiently to achieve one's goals. What is crucial is the ability to *raise* (and defend) *validity claims*, not the ability to act teleologically.[64]

Of course, none of this is meant to claim that animals are *in principle* unable to use language to make validity claims or that this inability can be known a priori. The question of whether certain animals are capable of this kind of language use is an entirely empirical one, to be left to linguists and biologists and animal researchers. If it turns out that some are, then those animals will be moral subjects in the sense I am defending. The same would be true in theory even of nonanimals—insects or plants or for that matter lakes or mountains—although again without resorting to metaphor this seems so unlikely as almost to be unimaginable. A lake may indeed *need* rain of the proper pH to thrive, and its blighted appearance in response to acid rain may quite clearly indicate this, but the lake does not *assert* the (discursively criticizable) *proposition* that it has this need, nor does it deny the normative rightness of a state of affairs in which that need is not fulfilled.

The point here is not, as anti-anthropocentrists sometimes argue, that we humans, who happen to be skilled at language, illegitimately and chauvinistically inflate that particular talent into the single morally significant one (as opposed to, say, being able to spin webs or to digest food by rumination or to fly).[65] The point is that normativity is bound up with language as it were from the inside, for the reasons Habermas has expounded, and that therefore any axiological discussion *at all* must itself have already taken for granted language's moral significance. Such critics are again in a performative contradiction: insofar as they employ argumentation in language to make their point, they too have accepted language's unique moral role. An implicit reference to discourse and an acknowledgment that those who can engage in it are the ultimate arbiters of normative questions are there already in the phrasing of the objection.

And by the same token it will not do to respond by proposing that the interests of mute natural entities or of nature as a whole can be *represented* in a practical discourse by humans deputized to speak "for" them. For then the question gets pushed back into one having to do with who will be so deputized and on what basis: which humans will be best able to engage in the delicate hermeneutic process of determining the interests and desires of creatures who themselves have no ways of expressing those interests and desires? And note that the problem is not simply, as it is in the case of children or mental incompetents, of determining what they *would* say if they were capable of rational speech. For in those latter cases we have some model to fall back upon in building our counterfactuals (i.e., normal adult humans); the reasoning involves extrapolating from an abnormal or immature case to the standard one, whereas in the case of animals or other natural entities it involves extrapolating *away* from the normal case. To imagine what an animal or tree or lake would say if it could speak is not really to imagine the animal or tree or lake at all, but rather some mythological creature in which human communicative capacity has been magically introduced into a nonhuman form.

Nor will it work to resolve the problem of representation by appealing to the judgments of scientific "experts," because scientific expertise is itself both discursively constituted and discursively confirmed. Here Habermas's argument and mine would diverge, although our conclusions would be the same. He would presumably object to the conflation of expertise in making descriptive truth-claims about nature with expertise in making the normative judgments that are really at issue here. But I am willing to accept that normative and scientific judgments are related, wanting only to point out that the relationship is double-edged: normative expertise is as relevant to scientific expertise as vice-versa. One cannot, that is, *identify* the experts on natural entities independently of the question of how one thinks those entities are to be treated. The choice of research topic, of "paradigm," even of scientific method all already involve a normative component. Think of the differences among researchers who might use vivisection, "master molecule" theories, genetic engineering, field observation, the Gaia hypothesis, Native American spirituality, creationism, etc. as basic to their biological work. Which of these are the experts? How is that to be decided, except discursively?

The point is that the attempt to include natural entities in a normative discourse by having them represented by experts is caught in a circle, because the experts cannot be identified except through that discourse. We cannot "represent" such entities in a practical discourse about how they are to be treated without having already made decisions about just that very issue. The appeal to expertise is just another form of naturalism, of the attempt (that is) to find some normatively relevant "nature in itself" above or below or behind or prior to social communicative practices that could serve to found such practices; it fails, not (as Habermas would have it) because scientific and normative discourse are distinct but precisely because they aren't—because the truth about nature is always itself already so infused with the social and hence the normative that it cannot at the same time serve as an *independent* foundation for any normative claims.

These conclusions, which one might well want to call "anthropocentrist," seem to me inescapable once one accepts the arguments that ground discourse ethics.[66] But it is important here to distinguish two senses that the word *anthropocentrism* might have. As already suggested, to assert that *value can be determined only by humans* is not to assert that *only humans have value*. Nor is it to assert that all value is determined only relative to human "interests," narrowly construed. What count as good reasons in a normative discourse can be decided only by participants in the discourse, but there is nothing intrinsic in the idea of such a discourse to suggest that the sole reasons they would count as good are those that work for their own personal advantage nor even for that of their species. Indeed, recent discussions of environmental issues suggest that for many engaged in normative discussions today humility and respect in the face of the multiplicity of species and the complexity of ecosystems are among the core values to be avowed.

Thus "anthropocentrism" here refers to the centrality of discursive participants in determining value, not to the centrality of humans as bearers of value. Recognition of the unique moral status of humans as potential participants in discourse—as the *subjects* of morality, as I have been saying—is perfectly compatible with the denial of any unique status for humans as the *objects* of morality. We may well decide, and may well have good reasons to decide, that all higher animals, or all animals, or even all living creatures, deserve equal respect and treatment, or that we need to find a way to live in nature that does not treat everything other than the human as mere means for the satisfaction of our needs. The point simply is that it is *we* humans who either will or will not decide this—because the decision can only be made discursively. The reasons for the decision must be accepted as good reasons by *us*; there is no one else around to accept or reject them.

4. AN ETHICS OF THE BUILT WORLD

As I have already suggested, I think that Habermas with his introduction of a communication-based account of ethics has made a substantial contribution to discussions of the ethical status of nature. This is so first of all in the sense just outlined: I think his account permits a clear explanation and defense of a justifiable "anthropocentrism," while allowing a careful distinction between this and the objectionable kind that can imagine no value in nonhuman entities and that sees our relation to the external environment in entirely instrumental terms. But secondly, and more broadly, I think Habermas's view connects with the considerations to which we have repeatedly been brought in previous chapters, offering a better understanding of what might be meant by saying that questions about the environment have to be seen as *social* questions. To say that they are social turns out now particularly to mean that they can only be answered in a discourse of the sort to which Habermas believes that all normative claims implicitly appeal. The question of how we are to approach and interact with nature can be answered only by us, in our own discussions with each other; no solution to it can be read off from nature "itself" in the manner that Marcusean naturalism believed was possible, nor from any sort of transcendental considerations either.

What is curious is that Habermas himself, far from seeing the sense in which his account of discourse ethics provides significant resources for (re)conceptualizing questions of environmental ethics, apparently thinks that nature stands as a difficulty for the account, and repeatedly returns to it as a problematic limit case. The reason for this, I think, lies in his continued commitment to the kind of dualism analyzed in the previous chapter. The charts in "Reply to My Critics" and *The Theory of Communicative Action* make it plain that nature for Habermas *must* be separated from the normative realm; that's why he finds it hard to imagine anything like a rationalizable "norm-conformative attitude towards the objective world."[67] Nature for him is the world investigated by a value-free science and manipulated by purposive-rational action, a world immunized in various ways from any admixture of the communicative or the social, and hence from the normative as well.[68] Once that separation is made, the fact that people do have a clear sense of ethical responsibilities regarding the environment doubtless looms as a serious problem. But the reinterpretation I have been proposing would remove both that separation and the ensuing problem as well: if nature is *part* of the social realm, which is to say part of the realm we come both actively to construct through our communicatively oriented practices and normatively to evaluate through our discourse, then the difficulty disappears.

It is instructive to note how much trouble Habermas has in envisaging what a normative discourse about nature would actually be like. As we saw in "Remarks on Discourse Ethics," he imagines it either as merely a derivative form of "moral" argumentation in his special sense—where we treat individual animals as "analogous" to humans—or else (as in the case of plants or species) he assimilates it if not to prudential discourse then to the "ethical" kind he associates with existential questions about "who we want to be."[69] But, as I have already suggested, in the first case this grants moral status to animals only by treating them as something other than nature (as quasi-humans), while in the second case the question remains only what is good for *us*. In neither case is there a serious discourse about *the environing world as such*; it's either a discourse "with" quasi-human interlocutors, or it's a discourse about "us" (humans), about what we need and who we are and desire to become. This *is* anthropocentrism in a criticizable sense. None of these discourses offers any way to grasp the possibility of constituting the environment *as valuable* or of imagining any sort of normative connection to it that is not based on one of simple (or even "quasi-")identity.

That a discourse intended to examine the normative status of nature cannot be a *moral* discourse in Habermas's technical use of this term follows immediately, I think, from the considerations of the previous section: natural entities, not being potential participants in a discourse, are not "ends in themselves" and hence are not covered by considerations of justice.[70] But it scarcely seems right to call it an *ethical* discourse in his technical sense either. The passage quoted earlier (p. 159) speaks vaguely of "ethical reasons" for environmental concern that go beyond the rights of animals, reasons that might follow from "members of a civilized global society" asking themselves "how we want to live on this planet and how . . . we want to treat other species." But it is not at all clear how those latter questions are to be answered. Habermas seems to view them as merely rhetorical, apparently taking it for granted as simply obvious that a "civilized" society would preserve the natural world. Yet an argument is needed here, and none is provided. Furthermore, his use of the term "ethical" with its basically existential meaning for him suggests that the underlying idea is again merely that "*we* would not like to be the sort of people who harm the environment"; the difference between this and Kant's infamous argument that cruelty to animals is wrong only because it coarsens those who engage in it and makes them more likely to be cruel to humans seems slight. What is wrong with environmental damage, presumably is not (only) what it would do to *us,* but what it would do to the world we inhabit.

Habermas's dilemma thus turns out to look like this: if entities in nature are viewed as quasi-interlocutors, then they are morally relevant but are no longer natural, but if they are really viewed as natural (and so independent of the social order), then they are no longer in themselves morally relevant, serving only as touchstones against which we can develop and test our own "existential self-understanding."[71] But this is the same dilemma we have been tracing throughout this book: the conflict between a view of nature as social on the one hand and as independent of the social (and hence of the normative) on the other that we have seen causing difficulties for each of the figures we have examined. Discourse ethics confirms what I have been arguing, which is that a nature truly independent of the social could have no moral significance; normativity is connected to language, and so to sociality (and to practice). But given Habermas's dualism a "social nature" is an oxymoron, and so he can grant ethical status to nature only by assimilating it (or more precisely animals) to the quasi-human. The antinomical result is to make a truly *environmental* ethics impossible.

What Habermas needs, but cannot envision because of his dualism, is a third possibility: a way to assert the sociality of nature without turning nature into a co-subject.[72] But there *is* such a possibility—a way to see nature as social, and hence as having ethical import, without imagining it as therefore a participant in discourse—and it is the view of nature I have been urging in the previous chapters. Nature, I have argued, is not independent of the subjective, but this does not mean that it is another subject: rather it is something we *constitute* in our social (and communicatively organized) practices. To grasp that fact (in the kind of self-reflective act whose importance I have repeatedly emphasized) is to see the world we inhabit as something *for which we are responsible,* in both the causal and the moral sense of that word, and hence to reveal it as possessing a normative significance of just the kind that Habermas thinks discourse ethics has trouble explaining.

The "ethical" question of how nature should be treated, as I have argued, cannot be separated from the "scientific" question of what nature *is*, and vice-versa; and answering all such questions further involves implicit appeal to a discursive context. But it involves appeal to a practical context as well: the issues of what nature is and how we should treat it are themselves not independent of the ordinary practices, in the laboratory but outside it too, through which our "natural environment" is constantly being made and remade. It would be better at this point perhaps to drop the term *nature* and replace it with the more precise term *environment*. The subject matter of environmental ethics is the *Umwelt*, the world that surrounds us, a world that is always already the product of our previous practices, and changes as those practices change.

But then the fundamental question for such an ethics is not "how ought we to interact with Nature?" as though this latter were something independent of us and given from all eternity, that unmediated "nature in itself" I have been criticizing all along. Such a question could only be answered by the kind of naturalism whose difficulties we have traced and discourse ethics has confirmed. Rather the question to be asked is more correctly "what ought the environment to be?" meaning now: what sorts of transformative practices should we engage in, how should they be organized, what considerations should inform them? What, in other words, should the communicatively and practically constituted world we inhabit be like? *This* is what a "communicative theory of nature" would involve: the recognition that questions about nature implicitly refer to a set of communicatively organized processes in which humans transform the world around them and thereby constitute their environment, and that only for that reason are normative questions about that environment both meaningful and (discursively) answerable.

We can begin to see more clearly here the problem with Habermas's system of "precisely three" formal world concepts—"*the* world" of objective nature, "*our* world" of the social, and finally "*my* world" of inner experience.[73] For there's a world missing from this system, one we all inhabit and whose existence renders problematic the sharp distinction Habermas wants to draw among the others. We might call it the "built world": the world of our cities and technologies and landscapes, our national parks and highways and wilderness areas too, our bubble chambers, petri dishes, refrigerators, and the like.[74] This world is our *environment*, literally. Perfectly objective—*the* world we live in—it is also *our* world: we have built it. And the practices through which we have built it are socially and communicatively organized ones, which hence possess from the outset a normative component.[75]

Habermas, we saw, had great difficulty in imagining a normative relation to the nonhuman world: he either assimilated it to the quasi-human or relegated it to a realm against which we measured our ethical-existential development. But *this* world, the built one, is neither human nor absolutely Other than the human; our normative relation to it has to do with the question not of who *we* should be but of what *it* should be, though these two questions are doubtless connected. In *The Theory of Communicative Action*, Habermas says his rejection of the possibility of a "norm-conformative attitude" toward the objective world would be disconfirmed if a "specialized" and rationalizable form of argumentation could be found corresponding to that supposedly empty cell of the chart; he doubts that it could.[76] But there *is* such a form: argumentation about *what we ought to build*. Of course under conditions of reification such argumentation is distorted, focusing on the teleological or "strategic" issue of what would make the most money for a corporation, for instance, instead of with the properly normative (and political) questions it ought to invoke; in this sense the necessary "rationalization" processes are not yet complete.

We are responsible for what we build precisely because *we* build it, and because in building it we build the world and build ourselves as well; but too often nowadays we do not acknowledge that responsibility. To acknowledge it would be to see the question "what ought we to build?" as indeed a normative one, bearing some relation doubtless to what Habermas calls "ethics" or "aesthetics" but in less of an existentialist or narcissistic sense. Discourse about such a question would be discourse about what it would be *good* to build, what would make the world a better place, more beautiful and more livable for its inhabitants (human and nonhuman both), and what would make us—the language users whose first sentence lights the world up and releases value into it—better people. In such a discourse Habermas's careful dualisms and triads are exploded, as the technical and normative and expressive all promiscuously mix together: we ask "how can this be built?" and "what would it look like?" and "what would our lives be like in it?" and "how would it affect other entities in the world?" and "what would it do to the environment?" all at once here, and cannot answer one of these questions without raising all the others.[77]

In the first volume of *The Theory of Communicative Action*, Habermas claims that "mythical" worldviews fail to distinguish between nature and culture and that the "modern" differentiation between them marks a developmental-logical advance.[78] This is in the context of a general discussion of the "rationality debate" about whether modern standards of rationality might justifiably claim universal applicability. Habermas persuasively argues that they can, and that the superiority of modern over mythic attitudes lies in the significance of the move from a "closed" to an "open" worldview, which is to say from one incapable of criticizing its own beliefs to one self-reflexively able to acknowledge the contingent and potentially fallible character of those beliefs. The distinction between nature and culture appears then to Habermas as a step in this "decentration" process characteristic of modernization: as a society moves away from a sociocentric identification of its own view of the world with reality itself, it thus comes to distinguish "our world" from "the world."

But there is a non-sequitur here. To recognize that the truth of a worldview is not simply given and that one's own traditional beliefs must be seen as questionable does not require the positing of some realm that *is* given and beyond questioning. The crucial move is not from "our world" to "the world" but rather from uncritical communicative action to what Habermas calls discourse—to the recognition, that is, that all validity claims must be discursively testable, and to the acknowledgment that even those outside "our" culture and time are potential contributors to such discourse. Habermas's impulse here is the same one we saw in the last chapter: he thinks he can only avoid relativism by positing some objective natural world independent of the social. Only that, he seems to believe, can justify the move to an "observer's" perspective, thereby providing sufficient distance to allow one's own culture to be problematized and permit questions to be raised about the legitimacy of the validity claims it makes for itself. But sociocentrism is not avoided by an appeal to "nature," as we have seen, since all accounts of nature are discursive too, including those of natural science, and so find the social and the normative already admixed within them.

Yet relativism does not follow, because discourses (as Habermas knows) are oriented towards validity claims that transcend the local context in which they are raised.[79] Sociocentrism is avoided not by an appeal to nature but by an appeal to *discourse*, which is to say by an increase in reflexivity. For the Lukácsian view I defended in Chapter 2, the "modern" distinction between nature and culture that Habermas celebrates looks more like an instance of reification. It might still represent a developmental-logical advance over uncritical mythic identifications of the two, but only as the second moment in a dialectical process. For increasing reflexivity about the role of discourse (and of practice) in constituting not just truths about the world we inhabit but also the very structure of that world itself might lead in turn to a third view—to the recognition that what has been taken for granted as immutable and immediate "nature" must itself be seen as discursively and practically constituted. Nature and culture would here be reunited, so to speak, not on the basis of some externally given unitary world defended by appeals to magic or divine will, but rather as something for which communicatively rational humans bear mutual responsibility.[80]

My ambivalence about Habermas's views should be obvious. His dualism and more specifically his materialist insistence on positing a single objective world of nature independent of the social seem to me to generate insuperable problems for his overall position and to regress in terms of insight behind (a suitably reinterpreted) Lukács. His confidence that "the world" and "our world" can be distinguished seems simply the confidence of reification—of a world in which we systematically fail to see the marks of our own activity in the environment that surrounds us. Yet Habermas's conception of discourse ethics, and of the significance of a shift in focus to communication, are in my opinion insights of the highest importance, not least (as I have tried to show) for issues of "environmental ethics." They allow us to see that such issues are more appropriately understood as involving the question of what our environment ought to be, which then itself must be understood as a practical question in which humans ask themselves what sort of world to *construct*. His "ascetic" proceduralist refusal to see these questions as answerable anywhere except *in* discourse itself is crucial, too: substantive normative questions like these cannot be answered a priori, nor by considerations derived from the structure of language, nor by the naturalistic arguments of Marcuse or deep ecology either.[81] The question of our relations to "nature," which is to say to the world surrounding us, can only be answered by *us*, those whose responsibility the environment is, and only in a free discourse in which everyone capable of language can be imagined (if only counterfactually) to engage. The theory of such a discourse and its structures might be what a "communicative theory of nature" would involve; I do not pretend to have done more here than to sketch out some of that theory's possible content.

5. CONCLUDING REMARKS

At this point the themes we have been following throughout this book converge. I have tried to distinguish two alternative ways of thinking about nature that have been available to the tradition of Western Marxism: on the one hand, the Hegelian appeal to self-reflection that we traced in Lukács, which emphasized the sociality of nature and the role of practice in constituting the environment; and, on the other, a romantic critique (with roots in *Lebensphilosophie*) of science and reason as "domination" of a nature taken as independent of the social. Lukács flirted with the latter view, we saw, and Horkheimer and Adorno and later Marcuse as well remain deeply ensnared in it.[82] But Habermas's appeal to discourse and to a normativity grounded in moral argumentation itself, when taken as pointing to a "communicative theory of nature," returns us to something like the Hegelian view. The question of value in nature, such a theory suggests, is a question to be answered by a *nature-building process become self-conscious*, one that knows the world it inhabits to be its own construction and its own responsibility and so poses for itself—discursively—the question of what that world should be like.

Habermas, as I have already suggested, was right: we cannot do without technology, which means we cannot do without changing the world. We are part of nature, but *actively*: we make our environment human by remaking nature, and we have done so from the very first use of tools. But again, Marcuse was right, too—in doing so we express a certain social view of ourselves and the world, one that is both historically changing and also necessarily subject to demands for normative justification. In the society we live in today, marked as it is by conditions of reification, we do not see our transformative activity as such; viewing ourselves as private individuals, we seem confronted by a world quite alien to us, given and immutable and independent of our wishes or our values. As "rational" agents, all we can do, it seems, is to figure out as much as possible about significant aspects of that world and then attempt to manipulate them to best achieve our own personal goals; changing the world, however, is impossible. Like Odysseus, we adapt ourselves to the system in order to survive, trying to "control" it only by submitting to it entirely. Each individual is concerned with doing as well as possible within the confines of the system, unable to recognize that it is precisely the total of our individually "rational" actions that continuously reproduces it. In this sense to acknowledge our (common) responsibility for its power over us would be the key to breaking its spell.

The environment we inhabit—the *single* world that contains impossible bureaucracies, depoliticized electorates, economic exploitation, appalling racism *and* toxic wastes, a depleted ozone layer, acid rain, deforested jungles, a terrifying nuclear arsenal, and all the rest—is one we have produced through our practices, sad though it is to say this. Oriented toward individual success and individual profit, our social system provides no means for conscious and rational social decision-making about the practices we engage in; instead, they are left up to the anonymous workings of that "market" in which the reification being discussed here finds its purest form. The call for a self-conscious acknowledgment by humans of their responsibility for the world is a call first of all for a new set of practices, but secondly also for a new form of social organization where such democratic decision-making would be both possible and encouraged, where (that is) something like an ongoing Habermasian discourse would find a means of being institutionalized. Such a society would also possess, I believe, something like the kind of not-exactly-Marcusean "new science" and "new technology" I discussed earlier—a science and technology that knew their own social significance and no longer hid behind the "illusion of objectivity" Habermas once wanted to extol.[83]

The responsibility we have for the world we inhabit is a *practical* responsibility; we produce that world through our practices and can change it only by changing those practices. I have already argued earlier that practice is distinguished from theory by its difficulty and its fallibility: not all practices succeed.[84] To say we must take responsibility for the environment is of course not to say that we can make for ourselves any environment we wish. But it is to say that we must learn to find ways to turn the world-changing practices in which we are in any case always already engaged into the objects of our explicit and discursively justified communal choice. To do so would doubtless be to begin to engage in different practices; no discursively organized rational society could possibly countenance the wholesale devastation by which we are surrounded today. Only in such a society would there be a chance for the world we inhabit—the one world that includes the "natural" and the "social" both—to exhibit the beauty, the meaning, and the value we have always dreamt of finding there.

Notes

INTRODUCTION

1. Of course, Engels believed that the scientific method involved something called "dialectics," and that previous (non-Marxist) thinkers had failed to recognize this. But his main argument for the validity of the "dialectical method" was that it could be scientifically verified, which is to say that it turns out to be a result, not a methodological precondition, of scientific investigation. "Nature is the proof of dialectics," he writes in *Anti-Dühring;* and "modern science . . . has furnished this proof with very rich materials increasing daily, and thus has shown that, in the last resort, nature works dialectically" (Moscow: Progress Publishers, 1978, p. 33).

2. In doing so, of course, he overthrows the central tenets of Engels's account of Marxism's philosophical status. See below, Chapter 1, p. 15.

3. I have argued elsewhere that "alienation from nature" in the sense of Marx's early manuscripts ought to be understood in this way. See my "Marx and Alienation from Nature," *Social Theory and Practice* vol. 14, no. 3 (Fall 1988), pp. 367–387.

4. One recent and welcome exception is James Bohman's *New Philosophy of Social Science* (Cambridge: MIT Press, 1991), which contains important discussions of the new "sociology of science." Bohman is considerably more critical than I of that work, although we share a deep worry about the relativism implicit (or explicit) in much of it. I think the relativism can be avoided without giving up what seem to me the important discoveries associated with the "sociological turn" in the philosophy of science: much of what follows is an attempt to show how the tradition of (quasi-)Hegelian (quasi-)Marxism provides a set of conceptual resources that make that possible.

5. Latour and Rouse (and others, too) certainly consider the political implications of their account of science but find themselves hamstrung by just

the relativism mentioned in the previous note—and (at least in Rouse's case) by a broadly Foucauldian conception of power and the political that is so vague as to be useless for a real critical theory. See my "Science, Practice, and Politics," in *Social Epistemology*, vol. 5, no. 4 (1991), pp. 267–292. Latour's recent *We Have Never Been Modern*, trans. Catherine Porter (Cambridge: Harvard University Press, 1993), with its interesting if highly ambiguous notion of a "democracy extended to things" (p. 142), moves closer to the kind of conception I will end up defending in Chapter 6.

CHAPTER 1. THE PROBLEM OF NATURE IN LUKÁCS

1. Andrew Feenberg, *Lukács, Marx, and the Sources of Critical Theory* (Totowa, N.J.: Rowman and Littlefield, 1981), p. 204. Andrew Arato, in his "Lukács' Theory of Reification," *Telos* 11 (Spring 1972), remarks more mildly that *History and Class Consciousness* is marked by "a rather confusing handling of the problem of nature" (p. 41).

2. Lucio Colletti, *Marxism and Hegel*, trans. Lawrence Garner (London: NLB, 1973), p. 181; Alfred Schmidt, *The Concept of Nature in Marx*, trans. Ben Fowkes (London: NLB, 1971), p. 96.

3. Schmidt, *The Concept of Nature in Marx*, p. 166.

4. Gareth Stedman Jones, "The Marxism of the Early Lukács: An Evaluation," *New Left Review* 70 (1971), p. 44; Colletti, *Marxism and Hegel*, p. 175.

5. Feenberg, *Lukács, Marx, and the Sources of Critical Theory*, p. 209.

6. See Andrew Arato and Paul Breines, *The Young Lukács and the Origins of Western Marxism* (New York: Seabury Press, 1979), pp. 241 (n. 9) and 119. Feenberg agrees that Lukács does not have a fully coherent theory of either nature or natural science; see *Lukács, Marx, and the Sources of Critical Theory*, p. 204.

7. Georg Lukács, *History and Class Consciousness*, trans. Rodney Livingstone (Cambridge, Mass.: MIT Press, 1971), p. xvii.

8. Ibid., p. xvi.

9. See Colletti, *Marxism and Hegel*, p. 176; Arato, "Lukács's Theory of Reification," p. 42; Schmidt, *The Concept of Nature in Marx*, pp. 69–70.

10. Feenberg, *Lukács, Marx, and the Sources of Critical Theory*, p. 204.

11. M. Marković, "The Critical Thought of Georg Lukács," in Tom Rockmore, ed., *Lukács Today: Essays in Marxist Philosophy* (Dordrecht: D. Reidel, 1988), p. 25.

12. *History and Class Consciousness*, p. 24, n. 4. Livingstone makes an uncharacteristic slip in the translation here, leaving out the two words "knowledge of" in the second sentence. But Lukács wrote "auf die Erkenntnis der

Natur" (and "Naturerkenntnis" in the next sentence, which Livingstone does translate correctly). See *Geschichte und Klassenbewusstsein* (Neuwied: Luchterhand, 1968), p. 175, n. 1. The difference is not unimportant because as we will see a lot depends on whether "nature" and "our knowledge of nature" can be coherently separated. See also below, p. 19.

13. See, e.g., the Preface to the second edition of *Anti-Dühring*, p. 16.

14. *History and Class Consciousness*, p. 3. Emphasis in original.

15. The phrase is from a set of supplementary texts published as an appendix in the German edition of the essay on Feuerbach. See *Ludwig Feuerbach und der Ausgang der klassischen deutschen Philosophie* (Berlin: Dietz Verlag, 1981), p. 76.

16. Colletti sees this as the only significant difference between "Western Marxism" and the "dialectical materialism" founded by Engels, which otherwise he finds to be linked by their mutual commitment to a neo-Hegelian and romantic "critique of the intellect." See *Marxism and Hegel*, pp. 193–195. I take this difference to be more fundamental, though, and will argue below that it helps to mark a break between Lukács and the *Lebensphilosophische* influences on his thought.

17. See Section 3.

18. *History and Class Consciousness*, p. 7.

19. See ibid., pp. 19, 86. Hegel's use of the term occurs in the *Philosophy of Right*, paragraph 151.

20. *History and Class Consciousness*, p. 10. Translation modified: see *Geschichte und Klassenbewusstsein*, p. 182. For a discussion of the neo-Kantian roots of Lukács's views, see Tom Rockmore, *Irrationalism: Lukács and the Marxist View of Reason* (Philadelphia: Temple University Press, 1992).

21. It also depends on being able coherently to draw a distinction between a science's *method* and its *object*, so that a given method might be appropriate to one sort of object but not another.

22. *History and Class Consciousness*, p. 207. Emphasis in original. See Feenberg, *Lukács, Marx, and the Sources of Critical Theory*, p. 209.

23. *History and Class Consciousness*, p. 234. Translation slightly modified: see *Geschichte und Klassenbewusstsein*, p. 410. See also *History and Class Consciousness*, p. 130.

24. Feenberg, who calls the claim that Lukács's account of nature is an idealist one "the 'myth' of Lukács' famous book," interprets this passage as referring only to "what passes for nature" (his translation for "was . . . als Natur gilt"), not to "nature in itself." See *Lukács, Marx, and the Sources of Critical Theory*, pp. 206–7. But such a distinction between nature "for us" and "in itself"—which we will meet again in Habermas—seems particularly out of place in this context, given Lukács's thoroughgoing critique of the Kantian doctrine of the *Ding an sich*. See p. 29 below.

25. Is that what the hint that an epistemological dialectics of nature has only been impossible "hitherto" means?

26. When he writes at the beginning of the reification essay that "there is no problem that does not ultimately lead back to" the questions raised by Marx about commodities and that "there is no solution that could not be found in the solution to the riddle of commodity-*structure*" (*History and Class Consciousness*, p. 83), he seems to mean this fairly literally, as the reader soon discovers.

27. The author must own up to an embarrassment here, as he finds himself struggling to come up with euphemisms for words like "capitalism." I have much sympathy for parts of Lukács's argument—indeed I will be suggesting that it is partly the failure to take this argument seriously, a failure that begins with Lukács's own turn to dualism, that has led Western Marxist accounts of nature and science astray. But I think what is valuable in his position is independent of his traditional Marxist employment of categories like "capitalism," "bourgeoisie," "proletariat," etc.—not to speak of his execrable Bolshevism and his spineless opportunism in later years. Such categories can in any case no longer be taken entirely seriously; to update them adequately would require an analysis far beyond what I propose to offer here. I take his account more broadly simply as first a critique of *existing society* and second a call for a radical *transformation* of it. That he calls that society "capitalist" and calls the subject of that transformation "proletarians" is to me more or less irrelevant. I will use these terms in what follows, because they are the ones he employs, but I place no serious theoretical stock in them at all.

28. Here, incidentally, Lukács goes beyond the mere "independent rediscovery" of ideas developed in the unpublished work of the young Marx that is often described as his main accomplishment. Marx never really attempted to settle accounts with the philosophical tradition before Hegel (and it is not clear how well he knew it).

29. *History and Class Consciousness*, p. 117. (The context is somewhat different.)

30. Hence it is not merely Marxism that is the culmination of classical German philosophy, it is the instant of the revolutionary seizure of power itself.

31. Karl Marx and Frederick Engels, *Collected Works* (New York: International Publishers, 1975) vol. 3, p. 144. See *History and Class Consciousness*, p. 2.

32. A final remarkable implication is worth mentioning here, too, having to do with the way a theory like this would have to be justified. For as suggested earlier, the subject in coming to know itself through practice does not simply become theoretically aware of something that was always true; it in a certain sense *makes* it true. This suggests that the truth value of the theory

that claims to describe that subject's activity (which is to say, of Lukács's own version of Hegelian Marxism) remains at best uncertain until such time as the practical act of self-recognition it calls for actually takes place. This is the deep voluntarist moment in Lukács's theory: the theory itself *becomes* true only at the moment of the proletarian seizure of power. Prior to that its status is quite different from that of a mere theoretical "prediction" that such a seizure will or must take place. See, e.g., *History and Class Consciousness*, pp. 189, 204. (Paul Piccone has pointed out the inverse of this: that the *failure* of the Bolshevik revolution to bring about anything like "proletarian self-recognition" must appear in Lukács's account precisely as a falsification of that very account. See Piccone's "The Crisis of One-Dimensionality," *Telos* 35 [Spring 1978], p. 44.)

33. I should emphasize the words "as Lukács understands it" in the previous sentence. Later (see Chapter 2, Section 3) I will argue that actual scientific practice is not contemplative at all. Lukács here is accepting what science says about its practice, rather than looking at what it actually does. This is not the last time in the history of Western Marxism such a thing occurs.

34. *History and Class Consciousness*, p. 132; emphasis in original. Again, I shall argue later that Engels is much nearer the truth than Lukács on this.

35. This is so *despite* the strong influences of neo-Kantianism on Lukács's thought. See note 20. Cf. Arato, "Lukács's Theory of Reification," p. 40.

36. This is not to say that they are *wholly* wrong. I will argue later that one of the sources for the ambiguities in Lukács's thought is an unresolved tension between Hegelian and *Lebensphilosophische* lines of argument. See Chapter 2, Section 2.

37. "It is not the primacy of economic motives in historical explanation that constitutes the decisive difference between Marxism and bourgeois thought, but the point of view of totality. . . . *The primacy of the category of totality is the bearer of the principle of revolution in science.*" *History and Class Consciousness*, p. 27; emphasis in original. Postmodernism has taught us a whole series of concerns about such a remark that Lukács never dreamed of; my point here is simply that on his own terms methodological dualism seems to be ruled out. We will return to the question of "totality" in Chapter 2. Cf. Martin Jay, *Marxism and Totality* (Berkeley: University of California Press, 1984), Chap. 2.

38. Hence "the more highly developed [such a system] becomes and the more scientific, the more it will become a formally closed system of partial laws. It will then find that the world lying beyond its confines, and in particular the material base which it is its task to understand, *its own concrete underlying reality* lies, methodologically and in principle, *beyond its grasp.*" *History and Class Consciousness*, p. 104; emphasis in original.

39. Arato notes this, in "Lukács's Theory of Reification," p. 46, but tries to defuse it by claiming much more modesty for Lukács's account of classical German thought than I think is textually warranted. He sees Lukács as "concerned with a limited number of problems" and as taking the difficulties of Kant and the post-Kantian tradition only as "symbolic" of or "related to" these problems. But the explicit claim in *History and Class Consciousness* is that "modern critical philosophy springs from the reified structure of consciousness" (pp. 110–111) and that "at this stage in the history of mankind there is no problem that does not ultimately lead back" to the question of commodities (p. 83). Even allowing for some hyperbole here, nothing in the reification essay suggests that it is to be read as anything other than a direct response to the problems of classical German philosophy.

40. *History and Class Consciousness*, p. 124; emphasis in original. See also (on "is" and "ought") pp. 160–161.

41. I will return to this point later; see Chapter 2, Section 2.

42. See especially the essays "Class Consciousness," "Legality and Illegality," and "Towards A Methodology of the Problem of Organization."

43. Feenberg, *Lukács, Marx, and the Sources of Critical Theory*, p. 241.

44. See ibid., pp. 210–211 (and p. 205). See also Arato, "Lukács's Theory of Reification," pp. 37–43 (especially p. 41). Arato's discussion reappears in an abbreviated form in Arato and Breines, *The Young Lukács*, pp. 119–121.

45. Feenberg, *Lukács, Marx, and the Sources of Critical Theory*, p. 205. Feenberg's book, which is the best work I know of on this aspect of Lukács's thought (and Marx's, too), keeps circling around the conclusion I am drawing here, but can never finally accept it. The position I will defend has much in common with the "Fichtean" version of Lukács that Feenberg sketches, and then criticizes, on pp. 205–206.

46. See above, p. 27.

CHAPTER 2. NATURE AND REIFICATION

1. In Rockmore, *Lukács Today*, pp. 167–195.

2. Ibid., p. 171. (The more usual translation for *vorhanden* is "present-at-hand.") See Lucien Goldmann, *Lukács and Heidegger*, trans. William Q. Boelhower (London: Routledge and Kegan Paul, 1977).

3. Lukács writes of "that legendary 'critic' in India who was confronted with the ancient story according to which the world rests upon an elephant. He unleashed the 'critical' question: upon what does the elephant rest? On receiving the answer that the elephant stands on a tortoise 'criticism' declared itself satisfied. It is obvious that even if he had continued to press apparently 'critical' questions, he could only have elicited a third miraculous animal. He

would not have been able to discover the solution to the real question." *History and Class Consciousness*, p. 110.

4. Ibid., p. 204.

5. See Chapter 1, pp. 24–25.

6. This is how Lukács attempts to solve the problem of explaining why the proletarian standpoint, both epistemological and moral-political, is superior to the bourgeois (contemplative) one: although neither can claim access to a class-neutral knowledge of what the world is (immediately) in itself, still the proletariat *knows* this, whereas the bourgeoisie remains "held fast in the mire of [the illusion of] immediacy" (*History and Class Consciousness*, p. 163). Armed with this knowledge, furthermore, the proletariat then proceeds in its revolutionary activity to construct for itself a world where its standpoint *becomes* true. (But see below, pp. 41–42.)

7. Arato writes, in "Lukács's Theory of Reification," against this kind of reading that "the concept of second nature has no sharpness when [first] nature itself seems to be presented as social" (p. 42). This sounds right but isn't: it's really just the Kantian move, which cannot understand how there could be a phenomenal world without a noumenal one underneath to "ground" it. No sharpness is lost if we see the critique of reification as a critique of the very idea of "nature" as distinct from the social, instead of as a critique of the blurring of the boundary between the two.

8. Cf. Latour, *We Have Never Been Modern*, pp. 51–55.

9. Karl Marx, *Capital*, vol. 1 (New York: Modern Library, n.d.), p. 85.

10. See my "Marx and Alienation from Nature," pp. 374–375.

11. See William Cronon, *Changes in the Land* (New York: Hill and Wang, 1983); René Dubos, *The Wooing of Earth* (New York: Charles Scribner's Sons, 1980); J. Donald Hughes, *Ecology in Ancient Civilizations* (Albuquerque: University Press of New Mexico, 1975).

12. On Niagara Falls, see George A. Seibel, *Ontario's Niagara Parks* (Ontario: Niagara Parks Commission, 1987), pp. 166–173, and Martin H. Krieger, "What's Wrong With Plastic Trees?" *Science* 179 (February 2, 1973), pp. 447–448. On the Mississippi, see John McPhee, *The Control of Nature* (New York: Farrar, Strauss, and Giroux, 1989). On Yellowstone, see Alston Chase, *Playing God in Yellowstone* (San Diego: Harcourt, Brace, Jovanovich, 1987).

13. Feminist critiques of science have done much in recent years to demonstrate this. See (among others) Evelyn Fox Keller, *Reflections on Gender and Science* (New Haven: Yale University Press, 1985); Sandra Harding, *The Science Question in Feminism* (Ithaca: Cornell University Press, 1986); Donna Haraway, *Primate Visions* (New York: Routledge, 1989); Helen Longino, *Science as Social Knowledge* (Princeton: Princeton University Press, 1990); Carolyn Merchant, *The Death of Nature* (San Francisco: Harper and Row, 1980).

14. And the "nature" we get to always turns out to be different from the one we "meant." See Jacques Derrida, "Différance," in *Margins of Philosophy*, trans. Alan Bass (Chicago: University of Chicago Press, 1982), pp. 1–27.

15. See, e.g., Joseph Rouse, *Knowledge and Power* (Ithaca: Cornell University Press, 1987), pp. 160–162.

16. See G. W. F. Hegel, *The Phenomenology of Spirit*, trans. A. V. Miller (Oxford: Oxford University Press, 1979), p. 103.

17. *History and Class Consciousness*, p. 112.

18. See Chapter 1, p. 30.

19. *History and Class Consciousness*, p. 122. Emphasis in original.

20. Ibid., p. 145.

21. See ibid., p. xvii.

22. Feenberg has noticed this important difference between Lukács and the young Marx. See *Lukács, Marx, and the Sources of Critical Theory*, p. 212: "Marx too sought to transcend philosophy and to develop a new system of reason based on the practical identity of subject and object, just as did Lukács in a later period. However, Marx starts out not from historical practice as the proximate domain of identity but from the labor process, and he is therefore able to grasp the natural subject and object in a dialectical interaction." Arato makes a similar point in "Lukács's Theory of Reification," p. 58.

23. The closest he comes is when he quotes a central passage from Marx's chapter on fetishism, and even here the point is not particularly emphasized. See *History and Class Consciousness*, p. 87. See also pp. 165–166, again following a quotation from Marx, and again without any special emphasis.

24. Ibid., p. xvii. Translation modified: see *Geschichte und Klassenbewusstsein*, p. 19.

25. Feenberg, *Lukács, Marx, and the Sources of Critical Theory*, pp. 206–210.

26. Of course Lukács's own personal intellectual roots in Kierkegaard, Dostoevsky, and similar authors are well-known. See, for example, his "Gelebtes Denken: Notes Towards an Autobiography," in Georg Lukács, *Record of a Life*, trans. Rodney Livingstone, ed. István Eörsi (London: Verso, 1983), pp. 150–151. See also Lee Congdon, *The Young Lukács* (Chapel Hill: University of North Carolina Press, 1983), pp. 139–143, and Arpad Kadarkay, *Georg Lukács: Life, Thought, and Politics* (London: Basil Blackwell, 1991), Chap. 9, both of which explicitly describe Lukács's famous overnight "conversion" to Marxism in terms of a Kierkegaardean leap.

27. *History and Class Consciousness*, pp. 224–225. Livingstone translates *hüllenlosen Wahrheit* as "unvarnished truth." See *Geschichte und Klassenbewusstsein*, p. 399.

28. *History and Class Consciousness*, pp. 164–167 (*Geschichte und Klassenbewusstsein*, pp. 349–351).

29. *History and Class Consciousness*, pp. 166–168.

30. Ibid., p. 165.

31. This is true especially of the categories of appearance and essence; see, for example, ibid., p. 8, where a distinction is drawn between the "real existence" and the "inner core" of facts. And see, too, p. 64, where Lukács writes that as capitalism develops, its "objective limits . . . do not remain purely negative. . . . On the contrary, those limits acquire a historical embodiment with its own consciousness and its own actions: the proletariat"—thus in typical Hegelian fashion making a real subject into the "embodiment" of an abstraction. And similarly on p. 296 he writes that "at every crucial stage of the revolution" the problem of the relation of theory to practice "reappears, always in a more advanced form and with reference to different phenomena. For a problem always makes its appearance first as an abstract possibility and only afterwards is it realised in concrete terms." To which the only possible response is: sez who?

32. On these roots of Lukács's thought, see Rockmore, *Irrationalism*, Chaps. 3 and 4; Arato and Breines, *The Young Lukács*, Chaps. 1–5; Goldmann, *Lukács and Heidegger*, introduction; Jones, "The Marxism of the Early Lukács," pp. 37–44; Jay, *Marxism and Totality*, Chaps. 1 and 2; George Lichtheim, *George Lukács* (New York: Viking Press, 1970), Chaps. 1 and 2.

33. See Chapter 1, p. 16.

34. *History and Class Consciousness*, p. 203; *Geschichte und Klassenbewusstsein*, p. 391. Emphasis in original.

35. See *History and Class Consciousness*, pp. 101–104.

36. Ibid., p. 27. See also p. 34, where Lukács rather hyperbolically writes that "whatever the subject of debate, the dialectical method is concerned always with the same problem: knowledge of the historical process in its entirety."

37. See ibid., pp. 88–90.

38. Ibid., p. 92; *Geschichte und Klassenbewusstsein*, p. 267.

39. See Chapter 1, Section 4. Of course by 1967 he had changed his mind about this: see *History and Class Consciousness*, p. xx.

40. See Rouse, *Knowledge and Power*, p. 23; Bruno Latour, "Give Me a Laboratory and I will Raise the World," in Karin Knorr-Cetina and Michael Mulkay, eds., *Science Observed* (London: Sage, 1983), pp. 141–170; Ian Hacking, *Representing and Intervening* (Cambridge: Cambridge University Press, 1983), Chap. 13; Thomas Kuhn, *The Structure of Scientific Revolutions* (Chicago: University of Chicago Press, 1962), pp. 121 and 150.

41. See, for example, Rouse, *Knowledge and Power*, esp. Chap. 7. Behind Rouse's work stands Foucault, whose discussions of the connections between knowledge and power have clear implications for the natural sciences despite the latter's own quite Lukácsian attempt to limit them to the "human"

(while at the same time of course deconstructing that category entirely). Other important discussions of the "problematic" connection between natural science and an oppressive social order can be found in recent feminist and environmentalist discussions, as well as in the older phenomenological tradition going back to Husserl and Heidegger (and, as we shall see in the next chapter, in the Frankfurt School as well). See, for example, the works cited in note 13. Of course "capitalism" in such discussions is often replaced by "enlightenment," "modernity," "Western metaphysics," "patriarchy," and so on.

42. See Kuhn, *The Structure of Scientific Revolutions*, Chap. 11, and Bruno Latour and Steve Woolgar, *Laboratory Life*, 2nd. ed. (Princeton: Princeton University Press, 1986), Chaps. 2 and 3. Cf. Latour's later *Science in Action* (Cambridge: Harvard University Press, 1987), which examines these processes in further detail.

43. We shall see in Chapter 5 that Habermas takes this methodological self-deception as "the glory of the sciences."

CHAPTER 3. HORKHEIMER, ADORNO, AND THE DIALECTICS OF ENLIGHTENMENT

1. Max Horkheimer and Theodor W. Adorno, *Dialectic of Enlightenment*, trans. John Cumming (New York: Seabury Press, 1972), p. 3. Translation modified: see *Dialektik der Aufklärung* (Frankfurt: Fischer Verlag, 1969), p. 7. It is amazing to me that Horkheimer and Adorno have been as influential in the English-speaking world as they have, given the execrable quality of the translations to which their work has been subjected. Cumming's translation of *Dialectic of Enlightenment* is absolutely riddled with confusions, infelicities, flat-out errors, and a remarkable number of misprints. The book's reputation in this country for obscurity would be considerably lessened (though doubtless not removed entirely) if someone would produce a new translation; many apparently incomprehensible passages got that way only because the translator—perhaps intellectually overtaxed himself—botched them. Christian Lenhardt's translation of Adorno's *Aesthetic Theory* has its own significant problems; it is often so free as to seem more a close commentary on the text than a literal rendering of it. (See the exchange between Lenhardt and Bob Hullot-Kentor in *Telos* 65 [Fall, 1985], pp. 143–152.) And E. B. Ashton's translation of *Negative Dialectics* is not much better. On Adorno translations, see Fredrick Jameson, *Late Marxism: Adorno, or, the Persistance of the Dialectic* (London: Verso, 1990), pp. ix–x (although Jameson unaccountably praises Cumming). My procedure throughout has nonetheless been to begin with these translations, but to feel free to modify them (sometimes significantly) when necessary; such modifications are always indicated in the notes, along

with a reference to the German original. See also note 19, below, and note 15 to Chapter 4.

2. *Dialectic of Enlightenment*, p. xiii. Translation modified: see *Dialektik der Aufklärung*, p. 3.

3. This idea of course goes back to Weber, who stands in the background of this work as he does Lukács's before it and Habermas's after it.

4. *Dialectic of Enlightenment*, p. 4. Translation modified: see *Dialektik der Aufklärung*, p. 8.

5. See *Dialectic of Enlightenment*, pp. xv–xvi.

6. Ibid., p. 9.

7. Ibid., p. xvi.

8. See ibid., pp. 8, 11, 31, 180.

9. Ibid., p. 16.

10. Thus the result of this dynamizing of the myth-enlightenment polarity is that the status of "myth" in Horkeimer and Adorno's account becomes ambiguous, with at least three possible meanings. It seems first to represent a lost past of unity with nature, mourned for and nostalgically invoked by the critique of enlightenment. But second, as "already enlightenment," it turns out already to involve the dream of control of nature (e.g., through sacrifice) and so to be itself subject to the same critique. And then third, as that to which enlightenment at the end of its fatal dialectic "reverts," it appears not as a harmonious unity of humans with nature at all but rather as the return of the dangerous natural forces that stand in the way of human happiness. The result is a characteristic Adornoesque paradox, in which the present order is criticized in the name of a nostalgia for a lost past which however is then admitted never to have existed, nor in fact to have been so different from the present after all. This ambiguity about the status of nature will return several times in what follows: see for instance below, pp. 62–63.

11. See *Dialectic of Enlightenment*, pp. 32–36 and 58–60.

12. Ibid., p. 57. Translation modified: see *Dialektik der Aufklärung*, p. 54.

13. Jameson is simply wrong to deny the significance of Freud to this work (see *Late Marxism*, pp. 26 and 254, n. 4); *Civilization and Its Discontents* stands behind every page of the chapter on Odysseus, as it does (along with *Beyond the Pleasure Principle*) behind many pages of the chapter on anti-Semitism as well. See below, p. 63.

14. *Dialectic of Enlightenment*, p. 57. Translation modified: see *Dialektik der Aufklärung*, p. 53.

15. See *Dialectic of Enlightenment*, pp. 60 and 64–69.

16. Ibid., p. 43. He is, of course, a bourgeois in another crucial sense as well, precisely in his relation to the oarsmen. He is the only one permitted to hear and enjoy the fatal song, while they, lacking the luxury of leisure, must

stop their ears with wax and continue their task. The resulting master-slave dialectic almost literally recapitulates Hegel's discussion: it is the master himself who is in "bondage"—both to the mast and to the song—while the slaves, unable to hear anything, are "free," and make the ship's escape possible. Odysseus's safety is entirely dependent on his crew, but his dependence takes the curious form of domination (he forbids them to hear the song) and alienation (they must not heed his cries for freedom). On all this see Jameson, *Late Marxism*, Part II.

17. *Dialectic of Enlightenment*, p. 59.

18. Ibid., p. 57. Translation modified: see *Dialektik der Aufklärung*, p. 53.

19. It is (typically) lost, though, in Cumming's translation, which renders the single word *List* in numerous different ways—as "cunning," as "artifice," as "nimble wit," etc.—thereby obscuring both the fact that a single concept is being employed and the important double reference to the Homeric "cunning of Odysseus" and the Hegelian "cunning of reason."

20. *Dialectic of Enlightenment*, p. 59. Translation modified: see *Dialektik der Aufklärung*, p. 55.

21. *Dialectic of Enlightenment*, pp. 58–59. Cf. Hegel's (Encyclopedia) *Logic*, paragraph 209.

22. *Dialectic of Enlightenment*, p. 57. Translation modified: see *Dialektik der Aufklärung*, p. 53.

23. *Dialectic of Enlightenment*, p. 13. Translation modified: see *Dialektik der Aufklärung*, p. 15.

24. See *Dialectic of Enlightenment*, pp. 26–27.

25. Compare Lukács's critique of this point; see p. 24 in Chapter 1.

26. *Dialectic of Enlightenment*, p. 85.

27. Ibid., p. 84. Translation modified: see *Dialektik der Aufklärung*, p. 77.

28. They also make the intentionally shocking suggestion that one finds in the schematism the paradigm for what the culture industry would do later on. See *Dialectic of Enlightenment*, pp. 84, 124.

29. Ibid., p. 84.

30. Ibid., p. 26.

31. Ibid., p. 26. Translation modified: see *Dialektik der Aufklärung*, p. 27.

32. *Dialectic of Enlightenment*, p. 94.

33. See ibid., p. 88. See also p. 104: "Even injustice, hatred, and destruction are regulated, automatic procedures, since the formalization of reason has caused all goals to lose, as delusion, any claim to necessity and objectivity."

34. Ibid., p. 89. Translation modified: see *Dialektik der Aufklärung*, pp. 80–81.

35. *Dialectic of Enlightenment*, p. 118.

36. Ibid., p. 87. Translation modified: see *Dialektik der Aufklärung*, p. 79.

37. See *Dialectic of Enlightenment*, pp. 99–101.

38. Ibid., p. 93. Translation modified: see *Dialektik der Aufklärung*, p. 84.

39. See *Dialectic of Enlightenment*, p. 84; see also p. 93.

40. See, for example, ibid., p. 11: the process of enlightenment is one "in which ever and again, with the inevitability of necessity, every specific theoretic view succumbs to the destructive criticism that it is only a belief, until the very notions of spirit, of truth, and indeed of enlightenment itself, have turned into animistic magic." Translation modified: see *Dialektik der Aufklärung*, p. 14.

41. *Dialectic of Enlightenment*, p. 93. Translation modified: see *Dialektik der Aufklärung*, p. 84.

42. *Dialektik der Aufklärung*, p. 104. (Cumming writes "irremediable"; *Dialectic of Enlightenment*, p. 115).

43. *Dialectic of Enlightenment*, p. 93.

44. Ibid., p. xvi. Translation modified: see *Dialektik der Aufklärung*, p. 5.

45. "Nature" here refers above all to the inner nature of humans themselves—the "impulse towards complete, universal, and undivided happiness" that Odysseus must learn to repress; but clearly the effect of enlightenment on external nature also is part of what Horkheimer and Adorno lament. This is the sense in which they are rightly seen as precursors of contemporary environmental thought. This becomes even more explicit, of course, in Marcuse: see Chapter 5.

46. *Dialectic of Enlightenment*, pp. 179–200.

47. The sense of smell, Horkheimer and Adorno write (following Freud), brings the subject closest to nature and so is both despised but also secretly enjoyed; this is the hidden significance, they suggest, of the anti-Semite's image of the Jew as specifically defined by a nose. "Civilized" people may not sniff—with one exception: "Anyone who seeks out 'bad' smells in order to destroy them may imitate sniffing to his heart's content. . . . The civilized man 'disinfects' the forbidden impulse by his unconditional identification with the authority which has prohibited it; in this way the action is made acceptable. . . . This is the schema of the anti-Semitic reaction." *Dialectic of Enlightenment*, p. 184. Cf. Sigmund Freud, *Civilization and Its Discontents* (New York: Norton, 1961), pp. 46, n. 1, and 53, n. 3.

48. *Dialectic of Enlightenment*, pp. 112. Translation modified: see *Dialektik der Aufklärung*, p. 101.

49. *Dialectic of Enlightenment*, p. 183. Translation modified: see *Dialektik der Aufklärung*, p. 164.

50. *Dialectic of Enlightenment*, p. 187. Translation modified: see *Dialektik der Aufklärung*, p. 167.

51. See above, pp. 57–59.

52. *Dialectic of Enlightenment*, pp. 189–190.
53. Ibid., p. 188.
54. Ibid., p. 189. (*Dialektik der Aufklärung*, p. 170.)
55. *Dialectic of Enlightenment*, p. 193. Translation modified: see *Dialektik der Aufklärung*, p. 173.
56. *Dialectic of Enlightenment*, p. 194. Translation modified: see *Dialektik der Aufklärung*, pp. 173–174.
57. *Dialectic of Enlightenment*, p. 194.
58. Ibid., p. 195. Translation modified: see *Dialektik der Aufklärung*, p. 174. Cumming renders *Besinnung* here as "reflection," which although not incorrect may perhaps misleadingly connote an element of self-awareness not found in the German term; *reflektierte* (which he awkwardly translates as "considered"), of course, does possess that connotation. I will criticize Horkheimer and Adorno's position later for *not* granting sufficient attention to "reflection" in the second sense. See Chapter 4, Section 2.
59. *Dialectic of Enlightenment*, pp. 217–218. Translation modified: see *Dialektik der Aufklärung*, p. 194.
60. It is with respect to this problem of normative grounding that Habermas offers his critique of Horkheimer and Adorno, and develops his own theory of "discourse ethics". See Chapter 6, Section 1.
61. I used to keep a list, as I was reading works of the Frankfurt School, of "Things Horkheimer and Adorno Don't Like." Among the items culled just from *Minima Moralia* (admittedly a particularly cranky example): teenagers with hands in their pockets (p. 110), "insufferable" room service in hotels (p. 117), fast trains (p. 119), comedies about death (p. 233), people who say "hello" to each other instead of tipping their hats (p. 41), telling jokes (p. 141), "exuberant health" (p. 77), and in general "all the amusements tolerated by this society" (p. 130). All references are to *Minima Moralia*, trans. E. F. N. Jephcott (London: NLB, 1974). One of my favorites was the discussion of "modern sport" in *Dialectic of Enlightenment*, where they complain about the fact that "the inadequately initiated spectator cannot divine the difference in the combinations, or the meaning of variations, by the arbitrarily determined rules" (p. 88). The image this conjures up—Horkheimer and Adorno Go To The Ballpark—is a delicious one, but it is pretty hard to take it seriously as cultural critique.

CHAPTER 4. ADORNO AND NATURE AS THE NONIDENTICAL

1. See my "Marx and Alienation from Nature" for a further development of the distinction between these two senses of alienation.
2. See Chapter 2, Section 1.

3. Theodor W. Adorno, *Negative Dialectics*, trans. E. B. Ashton (New York: Continuum, 1973), p. 5. Translation modified: see *Negative Dialektik* (Frankfurt: Suhrkamp, 1975), p. 17.

4. See (e.g.) *Negative Dialectics*, p. 318.

5. *Negative Dialectics*, p. 8. Translation modified: see *Negative Dialektik*, pp. 19–20.

6. *Negative Dialectics*, p. xx.

7. See ibid., pp. 158–161.

8. See ibid., p. 365, also p. 141.

9. Ibid., p. 13. Translation modified: see *Negative Dialektik*, p. 25.

10. *Negative Dialectics*, p. 136. Translation modified: see *Negative Dialektik*, p. 140.

11. *Negative Dialectics*, p. 106. Translation modified: see *Negative Dialektik*, p. 112.

12. See *Negative Dialectics*, p. 141, which speaks of "the seemingly unbearable thesis that subjectivity presupposes facts while objectivity presupposes the subject."

13. *Negative Dialektik*, pp. 139–140. (*Negative Dialectics*, pp. 135–136).

14. *Negative Dialectics*, p. 183. Translation modified: see *Negative Dialektik*, p. 184. See also p. 179: "It is not true that the object is a subject, as idealism has been drilling into us for thousands of years, but it is true that the subject is an object."

15. *Negative Dialectics*, p. 186. Translation modified: see *Negative Dialektik*, pp. 186–187. At least Ashton translates *Vermittlung* correctly here; elsewhere he renders this crucial word by "indirectness," "transmission," and the like, choices that have the effect of turning the already difficult prose of Adorno into gibberish. Compare, for instance, *Negative Dialectics*, p. 99 with *Negative Dialektik*, p. 106.

16. See *Negative Dialectics*, pp. 22–23. See also p. 172.

17. Ibid., p. 185. Translation modified: see *Negative Dialektik*, p. 186.

18. *Negative Dialectics*, pp. 189–190.

19. See ibid., p. 374.

20. Adorno sees such rage even in Marx's call in the *Theses on Feuerbach* for a philosophy that would change the world rather than interpret it. With this call, he writes, Marx "underwrote something as arch-bourgeois as the program of an absolute control of nature. What is felt here is the effort to take things unlike the subject and make them like the subject—the real model of the principle of identity, which dialectical materialism disavows as such" (*Negative Dialectics*, p. 244).

21. *Negative Dialectics*, p. 191.

22. Ibid., p. 374. Translation modified: see *Negative Dialektik*, p. 367.

23. *Negative Dialectics*, p. 190.

24. Gillian Rose, *The Melancholy Science: An Introduction to the Thought of Theodor W. Adorno* (New York: Columbia University Press, 1978), p. ix. See also p. 43, where Rose writes that reification "is the centrifuge of all his major works" after 1932—although I must say that the meaning of the centrifuge metaphor escapes me.

25. Rose never claims that Adorno's conception of reification is the same as Lukács's, and acknowledges the sharp critique in Adorno's work of what he sees as Lukács's idealism; given that "reification" appears as a central concept in Lukács's work and nowhere else in the Marxist tradition, Western or otherwise, though, it seems curious to speak of a theory of reification that is other than Lukács's. (See on this also Martin Jay, *Marxism and Totality*, pp. 267–271.) And when Rose attempts to develop that theory herself, the results are at best muddled. Thus when she writes (*Melancholy Science*, p. 47) that "to be non-reified . . . is really to be a property of a thing, or, by analogy, to be a use-value" one scarcely knows what is meant: the very words *reification*, *Verdinglichung*, speak of the turning of that which is not a thing into a thing, and so imply that to be nonreified is to be recognized as not a thing (nor a property of a thing) at all. Reification (Marx's "fetishism") does not involve the illusion that use-values are not properties of commodities—even "bourgeois political economy" always recognized that they were. Marx was pointing out not that use-values were inherent properties of objects but rather that *exchange-values were not*—that in exchange-value human action (labor) appears in the form of a thing, and so is *reified*. When in the next sentence Rose adds that for Adorno "something is non-reified when the concept is identical with its object" she makes a claim that seems to equate nonreification with precisely that identity thinking Adorno is most concerned to criticize.

26. See Rose, ibid., p. 44.

27. *Negative Dialectics*, p. 149.

28. Ibid.

29. Ibid., p. 150. See *Negative Dialektik*, p. 153.

30. See Chapter 2, Section 2.

31. One of those themes, though, and a central one for Lukács, does to be sure seem quite foreign to Adorno: the notion of "totality." Martin Jay among others has argued that it is with respect to this notion above all that Lukács differs from the later tradition of the Frankfurt School; see his *Marxism and Totality*, Chap. 8. It is true that whereas Lukács criticizes contemplation for its inability to grasp social reality as a whole, Adorno sees the very intention to totality as identity thinking at its worst. But this difference can be overstated: in both views a reductionist *Verstand* is criticized for its failure to comprehend the complexity and contradictory character of the whole and the role of internal relations in constituting it. The difference is only that Lukács,

unlike the more sceptical Adorno, still imagines the possibility of a dialectical thinking that could grasp that complexity and those contradictions as a "totality."

32. See Colletti, *Marxism and Hegel*, Chap. 10.

33. "Alle Verdinglichung ist ein Vergessen," *Dialektik der Aufklärung*, p. 206. Cumming misleadingly translates *Verdinglichung* as "objectification" (*Dialectic of Enlightenment*, p. 230).

34. The remark about all reification being a forgetting comes at the end of a horrifying little meditation, in the "Notes and Drafts" section of *Dialectic of Enlightenment*, about the possibility that surgical anesthetics, rather than actually blunting pain or even consciousness, simply paralyze the patient and then produce amnesia, so that each surgical operation produces agonies of pain which are then however promptly forgotten. This thought becomes a metaphor for enlightenment's doomed attempt to dominate nature, which ends up turning nature into a source of horror. (The idea here has the same structure as the "dialectics of enlightenment" examined in Chapter 3, and in particular is almost a direct reformulation, in an altered context, of the story of Odysseus and the Sirens.) See *Dialectic of Enlightenment*, pp. 229–230.

35. Indeed, this is central to enlightenment's project of "disenchantment"; it is the "extirpation of animism" Horkheimer and Adorno speak of on p. 5 of *Dialectic of Enlightenment*. See also p. 6: "Enlightenment has always taken the basic principle of myth to be anthropomorphism, the projection onto nature of the subjective."

36. See p. 71.

37. See the closing pages of Chapter 3.

38. *Negative Dialectics*, p. 365.

39. Ibid., pp. 285–286. Translation modified: see *Negative Dialektik*, p. 281.

40. *Negative Dialectics*, p. 203.

41. Earlier we saw Lukács returning to an appeal to immediacy in the same way; see Chapter 2, Section 2.

42. See Chapter 3, p. 58.

43. Or a moment at which we once did catch such a glimpse. Adorno is fond of Benjaminian appeals to memory as the faculty that allows us to grasp the nonidentical: see note 10 to Chapter 3.

44. See Chapter 2, pp. 34–35.

45. This is central, for example, to Hegel's critique of the Kantian doctrine of noumena, and leads him to say that "one can only read with surprise the perpetual remark that we do not know the thing-in-itself. On the contrary there is nothing we can know so easily" ([Encyclopedia] *Logic*, par. 44). Or compare the remark at par. 60 regarding the Kantian notion of knowledge as necessarily limited to phenomena: "No one knows, or even feels, that anything is a limit or defect, until he is at the same time above and beyond it."

46. See note 58 to Chapter 3.

47. See Chapter 1, Section 4.

48. See Chapter 3, Section 3.

49. *Dialectic of Enlightenment*, pp. 254–255. Translation modified; see *Dialektik der Aufklärung*, p. 227.

50. T. W. Adorno, *Aesthetic Theory*, trans. C. Lenhardt (London: Routledge and Kegan Paul, 1984), p. 91; *Ästhetische Theorie* (Frankfurt: Suhrkamp, 1973), p. 98.

51. See *Aesthetic Theory*, pp. 91–94.

52. Ibid., p. 94. Translation modified: see *Ästhetische Theorie*, p. 100.

53. *Aesthetic Theory*, p. 101. Translation modified: see *Ästhetische Theorie*, p. 107. See also Appendix 1 to *Aesthetic Theory*, p. 408, where Adorno speaks of "a critique of all natural moments to the degree to which they have been hypostatized, for none of them is eternal."

54. The domination of nature is itself one such presupposition: before nature was dominated it could appear to humans only as a source of fear, not wonder and pleasure, and certainly not as "aesthetic." See *Aesthetic Theory*, p. 96.

55. Ibid., p. 102. Translation modified: see *Ästhetische Theorie*, p. 108.

56. *Aesthetic Theory*, p. 104. Translation modified: see *Ästhetische Theorie*, p. 111. On *Vorrang des Objekts*, see above, pp. 74–75.

57. *Aesthetic Theory*, p. 110.

58. Ibid., p. 109. Translation modified: see *Ästhetische Theorie*, p. 115.

59. *Aesthetic Theory*, p. 108. Translation modified: see *Ästhetische Theorie*, p. 114.

60. *Aesthetic Theory*, pp. 387–388. Translation modified: see *Ästhetische Theorie*, p. 410. Lenhardt thinks the reference to Kant here is a slip by Adorno and replaces it by one to Hegel (see *Aesthetic Theory*, p. 507, n. 5), but I am not persuaded.

61. See, for example, *Aesthetic Theory*, p. 192. See note 10 to Chapter 3; cf. also Jay, *Marxism and Totality*, pp. 235–236. Anamnesis returns as a theme in Marcuse: see Chapter 5, pp. 135 and 138–139.

62. *Aesthetic Theory*, p. 95. Translation modified: see *Ästhetische Theorie*, p. 102. He continues: "Longing [*Sehnsucht*] may be assuaged or betrayed by those traces and false gratification gained in this way may even be evil; yet it legitimates itself by its outright denial of the present state of things."

63. *Aesthetic Theory*, p. 96. Translation modified: see *Ästhetische Theorie*, p. 103.

64. *Aesthetic Theory*, p. 101. Translation modified: see *Ästhetische Theorie*, p. 107.

65. *Aesthetic Theory*, p. 311. Translation modified: see *Ästhetische Theorie*, p. 325.

66. *Aesthetic Theory*, pp. 99–100. Translation modified: see *Ästhetische Theorie*, p. 106.

67. *Aesthetic Theory*, p. 33. Translation modified: see *Ästhetische Theorie*, p. 41.

68. *Aesthetic Theory*, p. 114.

69. Ibid., p. 107. Translation modified: see *Ästhetische Theorie*, p. 113.

70. *Aesthetic Theory*, pp. 80–81.

71. Ibid., p. 81.

72. *Aesthetic Theory*, pp. 116ff. (Lenhardt translates *Mehr* as "plus.") See *Ästhetische Theorie*, p. 122ff.

73. *Aesthetic Theory*, p. 117. Translation modified: see *Ästhetische Theorie*, p. 122.

74. See *Aesthetic Theory*, p. 128. Translation modified: see *Ästhetische Theorie*, p. 134.

75. Ibid. See also p. 389: "Artworks are things which tend to shed their thinglike quality. . . . One of the key characteristics of works of art is . . . their ability to undo their own reified shapes in such a way that reification becomes the medium of its own negation."

76. Ibid., pp. 256–257.

77. Ibid., p. 256. Translation modified: see *Ästhetische Theorie*, p. 267.

78. See *Aesthetic Theory*, p. 191; I have altered the translation Jameson gives in *Late Marxism*, p. 214. See *Ästhetische Theorie*, p. 199.

79. See *Aesthetic Theory*, pp. 199–200; also p. 114.

80. Ibid., p. 200. Translation modified: see *Ästhetische Theorie*, p. 208.

81. See above p. 34.

82. As we have seen earlier, the only real content Adorno offers involves an appeal to the somatic, which is to say to immediacy. See pp. 80–81.

83. I will return to this point in my discussion of Habermas in Chapter 6.

84. *Aesthetic Theory*, p. 17. Translation modified: see *Ästhetische Theorie*, p. 26. He even writes in the draft introduction to *Aesthetic Theory* that although idealism is wrong about ordinary objects in general, it is actually right about works of art. See pp. 471–473, also 481.

85. *Aesthetic Theory*, p. 173. Translation modified: see *Ästhetische Theorie*, p. 180.

86. *Aesthetic Theory*, p. 17. Translation modified: see *Ästhetische Theorie*, p. 26.

87. *Aesthetic Theory*, p. 343. Translation modified: see *Ästhetische Theorie*, p. 359. He associates this violence with "the barbaric appetite of the species," not (say) with any particular social order.

88. *Negative Dialectics*, pp. 200–201.

89. Ibid., p. 192; see *Negative Dialektik*, pp. 192–193.

90. See above, pp. 71–75.

91. This argument, of course, goes back to Berkeley—which doesn't keep it from being valid.

92. See Chapter 3, pp. 54–55.

93. See *Dialectic of Englightenment*, pp. 59–60.

CHAPTER 5. MARCUSE, HABERMAS, AND THE RETREAT TO NATURE

1. See (e.g.) Herbert Marcuse, *Eros and Civilization* (New York: Vintage Books, 1962), pp. 136–143.

2. Ibid., p. 142; cf. also p. 95. See C. Fred Alford, *Science and the Revenge of Nature: Marcuse and Habermas* (Tampa: University of South Florida Press, 1985), pp. 37–43.

3. For discussions of Marcuse's ambivalent relation to technology, see especially William Leiss, *The Domination of Nature* (Boston: Beacon Press, 1974), pp. 207–212; Alford, *Science and the Revenge of Nature*, Chaps. 3 and 4; Andrew Feenberg, "The Bias of Technology" in Robert Pippen, Andrew Feenberg, and Charles P. Webel, eds., *Marcuse: Critical Theory and the Promise of Utopia* (South Hadley, Mass.: Bergin and Garvey, 1988), pp. 225–226; Douglas Kellner, *Herbert Marcuse and the Crisis of Marxism* (Berkeley: University of California Press, 1984), pp. 323–330.

4. Thus in *Eros and Civilization* alongside the talk of "the inevitably repressive workworld" (p. 178) and the assertion quoted above that it is only "the sphere outside labor which defines freedom and fulfillment" one can also find Marcuse speaking very differently—e.g., of "a change in the character of work by virtue of which the latter would be assimilated to play" and so "would tend to become gratifying in itself without losing its *work* content" (pp. 195–196). Sometimes it seems as though a distinction is being drawn between "labor" (which is toil, and repressive) and "work" (which is eroticized, and has been turned into play), but this suggestion is never systematically carried through. See, for example, p. 194.

5. See "The End of Utopia," in Herbert Marcuse, *Five Lectures*, trans. Jeremy J. Shapiro and Shierry M. Weber (Boston: Beacon Press, 1970), pp. 62–63.

6. "Industrialization and Capitalism in the Work of Max Weber," in Herbert Marcuse, *Negations*, trans. Jeremy J. Shapiro (Boston: Beacon Press, 1968), pp. 225, 224. Emphasis in original.

7. For useful discussions of Marcuse's later views, see Alford, *Science and the Revenge of Nature*, especially Chap. 4, as well as Leiss, *The Domina-*

tion of Nature, Appendix, and Kellner, *Herbert Marcuse and the Crisis of Marxism*, pp. 330–338.

8. See Herbert Marcuse, *One-Dimensional Man* (Boston: Beacon Press, 1964), pp. 156–169. Andrew Feenberg's *Critical Theory of Technology* (New York: Oxford University Press, 1991) offers an excellent and sophisticated defense of a similar view.

9. This is, of course, just another version of the "dialectic of enlightenment" outlined in Section 2 of Chapter 3.

10. *One-Dimensional Man*, pp. 25–27. But even here Marcuse's ambivalence is apparent, as he begins to argue that it is the *incompleteness* of an automation that has not yet entirely done away with the need for human oversight that causes this mechanization. By pp. 35–37, he is once again touting "complete" automation as leading to "the historical transcendence towards a new civilization" of unparalleled human freedom.

11. Ibid., p. 23.

12. Ibid., pp. 166–167; see also pp. 230–233. "This development," Marcuse writes (p. 233), "confronts science with the unpleasant task of becoming *political*—of recognizing scientific consciousness as political consciousness." (All emphases in original.) As we will see, it is precisely this kind of self-reflexive recognition that Habermas wants to avoid. See Section 4 below.

13. See Herbert Marcuse, *An Essay on Liberation* (Boston: Beacon Press, 1969), pp. vii–ix; *Counterrevolution and Revolt* (Boston: Beacon Press, 1972), pp. 31–33, 74–78. See Kellner, *Herbert Marcuse and the Crisis of Marxism*, Chap. 9.

14. *Counterrevolution and Revolt*, p. 60. Emphasis in original.

15. Ibid., p. 74.

16. Ibid., p. 67.

17. *An Essay on Liberation*, p. 31. Emphasis in original.

18. See "The End of Utopia," p. 68.

19. *Counterrevolution and Revolt*, pp. 2–3.

20. *One-Dimensional Man*, p. 236. See Leiss, *The Domination of Nature*, p. 212.

21. *Counterrevolution and Revolt*, p. 66; the phrase appears in Adorno, *Ästhetische Theorie*, p. 107. (It is translated differently in *Aesthetic Theory*, p. 101.) "Paradoxical" might be too weak a word here; I will argue below (in Section 5) that there is something finally incoherent about the notion of a "transformation" of nature that nonetheless reveals its "inherent" qualities.

22. *Eros and Civilization*, p. 151. Emphasis in original.

23. *An Essay on Liberation*, pp. 45, 31. Cf. *Eros and Civilization*, p. 173: "the play impulse would literally transform the reality."

24. See *One-Dimensional Man*, pp. 231–233, where the ambiguity is quite clear.

25. See Alford, *Science and the Revenge of Nature*, pp. 43–45. Cf. the text to note 19 above: it is "the technical *and natural* environment" that individuals in a liberated society would create.

26. Jürgen Habermas, *Knowledge and Human Interests*, trans. Jeremy Shapiro (Boston: Beacon Press, 1968). The critique of Marcuse is developed in "Technology and Science as 'Ideology'," published in English in *Toward a Rational Society*, trans. Jeremy Shapiro (Boston: Beacon Press, 1970).

27. See Chapter 1, p. 18.

28. *Knowledge and Human Interests*, pp. 68–69.

29. "Appendix" to ibid., p. 308.

30. See ibid., pp. 191–198, and *Toward a Rational Society*, pp. 91–93. Habermas also asserts the existence of a third "emancipatory" interest in "self-reflection," associated with "critical" sciences such as psychoanalysis and critical social theory itself. Always a bit of a deus ex machina, this third interest will not concern us here; I take it already to have been sufficiently criticized, not least by Habermas himself. See, for example, "A Postscript to *Knowledge and Human Interests*," *Philosophy of Social Science* 3 (1973), pp. 182–185. See also Thomas McCarthy, *The Critical Theory of Jürgen Habermas* (Cambridge, Mass.: MIT Press, 1978), pp. 92–110.

31. *Knowledge and Human Interests*, pp. 194–195. See Jürgen Habermas, *Erkenntnis und Interessse* (Frankfurt: Suhrkamp, 1979), p. 240.

32. See *Knowledge and Human Interests*, pp. 125–129, 175–176, 304–308 ("Appendix").

33. *Toward a Rational Society*, p. 88. We will return to this important point below.

34. Ibid., p. 87.

35. Ibid., p. 94.

36. On this, see two other essays in *Toward a Rational Society*: "Technical Progress and the Social Life-World" (pp. 50–61) and "The Scientization of Politics and Public Opinion" (pp. 62–80).

37. Ibid., pp. 112–113. Emphasis in original.

38. Ibid., p. 88.

39. I shall return to the question of the "communicative" status of nature and natural entities in the next chapter. Habermas, I will argue, is right that nature cannot be a communicative *partner*, but wrong to think that this means it can only be the object of instrumental manipulation; as that which we transform in our practices, it is something *about which* we communicate with each other, and so it does possess an ethical status. See Section 4 of Chapter 6.

40. For critical discussion of the schema of *Knowledge and Human Interests* see McCarthy, *The Critical Theory of Jürgen Habermas*, Chap. 2; Alford, *Science and the Revenge of Nature*, Chaps. 5 and 6; David Held, *Introduction*

to Critical Theory (Berkeley: University of California Press, 1980), pp. 389–398; Russell Keat, *The Politics of Social Theory* (Chicago: University of Chicago Press, 1981), Chap. 3; Richard Bernstein, *The Restructuring of Social and Political Theory* (Philadelphia: University of Pennsylvania Press, 1976), pp. 219–225; and "Introduction" to Richard Bernstein, ed., *Habermas and Modernity* (Cambridge, Mass.: MIT Press, 1985), pp. 8–15; Rick Roderick, *Habermas and the Foundations of Critical Theory* (New York: St. Martin's Press, 1986), pp. 62–73.

41. See Section 5 below, as well as Chapter 6. For Habermas's own self-critique, see especially the "Postscript to *Knowledge and Human Interests*" and "Some Difficulties in the Attempt to Link Theory and Praxis," published as the new introduction to *Theory and Practice*, trans. John Viertel (Boston: Beacon Press, 1973), pp. 14ff. (But note that in a 1984 interview Habermas is quoted as saying that "I still consider the outlines of the argument developed in the book [*Knowledge and Human Interests*] to be correct"; see Peter Dews, ed., *Habermas: Autonomy and Solidarity* [London: Verso, 1986], p. 152.)

42. Thomas McCarthy has analyzed this well—see McCarthy, *The Critical Theory of Jürgen Habermas*, pp. 110–125—and I am indebted to his account in what follows. See also Joel Whitebook, "The Problem of Nature in Habermas," *Telos* 40 (1979), pp. 48–50; Richard Bernstein, "Introduction" to *Habermas and Modernity*, p. 13; Henning Ottmann, "Cognitive Interests and Self-Reflection" in John B. Thompson and David Held, eds., *Habermas: Critical Debates* (Cambridge, Mass.: MIT Press, 1982), pp. 91–92.

43. *Knowledge and Human Interests*, pp. 35–36.

44. Ibid., p. 133; emphasis in original. See also the "Appendix" to the same work, p. 312: "the achievements of the transcendental subject have their basis in the natural history of the human species."

45. See ibid., p. 34.

46. Habermas would later admit this. See "Some Difficulties in the Attempt to Link Theory and Praxis," p. 14.

47. See ibid., pp. 21–22. See also McCarthy, *The Critical Theory of Jürgen Habermas*, pp. 121–124, and Whitebook, "The Problem of Nature in Habermas," pp. 59–61.

48. In his later work Habermas attempts to resolve this problem by appeal to the notion of a "reconstructive science"—he has in mind Piagetian psychology or Chomskyan linguistics—in which investigators reflect upon the necessary implicit competencies that make possible the observed behavior of actors. Yet the epistemological status of such a reconstructive science is hardly any clearer than the ontological status of an "interest" in the theory of *Knowledge and Human Interests*, and for similar reasons. See, for example, the important criticisms offered by Thomas McCarthy in his "Rationality and

Relativism: Habermas's 'Overcoming' of Hermeneutics" in Thompson and Held, *Habermas: Critical Debates*. Part of Habermas's point, of course, is that philosophy can no longer claim for itself the kind of certainty that talk of "transcendentalism" suggests; its real role, he argues, is as "stand-in" for the sciences, offering empirical hypotheses for later scientific investigation, and hence all its theories must be understood fallibilistically. See on this his *Moral Consciousness and Communicative Action*, trans. Christian Lenhardt and Shierry Weber Nicholsen (Cambridge, Mass: MIT Press, 1990), pp. 15–16, as well as his critique of Apel in the same work, pp. 95–98, and in *Justification and Application*, trans. Ciaran P. Cronin (Cambridge, Mass.: MIT Press, 1993), pp. 83–84. About this he is doubtless right; yet the question here is not whether our claims regarding the "interest-structures" underlying knowledge are fallible or not—surely they are. It is whether they themselves can be coherently understood as *structured by interests*.

49. Jürgen Habermas, "Reply to My Critics," in Thompson and Held, *Habermas: Critical Debates*, p. 274.

50. *Knowledge and Human Interests*, p. 137.

51. Ibid., p. 127. Emphasis in original.

52. Ibid., p. 91.

53. "Appendix" to ibid., p. 308.

54. Ibid., p. 161. Translation modified: see *Erkenntnis und Interesse*, p. 204.

55. See *Knowledge and Human Interests*, p. 144.

56. One is reminded of Charles Taylor's amusing image of "old-guard Diltheyans, their shoulders hunched from years-long resistance against the encroaching pressure of positivist natural science, suddenly pitch[ing] forward on their faces as all opposition ceases to the reign of universal hermeneutics." See his "Understanding in Human Science," *Review of Metaphysics* 34 (1980), p. 26; Rouse quotes this remark on p. 47 of *Knowledge and Power*.

57. Mary Hesse, "In Defence of Objectivity," in *Revolutions and Reconstructions in the Philosophy of Science* (Bloomington: Indiana University Press, 1980), esp. pp. 169–173. For Habermas's account of hermeneutics, see especially *Knowledge and Human Interests*, pp. 161–176.

58. Cf. Richard Bernstein, *Beyond Objectivism and Relativism* (Philadelphia: University of Pennsylvania Press, 1983), especially pp. 52–86.

59. Later Habermas will attempt to maintain his dualism by asserting that even a "hermeneutic" natural science is methodologically distinct from the *Geisteswissenschaften* because the social sciences are subject to a *double* hermeneutic, since not only the process of investigation but also the object being investigated possess a meaningful character, See pp. 130–131 below.

60. *Knowledge and Human Interests*, pp. 86–90.

61. Ibid., p. 95. Emphasis in original.

62. Ibid., p. 97.

63. Ibid., p. 95.

64. Karl Popper, *The Logic of Scientific Discovery* (New York: Harper and Row, 1968), pp. 104–105.

65. Ibid., p. 104.

66. Jürgen Habermas, "The Analytical Theory of Science and Dialectics," in Theodor Adorno et. al., *The Positivist Dispute in German Sociology*, Glyn Adey and David Frisby, trans. (London: Heinemann, 1976), pp. 149–152.

67. Ibid., pp. 152–162.

68. *Knowledge and Human Interests*, p. 137. Translation modified: see *Erkenntnis und Interesse*, pp. 175–176.

69. Jürgen Habermas, "A Positivistically Bisected Rationalism," in Adorno, et. al., *The Positivist Dispute*, pp. 203–204.

70. See ibid., pp. 204–207.

71. See ibid., p. 206.

72. Axel Honneth, in his very interesting *The Critique of Power*, trans. Kenneth Baynes (Cambridge, Mass.: MIT Press, 1991), makes a similar argument about the social-theoretic model of "institutional framework" and "subsystems of purposive-rational action" employed in Habermas's critique of Marcuse. These subsystems are never really autonomous, Honneth points out, but are rather always the subject of an ongoing social "negotiation" in which relations of domination—"class struggle"—play themselves out. See pp. 269–277.

73. "Appendix" to *Knowledge and Human Interests*, pp. 305–306. Translation modified: see Jürgen Habermas, *Technik und Wissenschaft als "Ideologie"* (Frankfurt: Suhrkamp, 1979), p. 152.

74. "That we disavow reflection," Habermas would write later, "*is* positivism." *Knowledge and Human Interests*, p. vii.

75. "Appendix" to ibid., p. 315.

76. Ibid., p. 196.

77. See Hesse, "In Defence of Objectivity," pp. 185–186, as well as her "Science and Objectivity" in Thompson and Held, *Habermas: Critical Debates*, pp. 105–108.

78. See Chapter 2, Section 1.

79. "Appendix" to *Knowledge and Human Interests*, p. 314.

80. This idea should be familiar: it follows from the (Hegelian) insights about self-reflection and self-knowledge to which I have several times referred and according to which those acts of mediation that know themselves as such are superior to those that do not. See Chapter 2, pp. 48–49, and Chapter 4, pp. 82–83.

81. See Chapter 6, p. 164.

82. "The notion of the self-understanding of science contradicts the notion of science itself," we saw Horkheimer and Adorno writing (*Dialectic of*

Enlightenment, p. 85; see Chapter 3, p. 57). But another way to say this would be to suggest that any science that *did* understand itself would have to be a new science. We will return to this idea in Section 6.

83. See also the new introduction to *Theory and Practice* ("Some Difficulties in the Attempt to Link Theory and Praxis"), as well as the essays "Wahrheitstheorien," originally published in 1973 and reprinted in Jürgen Habermas, *Vorstudien und Ergänzungen zur Theorie des Kommunikativen Handelns* (Frankfurt: Suhrkamp, 1984), and "What Is Universal Pragmatics?" in Jürgen Habermas, *Communication and the Evolution of Society*, trans. Thomas McCarthy (Boston: Beacon Press, 1979). I will consider the broader scope of Habermas's later views, and in particular his important conception of "discourse ethics," in Chapter 6.

84. "A Postscript to *Knowledge and Human Interests*," p. 168. Translation modified: see "Nachwort" in *Erkenntnis und Interesse*, p. 386. Emphasis in original. See also "Wahrheitstheorien," pp. 130–131.

85. "A Postscript to *Knowledge and Human Interests*," p. 169.

86. "Wahrheitstheorien," p. 171.

87. Ibid., pp. 174–175.

88. Kuhn, *Structure of Scientific Revolutions*, p. 115.

89. "A Postscript to *Knowledge and Human Interests*," p. 171. Emphasis in original.

90. See above, pp. 113–114.

91. See, for example, Latour, "Give Me a Laboratory and I will Raise the World," and *The Pasteurization of France*, trans. Alan Sheridan and John Law (Cambridge, Mass: Harvard University Press, 1988). See also Rouse, *Knowledge and Power*.

92. Rouse makes this point well, reminding us that science has arguably had a greater transformative impact on objective "experience" than it ever had on the supposedly timeless realm of discourse: science and technology, he writes, "have . . . transformed the globe more thoroughly than they have transformed our thinking about it; an eighteenth-century intellectual would be far more at home in our university classrooms than in our homes, factories, and cities." *Knowledge and Power*, p. 6.

93. "Wahrheitstheorien," p. 153. Cf. "A Postscript to *Knowledge and Human Interests*," p. 166, and see also p. 170: "*objectivity* of experience means that everybody can count on the success or failure of certain actions; the *truth* of a proposition stated in discourses means that everybody can be persuaded by reasons to recognize the truth claim of the statement as being justified." All emphases in original.

94. See "Wahrheitstheorien," pp. 134–135. See also "A Postscript to *Knowledge and Human Interests*," pp. 168–170.

95. "Wahrheitstheorien," p. 134. See also "Some Difficulties in the Attempt to Link Theory and Praxis," p. 20, where the distinction is drawn between "opinions about objects" and "statements about facts." And cf. "Reply to My Critics," p. 275.

96. Hesse, "Science and Objectivity," pp. 100–101. See also J. Thompson, "Universal Pragmatics," in Thompson and Held, *Habermas: Critical Debates*, pp. 130–131.

97. See Hesse's remarks on Habermas's notion of a "reconstructive science" in "Science and Objectivity," pp. 111–112.

98. Hesse, "In Defence of Objectivity," p. 181; see also her "Habermas's Consensus Theory of Truth," in *Revolutions and Reconstructions in the Philosophy of Science*, p. 225.

99. "A Postscript to *Knowledge and Human Interests*," p. 169; see also "Some Difficulties in the Attempt to Link Theory and Praxis," p. 20, and "Wahrheitstheorien," p. 135.

100. Cf. also Rouse, *Knowledge and Power*, Chap. 4.

101. Latour's notion of "laboratization" is also relevant here, for it suggests that the continuity goes in both directions. The point is not simply that the objects scientists interact with are just like those of "ordinary life," it is also that one consequence of what scientists do is to make the objects of ordinary life more and me like those of the laboratory. See "Give Me a Laboratory and I Will Raise the World."

102. See Latour and Woolgar, *Laboratory Life*, Chap. 2.

103. See Anthony Giddens, *New Rules of Sociological Method*, 2d ed. (Stanford, Calif.: Stanford University Press, 1993), p. 86. Cf. also Peter Winch, *The Idea of a Social Science and Its Relation to Philosophy* (London: Routledge and Kegan Paul, 1958), pp. 86–91, where a similar argument is offered.

104. Jürgen Habermas, *The Theory of Communicative Action*, trans. Thomas McCarthy (Boston: Beacon Press, 1984), vol. 1, p. 110. Emphasis in original. See also "Reply To My Critics," p. 274.

105. *The Theory of Communicative Action*, vol. 1, pp. 111–112.

106. See, for example, Rouse's discussion of the laboratory as "a locus for the construction of phenomenal microworlds" in *Knowledge and Power*, pp. 95–111. Of course the fact that the objects scientists employ ("observe") in their practices may be fruitfully subjected to an ethnographic analysis is precisely the (ironic) point of Latour and Woolgar's *Laboratory Life*.

107. See Chapter 2, p. 36.

108. Here is where I think Rouse, whose *Knowledge and Power* is the best philosophical examination of the idea of science as a practice continuous with all the other practices of everyday life and labor that I know of, errs. Just as Habermas imagines a discourse without practice in which "ordinary life-

praxis" has been left behind, so Rouse imagines that practices have nothing of the discursive in them. His mistake is to think that just because the tacit knowhow underlying our practices is necessarily unarticulated within those practices it must therefore be unarticul*able* as such and so can never be captured in discursive form. But just because we can never discursively grasp everything in the background of our practices *at once* it does not follow that there is any aspect of that background that cannot be discursively grasped *at all*. Any element of the background can potentially be put to discursive test, that is to the test of justification that Habermas proposes. In this sense discourse serves as a metapractice with a special epistemological role. See my "Science, Practice, and Politics," pp. 272–273.

109. See, for example, "What Is Universal Pragmatics?" p. 68; *The Theory of Communicative Action*, vol. 1, p. 100; *Moral Consciousness and Communicative Action*, p. 136. The dualism here of course has become a trilateralism, which only confirms Habermas's debt to Kant.

110. See Chapter 6, Section 4.

111. *Counterrevolution and Revolt*, p. 59.

112. See Chapter 2, Section 1.

113. See above, pp. 104–105. The last quotation is from *Counterrevolution and Revolt*, p. 64.

114. See Chapter 4, Section 1.

115. *Counterrevolution and Revolt*, p. 69. (Emphasis in original in this and each of the following three quotations.)

116. Ibid., pp. 69–70.

117. Ibid., p. 67.

118. Ibid., p. 62.

119. Indeed by the end of the discussion of Marx Marcuse concludes that the former's activist view "retains something of the *hubris* of domination" and needs to be modified (ibid., pp. 68–69). The "modification," it seems to me, in fact vitiates the whole argument. See Morton Schoolman, *The Imaginary Witness* (New York: New York University Press, 1984), pp. 125–127.

120. *Counterrevolution and Revolt*, p. 74.

121. Ibid., p. 69.

122. See Schoolman, *The Imaginary Witness*, Chap. 3, and pp. 284–286.

123. *Eros and Civilization*, p. 12.

124. See ibid., pp. 99–107.

125. Ibid., p. 146.

126. Ibid., p. 149.

127. On Eros and Nirvana, see (for example) ibid., pp. 27, 214–215, 247. See also "Freedom and Freud's Theory of Instincts" in *Five Lectures*, pp. 7–8. Cf. Schoolman, *The Imaginary Witness*, pp. 112–116.

128. *Eros and Civilization*, pp. 150–151.

129. Ibid., p. 151.

130. See Alford, *Science and The Revenge of Nature*, pp. 44, 55.

131. See *Eros and Civilization*, p. 173.

132. See above, pp. 94–95.

133. *Eros and Civilization*, p. 130.

134. Ibid.

135. Ibid., p. 132.

136. Of course the vision of art presented here is quite different from the one found in Adorno.

137. *Eros and Civilization*, p. 154.

138. Ibid., p. 135.

139. See, for example, ibid., pp. 181 or 186. The tipoff occurs when the "post-technological" utopia is admitted to be (surprisingly?) identical to a "pre-technological" one: see ibid., pp. 137–138 and also *One-Dimensional Man*, pp. 59–60.

140. To be sure, Marcuse sometimes tries to suggest the possibility of an "eroticization" of work, but when he describes it it doesn't really sound like work at all. Thus in *Eros and Civilization* eroticized work is portrayed in such a way that any administration or organization of it, indeed any planning or purpose to it, would return it to the realm of alienation; if such purposeless play happened to produce a useful object, or to change the world in any substantial manner, it would be entirely coincidental. See *Eros and Civilization*, pp. 194–199. In *An Essay on Liberation* a better formulation appears (at pp. 20–22 and especially p. 24), in which Marcuse envisages the moment of planning as itself being eroticized. Still, the fundamental ontological characteristic of labor as conscious world changing is something he never emphasizes.

141. See above, Chapter 4, Section 5.

142. Whether eroticism itself is thinkable (or, anyway, desirable) without otherness is itself not at all clear. What Marcuse has in mind sounds more like narcissism.

143. Cf. Alford's discussion of Christopher Lasch's critique of Marcuse in *Science and the Revenge of Nature*, pp. 45–48.

144. *An Essay on Liberation*, p. 7. See *Eros and Civilization*, Chap. 6.

145. See *An Essay on Liberation*, pp. 16–17; also *Counterrevolution and Revolt*, pp. 16–17, and "The End of Utopia," pp. 71–72. "What do we need a revolution for if we're not going to get a new human being?" asked Marcuse in a 1977 conversation with Habermas; see Marcuse et al., "Theory and Politics: A Discussion," *Telos* 38 (Winter 1978–79), p. 133.

146. *An Essay on Liberation*, pp. 10–11. Note the Lamarckianism here, which in fact is never far from the surface in Marcuse's biological talk, and which is typical of positions that systematically mistake the social for the natural.

147. "The End of Utopia," p. 67.

148. *An Essay on Liberation*, p. 21.

149. See for example "The End of Utopia," p. 65.

150. See Habermas, "Psychic Thermidor and the Rebirth of Rebellious Subjectivity," in Bernstein, *Habermas and Modernity*, pp. 74–77.

151. *An Essay on Liberation*, p. 63.

152. Another example: the last paragraph of *An Essay on Liberation* begins by calling once again for new and noncompetitive "incentives" to be "built into the instinctual structure" of humans as the basis for a free society, but ends by quoting "a young black girl" who speaks of such a society as one where "for the first time in our life, we shall be free to think about what we are going to do" (p. 91). There is no recognition shown that acting from instinct and "thinking what we are going to do" are *mutually exclusive*.

153. I would suggest that what might be called the *antidemocratic* aspects of Marcuse's thought—the talk of false needs, of repressive tolerance, of the "limits of democratic persuasion and evolution" (*An Essay on Liberation*, p. 17)—have their source in just this mistake. This is very clear in the 1977 discussion between Habermas and Marcuse; see "Theory and Politics," pp. 133–138.

154. This is, of course, exactly the point at which Adorno makes his own naturalistic appeal to the "somatic." See Chapter 4, pp. 80–81.

155. See Rouse, *Knowledge and Power*, p. 239.

CHAPTER 6. TOWARDS A COMMUNICATIVE THEORY OF NATURE

1. *The Theory of Communicative Action*, vol. 1, p. 392.

2. Discussions of Habermas's more recent work that I have found useful, beyond those mentioned earlier, include Seyla Benhabib, *Critique, Norm, and Utopia* (New York: Columbia University Press, 1986); David Ingram, *Habermas and the Dialectic of Reason* (New Haven, Conn.: Yale University Press, 1987); Stephen White, *The Recent Work of Jürgen Habermas* (Cambridge: Cambridge University Press, 1988); David M. Rasmussen, *Reading Habermas* (Cambridge, Mass.: Basil Blackwell, 1990); Kenneth Baynes, *The Normative Grounds of Social Criticism* (Albany: SUNY Press, 1992); Jane Braaten, *Habermas's Critical Theory of Society* (Albany: SUNY Press, 1991).

3. See Chapter 5, p. 110.

4. See *The Theory of Communicative Action*, vol. 1, Chap. 4, as well as Jürgen Habermas, *The Philosophical Discourse of Modernity*, trans. Frederick Lawrence (Cambridge, Mass.: MIT Press, 1987), Chap. 5. See also Honneth, *The Critique of Power*, esp. Part I.

5. *The Theory of Communicative Action*, vol. 1, p. 377.

6. Ibid., pp. 382–384.

7. *The Philosophical Discourse of Modernity*, p. 129.

8. See note 48 to Chapter 5. These last correspond roughly in content to *Moralbewusstsein und Kommunikatives Handeln* (Frankfurt: Suhrkamp, 1983) and *Erläuterungen zur Diskursethik* (Frankfurt: Suhrkamp, 1991). For a good account of the argument for discourse ethics, see Baynes, *The Normative Grounds of Social Criticism*, Chap. 3.

9. In this reflexivity, I would argue, one sees the linguistic version of the Hegelian appeal to self-reflection mentioned repeatedly above.

10. See "What Is Universal Pragmatics?" pp. 50–59. Cf. *The Theory of Communicative Action*, vol. 1, Chap. 3, especially pp. 295–310.

11. See Chapter 5, Section 5.

12. "What Is Universal Pragmatics?" pp. 59–68.

13. See *Moral Consciousness and Communicative Action*, p. 56.

14. Ibid., pp. 52–57.

15. See ibid., pp. 86–94.

16. Ibid., p. 93.

17. See ibid., pp. 94–98; also *Justification and Application*, pp. 83–86.

18. See, for example, *Moral Consciousness and Communicative Action*, pp. 93–94.

19. See, for example, ibid., pp. 108, 177–178, 204–205.

20. See *Justification and Application*, pp. 2–8.

21. See ibid., pp. 11, 23, 127. Habermas has struggled with the place for "ethics" in his theory for some time, partly in response to the sustained critique that deontological theories in general have received in recent years from neo-Aristotelian, communitarian, feminist, and postmodernist thinkers. I will not pursue this (important) issue further here; it will be clear later the extent to which I do not entirely share his scepticism about the possible role of consensus as a regulative ideal even outside the "moral" realm. For a useful discussion of some of the issues here, see Georgia Warnke, *Justice and Interpretation* (Cambridge, Mass.: MIT Press, 1993), Chap. 5.

22. The astute reader will have noticed that I have now criticized Lukács for having having failed to comprehend labor (Chapter 2, p. 40), Adorno for hating practice (Chapter 4, p. 94), Marcuse for being suspicious of activity (Chapter 5, p. 138), and now Habermas again for failing to discuss labor. The position I have been defending in this book is one where real concrete human activity or practice plays a focal role; my claim is that the failure of the thinkers I am examining adequately to grasp the epistemological and ontological significance of that activity is central to the problems they all face with regard to nature.

23. See Whitebook, "The Problem of Nature in Habermas"; Ottmann, "Cognitive Interests and Self-Reflection"; Thomas McCarthy, "Reflections on Rationalization in *The Theory of Communicative Action*" in Bernstein, *Habermas and Modernity*; John S. Dryzek, "Green Reason: Communicative Ethics for the Biosphere," *Environmental Ethics* 12 (Fall 1990), pp. 195–210.

24. See, for example, Whitebook, "The Problem of Nature in Habermas," p. 52; Dryzek, "Green Reason," pp. 202–204.

25. See *Moral Consciousness and Communicative Action*, pp. 46–47 (correcting an obvious misprint): "The objectivating attitude of the nonparticipating observer annuls the communicative roles of I and thou, the first and second persons, and neutralizes the realm of moral phenomena as such. The third-person attitude causes this realm of phenomena to vanish." (I will question Habermas's distinction between "worlds" later; see p. 168).

26. See "Reply to My Critics," pp. 241–250 and *The Theory of Communicative Action*, vol. 1, pp. 236–239.

27. "Reply to My Critics," pp. 243–244. Emphasis in original. Note incidentally that this is not a new concession: see "Technology and Science as 'Ideology,' " p. 88.

28. "Reply to My Critics," p. 244. See also the associated chart on p. 249. (The same charts appear in *The Theory of Communicative Action*, vol. 1, pp. 237–238).

29. "Reply to My Critics," pp. 244–245.

30. Ibid.

31. Ibid., p. 245.

32. "There remains a stain on the idea of a justice that is bought with the irrevocable injustice perpetrated on earlier generations," he writes. Ibid., p. 246.

33. Ibid., p. 247.

34. Thus he writes that the difficulties faced by discourse ethics with respect to nature "do not so much put in question the approach from which they arise as perform the function of throwing light on the limits of human reason." Ibid., p. 242.

35. Ibid., p. 248.

36. Ibid., pp. 248–249.

37. Ibid., p. 247.

38. See Whitebook, "The Problem of Nature in Habermas," pp. 61–64.

39. One also has the clear sense that several different writings (produced at different times?) have been spliced together here. The transitions at pp. 245 and 248 of "Reply to My Critics" are particularly rough.

40. Republished as "Questions and Counterquestions" in Bernstein, *Habermas and Modernity*.

41. See McCarthy, "Reflections on Rationalization," pp. 176–191.

42. Ibid., p. 179.

43. See "Questions and Counterquestions," p. 206.

44. Ibid., pp. 208–209.

45. "Questions and Counterquestions," p. 211. "All this is not really an argument," he adds, and leaves open the possibility that "McCarthy or others

will some day succeed in formulating the continuities between human history and natural history so carefully that they are weak enough to be plausible and yet strong enough to permit us to recognize man's place in the cosmos."

46. *Moral Consciousness and Communicative Action*, pp. 195–215. The original version of this essay appeared in *Erläuterungen zur Diskursethik*, pp. 9–30.

47. *Moral Consciousness and Communicative Action*, p. 211.

48. Ibid., p. 211. Emphasis in original. Compare also *Justification and Application*, p. 176, where Habermas calls for an "ascetic" approach to moral theory which recognizes that "philosophy cannot arrogate to itself the task of finding answers to substantive questions of justice or of an authentic, unfailed life, for it properly belongs to the participants."

49. *Justification and Application*, pp. 105–111.

50. See "Ökologische Ethik—innerhalb der Grenzen bloßer Vernunft," in H. J. Elster, ed., *Umweltschutz—Herausforderung unserer Generation* (Göttingen: Studienzentrum Weikersheim, 1984). Cf. also Patzig's essay "Der wissenschaftliche Tierversuch unter ethischen Aspekten" in Wolfgang Hardegg and Gert Preiser, eds., *Tierversuch und medizinische Ethik* (Hildesheim: Georg Olms AG, 1986).

51. See "Ökologische Ethik," p. 73.

52. *Justification and Application*, pp. 106–107.

53. Ibid., pp. 109–110. Emphasis in original.

54. Ibid., p. 110. Emphasis in original.

55. Ibid., p. 111; see also p. 108 on vegetarianism. But at p. 111 he admits that "it is a tricky moral question to determine in which situations" those limits are reached, and even concedes the possibility that "some vegetarians exhibit a moral sensibility that may prove to be the correct moral intuition under more auspicious social circumstances." It is certainly not at all clear that this argument is satisfactory. The distinction being drawn here between entities as individuals and entities as "exemplars of a species" is indeed a problematic one, and is not clearly justifiable in the context of Habermas's fundamentally individualistic account of morality. And it seems by his account that members of a society that chose *never* to engage in quasi-communicative interactions with animals—no pets, nothing but instrumental relations—would then possess no moral obligations toward them.

56. For discussion of the tensions between these positions, see Mark Sagoff, "Animal Liberation and Environmental Ethics: Bad Marriage, Quick Divorce," *Osgoode Hall Law Journal* 22, no. 2 (1984): 297–307; also J. Baird Callicott, "Animal Liberation: A Triangular Affair," *Environmental Ethics* 2, no. 4 (Winter 1980): 311–338.

57. *Justification and Application*, p. 111. Emphasis in original.

58. For a good history of this idea, see Roderick Nash, *The Rights of Nature* (Madison: University of Wisconsin Press, 1989). See also Peter Singer, *Animal Liberation* (New York: Avon Books, 1975) and Tom Regan, *The Case for Animal Rights* (Berkeley: University of California Press, 1983).

59. Patzig construes the problem in the latter way; see "Ökologische Ethik," p. 73. Cf. Jan Narveson, "Animal Rights Revisited," in H. Miller and W. Williams, eds., *Ethics and Animals* (Clifton, N.J.: Humana Press, 1983), pp. 45–59.

60. Jeremy Bentham, *An Introduction to the Principles of Morals and Legislation* (London: The Athlone Press, 1970), p. 283n. Emphasis in original. Patzig and Habermas both quote it, too: see (respectively) "Der wissenschaftliche Tierversuch," p. 77, and *Justification and Application*, p. 106.

61. In this sense the argument itself bears traces of reification: lacking self-reflection, it fails to see the constitutive role of language (and of reason) in its own account of the extralinguistic realm whose independence of the human it believes itself to be proclaiming. Compare the "Hegelian trick" mentioned earlier; see Chapter 4, p. 82, as well as note 91 in the same chapter.

62. Dryzek, "Green Reason," pp. 204–210.

63. See ibid., pp. 206–207. In this sense Dryzek has not yet really taken Habermas's "communicative turn."

64. Cf. *Philosophical Discourse of Modernity*, pp. 311–312.

65. Even Habermas sometimes interprets the position this way, as in the odd reference to the "narcissism" of anthropocentrism in the passage quoted earlier (p. 156) from the essay on "Morality and Ethical Life."

66. Of course a more correct term here would be something like *logocentrist*, but that would just get me in hotter water!

67. See Section 2 above.

68. On Habermas's dualism, cf. Latour, *We Have Never Been Modern*, p. 60.

69. See above, pp. 158–160.

70. I suspect that Habermas is right to locate the source of our "intuitions" about the rights of (higher) animals in our propensity to see them as quasi-interlocutors, although I tend to think this has more to do with a psychological tendency to project communicative capability onto nonlinguistic creatures than with a real moral insight.

71. See *Justification and Application*, p. 4.

72. This helps to elucidate both what is right and wrong about his critique of Marcuse: he is right to insist against the latter that nature does not speak and hence cannot be a "partner" to whom we owe moral obligations of the sort we owe to each other, but he is wrong to conclude from that that nature can have no normative status at all, functioning in essence only as an object for instrumental manipulation. See Chapter 5, p. 141.

73. See Chapter Five above, p. 132. Habermas says there are "precisely" three worlds in *Moral Consciousness and Communicative Action*, p. 136.

74. See Chapter 2, Section 1.

75. Latour speaks similarly of the "quasi-objects" that surround us, writing that they are "simultaneously real, like nature, narrated, like discourse, and collective, like society." *We Have Never Been Modern*, p. 6. To introduce this "built world," one might note, is to see the point at which Habermas's neat distinction between "philosophy of consciousness" and "philosophy of communication" begins to break down. To the extent that subject-object relations involve *building*, in a social context that is discursively grounded, they, too, are already communicative. This was really one of Hegel's central points—put differently, of course—which is why Habermas's lumping of him with those committed to a "philosophy of consciousness" seems particularly unfair.

76. *The Theory of Communicative Action*, vol. 1, p. 239.

77. I am reluctant to enter too deeply into Habermas's slightly compulsive system-building and chart-drawing mania; it is seductive but dangerous. So I will resist the temptation to try to find some particular space in his system for what I am describing here. There is clearly some relation to what he calls the "aesthetic," especially in the quite interesting discussion of art that he offers in "Questions and Counterquestions," pp. 199–203. What tends however to be emphasized in such discussions (whose roots in Benjamin and Adorno are clear) is the role of art as "revelatory," as "opening our eyes anew"; my own use of the concept of practice is meant to emphasize the moment not so much of disclosure as of *construction*.

78. See *The Theory of Communicative Action*, vol. 1, pp. 48–74.

79. *Justification and Application*, pp. 145–146.

80. The trouble, that is, with premodern society's failure to distinguish the natural from the normative is that it attempts to derive the latter from the former—which is the same move I criticized in Horkheimer and Adorno and in Marcuse too. Once nature is seen as socially constituted, then the normative status of nature derives *from* the social rather than seeming to underlie it.

81. See *Justification and Application*, p. 176.

82. See above, Chapter 2, p. 46; Chapter 4, p. 77; Chapter 5, p. 135.

83. See Chapter 5. pp. 142–143.

84. See Chapter 4, p. 96.

Works Cited

Adorno, T. W. *Aesthetic Theory*, trans. C. Lenhardt. London: Routledge and Kegan Paul, 1984.

——. *Ästhetische Theorie*. Frankfurt: Suhrkamp, 1973.

——. *Minima Moralia*, trans. E. F. N. Jephcott. London: NLB, 1974.

——. *Negative Dialectics*, trans. E. B. Ashton. New York: Continuum, 1973.

——. *Negative Dialektik*. Frankfurt: Suhrkamp, 1975.

——, Hans Albert, Ralf Dahrendorf, Jürgen Habermas, Harald Pilot, and Karl R. Popper. *The Positivist Dispute in German Sociology*, trans. Glyn Adey and David Frisby. London: Heinemann, 1976.

Alford, C. Fred. *Science and the Revenge of Nature: Marcuse and Habermas*. Tampa: University of South Florida Press, 1985.

Arato, Andrew. "Lukács's Theory of Reification." *Telos* 11 (Spring 1972): 25–66.

—— and Paul Breines. *The Young Lukács and the Origins of Western Marxism*. New York: Seabury Press, 1979.

Baynes, Kenneth. *The Normative Grounds of Social Criticism*. Albany: SUNY Press, 1992.

Benhabib, Seyla. *Critique, Norm, and Utopia*. New York: Columbia University Press, 1986.

Bentham, Jeremy. *An Introduction to the Principles of Morals and Legislation*. London: The Athlone Press, 1970.

Bernstein, Richard. *Beyond Objectivism and Relativism*. Philadelphia: University of Pennsylvania Press, 1983.

——. *The Restructuring of Social and Political Theory*. Philadelphia: University of Pennsylvania Press, 1976.

——, ed. *Habermas and Modernity*. Cambridge, Mass.: MIT Press, 1985.

Bohman, James. *New Philosophy of Social Science*. Cambridge, Mass.: MIT Press, 1991.

211

Braaten, Jane. *Habermas's Critical Theory of Society*. Albany: SUNY Press, 1991.

Callicott, J. Baird. "Animal Liberation: A Triangular Affair." *Environmental Ethics* 2 (Winter 1980): 311–338.

Chase, Alston. *Playing God in Yellowstone*. San Diego, Calif.: Harcourt, Brace, Jovanovich, 1987.

Colletti, Lucio. *Marxism and Hegel*, trans. Lawrence Garner. London: NLB, 1973.

Congdon, Lee. *The Young Lukács*. Chapel Hill: University of North Carolina Press, 1983.

Cronon, William. *Changes in the Land*. New York: Hill and Wang, 1983.

Derrida, Jacques. *Margins of Philosophy*, trans. Alan Bass. Chicago: University of Chicago Press, 1982.

Dews, Peter, ed. *Habermas: Autonomy and Solidarity*. London: Verso, 1986.

Dryzek, John S. "Green Reason: Communicative Ethics for the Biosphere." *Environmental Ethics* 12 (Fall 1990): 195–210.

Dubos, René. *The Wooing of Earth*. New York: Charles Scribner's Sons, 1980.

Elster, H. J., ed. *Umweltschutz—Herausforderung unserer Generation*. Göttingen: Studienzentrum Weikersheim, 1984.

Engels, Frederick. *Anti-Dühring*. Moscow: Progress Publishers, 1978.

———. *Dialectics of Nature*. New York: International Publishers, 1940.

———. *Ludwig Feuerbach und der Ausgang der klassischen deutschen Philosophie*. Berlin: Dietz Verlag, 1981.

Feenberg, Andrew. *Critical Theory of Technology*. New York: Oxford University Press, 1991.

———. *Lukács, Marx, and the Sources of Critical Theory*. Totowa, N.J.: Rowman and Littlefield, 1981.

Freud, Sigmund. *Beyond the Pleasure Principle*. New York: Norton, 1961.

———. *Civilization and Its Discontents*. New York: Norton, 1961.

Giddens, Anthony. *New Rules of Sociological Method*, 2d ed. Stanford, Calif.: Stanford University Press, 1993.

Goldmann, Lucien. *Lukács and Heidegger*, trans. William Q. Boelhower. London: Routledge and Kegan Paul, 1977.

Habermas, Jürgen. *Communication and the Evolution of Society*, trans. Thomas McCarthy. Boston: Beacon Press, 1979.

———. *Erkenntnis und Interesse*. Frankfurt: Suhrkamp, 1979.

———. *Erläuterungen zur Diskursethik*. Frankfurt: Suhrkamp, 1991.

———. *Justification and Application*, trans. Ciaran P. Cronin. Cambridge, Mass.: MIT Press, 1993.

———. *Knowledge and Human Interests*, trans. Jeremy Shapiro. Boston: Beacon Press, 1968.

———. *Moralbewusstsein und Kommunikatives Handeln*. Frankfurt: Suhrkamp, 1983.

———. *Moral Consciousness and Communicative Action*, trans. Christian Lenhardt and Shierry Weber Nicholsen. Cambridge, Mass.: MIT Press, 1990.

———. *The Philosophical Discourse of Modernity*, trans. Frederick Lawrence. Cambridge, Mass.: MIT Press, 1987.

———. "A Postscript to *Knowledge and Human Interests.*" *Philosophy of Social Science* 3 (1973): 157–189.

———. *Technik und Wissenschaft als "Ideologie."* Frankfurt: Suhrkamp, 1979.

———. *Theory and Practice*, trans. John Viertel. Boston: Beacon Press, 1973.

———. *The Theory of Communicative Action*, 2 vols., trans. Thomas McCarthy. Boston: Beacon Press, 1984 and 1987.

———. *Toward a Rational Society*, trans. Jeremy Shapiro. Boston: Beacon Press, 1970.

———. *Vorstudien und Ergänzungen zur Theorie des Kommunikativen Handelns*. Frankfurt: Suhrkamp, 1984.

Hacking, Ian. *Representing and Intervening*. Cambridge: Cambridge University Press, 1983.

Haraway, Donna. *Primate Visions*. New York: Routledge, 1989.

Hardegg, Wolfgang, and Gert Preiser, eds. *Tierversuche und medizinische Ethik*. Hildesheim: Georg Olms AG, 1986.

Harding, Sandra. *The Science Question in Feminism*. Ithaca, N.Y.: Cornell University Press, 1986.

Hegel, G. W. F. *The Logic of Hegel*, trans. William Wallace, 2d ed. London: Oxford University Press, 1904.

———. *The Phenomenology of Spirit*, trans. A. V. Miller. Oxford: Oxford University Press, 1979.

———. *Philosophy of Right*, trans. T. M. Knox. London: Oxford University Press, 1971.

Held, David. *Introduction to Critical Theory*. Berkeley: University of California Press, 1980.

Hesse, Mary. *Revolutions and Reconstructions in the Philosophy of Science*. Bloomington: Indiana University Press, 1980.

Honneth, Axel. *The Critique of Power*, trans. Kenneth Baynes. Cambridge, Mass.: MIT Press, 1991.

Horkheimer, Max, and Theodor W. Adorno. *Dialectic of Enlightenment*, trans. John Cumming. New York: Seabury Press, 1972.

———. *Dialektik der Aufklärung*. Frankfurt: Fischer Verlag, 1969.

Hughes, J. Donald. *Ecology in Ancient Civilizations*. Albuquerque: University Press of New Mexico, 1975.

Hullot-Kentor, Bob. "Adorno's *Aesthetic Theory*: The Translation." *Telos* 65 (1985): 143–147.

Ingram, David. *Habermas and the Dialectic of Reason*. New Haven, Conn.: Yale University Press, 1987.

Jameson, Frederick. *Late Marxism: Adorno, or, the Persistence of the Dialec-tic*. London: Verso, 1990.

Jay, Martin. *Marxism and Totality*. Berkeley: University of California Press, 1984.

Jones, Gareth Stedman. "The Marxism of the Early Lukács: An Evaluation." *New Left Review* 70 (1971): 27–64.

Kadarkay, Arpad. *Georg Lukács: Life, Thought, and Politics*. London: Basil Blackwell, 1991.

Keat, Russell. *The Politics of Social Theory*. Chicago: University of Chicago Press, 1981.

Keller, Evelyn Fox. *Reflections on Gender and Science*. New Haven, Conn.: Yale University Press, 1985.

Kellner, Douglas. *Herbert Marcuse and the Crisis of Marxism*. Berkeley: University of California Press, 1984.

Knorr-Cetina, Karin, and Michael Mulkay, eds. *Science Observed*. London: Sage, 1983.

Krieger, Martin H. "What's Wrong With Plastic Trees?" *Science* 179 (February 2, 1973): 447–448.

Kuhn, Thomas. *The Structure of Scientific Revolutions*. Chicago: University of Chicago Press, 1962.

Latour, Bruno. *The Pasteurization of France*, trans. Alan Sheridan and John Law. Cambridge, Mass.: Harvard University Press, 1988.

———. *Science in Action*. Cambridge, Mass.: Harvard University Press, 1987.

———. *We Have Never Been Modern*, trans. Catherine Porter. Cambridge, Mass.: Harvard University Press, 1993.

——— and Steve Woolgar. *Laboratory Life*, 2d ed. Princeton, N.J.: Princeton University Press, 1986.

Leiss, William. *The Domination of Nature*. Boston: Beacon Press, 1974.

Lenhardt, Christian. "Reply to Hullot-Kentor." *Telos* 65 (1985): 147–152.

Lichtheim, George. *George Lukács*. New York: Viking Press, 1970.

Longino, Helen. *Science as Social Knowledge*. Princeton, N.J.: Princeton University Press, 1990.

Lukács, Georg. *Geschichte und Klassenbewusstsein*. Neuwied: Luchterhand, 1968.

———. *History and Class Consciousness*, trans. Rodney Livingstone. Cambridge, Mass.: MIT Press, 1971.

———. *Record of a Life*, ed. István Eörsi, trans. Rodney Livingstone. London: Verso, 1983.

Marcuse, Herbert. *Counterrevolution and Revolt*. Boston: Beacon Press, 1972.

———. *Eros and Civilization*. New York: Vintage Books, 1962.

———. *An Essay on Liberation*. Boston: Beacon Press, 1969.

———. *Five Lectures*, trans. Jeremy J. Shapiro and Shierry M. Weber. Boston: Beacon Press, 1970.

————. *Negations*, trans. Jeremy J. Shapiro. Boston: Beacon Press, 1968.

————. *One-Dimensional Man*. Boston: Beacon Press, 1964.

————, Jürgen Habermas, Heinz Lubasz, and Tilman Spengler. "Theory and Politics: A Discussion." *Telos* 38 (1978–79): 124–153.

Marx, Karl. *Capital*, vol. 1. New York: Modern Library, n.d.

———— and Frederick Engels. *Collected Works*, vol. 3, 1843–1844. New York: International Publishers, 1975.

McCarthy, Thomas. *The Critical Theory of Jürgen Habermas*. Cambridge, Mass.: MIT Press, 1978.

————. *Ideals and Illusions*. Cambridge, Mass.: MIT Press, 1991.

McPhee, John. *The Control of Nature*. New York: Farrar, Strauss, and Giroux, 1989.

Merchant, Carolyn. *The Death of Nature*. San Francisco: Harper and Row, 1980.

Miller, H. and W. Williams, eds. *Ethics and Animals*. Clifton, N.J.: Humana Press, 1983.

Nash, Roderick. *The Rights of Nature*. Madison: University of Wisconsin Press, 1989.

Piccone, Paul. "The Crisis of One-Dimensionality." *Telos* 35 (1978): 43–54.

Pippen, Robert, Andrew Feenberg, and Charles P. Webel, eds. *Marcuse: Critical Theory and the Promise of Utopia*. South Hadley, Mass.: Bergin and Garvey, 1988.

Popper, Karl. *The Logic of Scientific Discovery*. New York: Harper and Row, 1968.

Rasmussen, David M. *Reading Habermas*. Cambridge, Mass.: Basil Blackwell, 1990.

Regan, Tom. *The Case for Animal Rights*. Berkeley: University of California Press, 1983.

Rockmore, Tom. *Irrationalism: Lukács and the Marxist View of Reason*. Philadelphia: Temple University Press, 1992.

————, ed. *Lukács Today: Essays in Marxist Philosophy*. Dordrecht: D. Reidel, 1988.

Roderick, Rick. *Habermas and the Foundations of Critical Theory*. New York: St. Martin's Press, 1986.

Rose, Gillian. *The Melancholy Science: An Introduction to the Thought of Theodor W. Adorno*. New York: Columbia University Press, 1978.

Rouse, Joseph. *Knowledge and Power*. Ithaca, N.Y.: Cornell University Press, 1987.

Sagoff, Mark. "Animal Liberation and Environmental Ethics: Bad Marriage, Quick Divorce." *Osgood Hall Law Journal* 22, no. 2 (1984): 297–307.

Schmidt, Alfred. *The Concept of Nature in Marx*, trans. Ben Fowkes. London: NLB, 1971.

Schoolman, Morton. *The Imaginary Witness*. New York: New York University Press, 1984.

Seibel, George A. *Ontario's Niagara Parks*. Ontario: Niagara Parks Commission, 1987.

Singer, Peter. *Animal Liberation*. New York: Avon Books, 1975.

Taylor, Charles. "Understanding in Human Science." *Review of Metaphysics* 34 (1980): 25–38.

Thompson, John B. and David Held, eds. *Habermas: Critical Debates*. Cambridge, Mass.: MIT Press, 1982.

Vogel, Steven. "Marx and Alienation from Nature." *Social Theory and Practice* 14, no. 3 (1988): 367–387.

———. "Science, Practice, and Politics." *Social Epistemology* 5, no. 4 (1991): 267–292.

Warnke, Georgia. *Justice and Interpretation*. Cambridge, Mass.: MIT Press, 1993.

White, Stephen. *The Recent Work of Jürgen Habermas*. Cambridge: Cambridge University Press, 1988.

Whitebook, Joel. "The Problem of Nature in Habermas." *Telos* 40 (1979): 41–69.

Winch, Peter. *The Idea of a Social Science and Its Relation to Philosophy*. London: Routledge and Kegan Paul, 1958.

Index

217